DATE DUE

DEMCO 38-296

Yemen and the United States

Yemen and the United States:
A study of a small power and super-state relationship 1962–1994

AHMED NOMAN KASSIM
ALMADHAGI

Tauris Academic Studies
I.B. Tauris Publishers
LONDON · NEW YORK

Published in 1996 by Tauris Academic Studies
an imprint of I.B.Tauris & Co Ltd
45 Bloomsbury Square,
London WC1A 2HY

175 Fifth Avenue,
New York NY 10010

In the United States of America
and in Canada distributed by
St Martin's Press, 175 Fifth Avenue,
New York NY 10010

A full CIP record for this book is available from the British
Library

A full CIP record for this book is available from the Library
of Congress

ISBN 1 85043 772 6

Library of Congress catalog card number 93–60679

Set in Monotype Ehrhardt by Ewan Smith, London

Printed and bound in Great Britain by
WBC Ltd, Bridgend, Mid Glamorgan

Contents

Acknowledgements

I wish to thank all those who assisted in the research and preparation of this thesis. I am most grateful to my supervisor, Professor Fred Halliday, who gave me much appreciated advice and support throughout all stages. I am indebted to the UK Foreign and Commonwealth Office for granting me an award which made it possible. 'Abdul-'Aziz 'Abdul-Ghani, former YAR prime minister, kindly gave me encouragement. Muhsin al-'Aini, former YAR prime minister and currently ROY ambassador to the US, facilitated my fieldwork. Under the Freedom of Information Act, the US Department of State provided me with documents necessary to accomplish this research. The American Institute for Yemeni studies (AIYS) kindly facilitated my research and made it possible for me to extend the period of my fieldwork in the US and in Yemen. Later, the AIYS funded my preparation and updating of the manuscript for publication.

I would like to thank the following non-Yemenis for the interviews granted and information provided: David Ransom, Marjorie Ann Ransom, George Lane, William Rugh, Robert Stookey, Robert Burrowes, Manfred Wenner, Tom Meurer, Laurie Johnston, William Stoltzfus, John E. Peterson, Sheila Carapico, Brinkley Messick, Curt Walters, Talcott Seelye, Peter H. Deinken, Jack McCreary, Vinyamin Bobov, Mark Katz, David Warburton, Mu'djib al-Malazi and 'Adnan al-Tarsisi.

Of the Yemenis who have assisted me I wish to thank 'Abdul-Karim al-Iryani, Muhammad 'Abdul-'Aziz Sallam, Muhammad Sa'id al-'Attar, 'Abd Allah al-Ashtal, Sayyid Mustafa Salem, 'Ali Muhammad 'Abduh, Moh'd An'am Ghalib, Muhammad Kaid Saif, 'Abdul-Salam Sabrah, Ahmad Muhammad al-Shami and Muhammad Ahmad Zabarah.

Abbreviations

ACC	Arab Cooperative Council
ANA	Aden News Agency
FBIS	United States Foreign Broadcast Information Service
FLOSY	Front for the Liberation of Occupied South Yemen
FOO	Free Officers Organization
FYM	Free Yemeni Movement
FYP	Free Yemeni Party
GCC	Gulf Cooperation Council
GPC	General People's Congress
HKJ	Hashemite Kingdom of Jordan
ICA	US International Cooperation Administration
IMF	International Monetary Fund
JANA	Libyan News Agency
KOY	Kingdom of Yemen (1918–48)
KSA	Kingdom of Saudi Arabia
ME	BBC, Summary of Word Broadcasts, Part IV, the Middle East
MKOY	Mutawakkilite Kingdom of Yemen (1948–62)
NDF	National Democratic Front in the Yemen Arab Republic
NLF	National Liberation Front (of South Yemen)
PDRY	People's Democratic Republic of Yemen
PFLO	People's Front for the Liberation of Oman
PFLOAG	People's Front for the Liberation of Oman and the Occupied Arab Gulf (1968–71); People's Front for the Liberation of Oman and the Arab Gulf (1971–74)
PRSY	People's Republic of South Yemen
RDP	Revolutionary Democratic Party
ROY	Republic of Yemen
SABA'	YAR News Agency
SAF	South Arabia Federation
SAG	South Arabia Government
UAR	United Arab Republic (Egypt 1959–71)
UPONF	Unified Political Organization of the National Front

USAID	United States Agency for International Development
USIA	United States Information Agency
USIS	United States Information Service
YAR	Yemen Arab Republic
YARCPO	YAR Central Planning Organization
YEPCO	Yemen Exploration and Production Company
YHOC	Yemen Hunt Oil Company
YOMINCO	Yemen Oil and Minerals Corporation
YSP	Yemeni Socialist Party

Note on transliteration

Except where names of places or individuals are conventionally rendered into English in other forms, the process of transliteration from Arabic used throughout the book is based on that of *The Encyclopaedia of Islam*.

Introduction

This study covers the relationship between the former Yemen Arab Republic (YAR) and the United States during the period between the 1962 North Yemeni revolution and the unification of the two Yemens on 22 May 1990 – when the YAR merged with the People's Democratic Republic of Yemen (PDRY) to form the Republic of Yemen (ROY) – and then takes up the ROY–US relationship between 1990 and 1994. Despite unification, there is a large measure of continuity between earlier YAR–US relations and ROY–US relations today. While relations between what was South Yemen (the PDRY) and the US were limited to the period between 1967 and 1969,[1] Sana'a's more continuous relations with Washington were inherited by the ROY, since Sana'a was the capital of the former YAR and is today the capital of the new united Yemen. The first phase of ROY–US relations thus exemplify ongoing interactions and encounters between Sana'a and Washington. The story of Sana'a–Washington relations, therefore, represents a case study of a relationship between a small state and a superpower lasting over three decades, a relationship encapsulated in Cold War politics, constrained by the US role in the Arab–Israeli conflict arena, affected by US interests in Arabian oil and ruptured by the 1990/91 Gulf crisis. It illustrates the role of small states or powers *vis-à-vis* larger ones, and the degree of freedom of manoeuvre which small states have in determining their foreign policy.

The study is organized chronologically and traces the historical development of Washington–Sana'a relations. Chapter 1 is a survey of North Yemen–US contacts before the revolution of 26 September 1962 and provides the background to issues at the core of the book. The next three chapters cover in detail the different phases of diplomatic relations between the YAR and the US from 1962 to 1990. These relations fall into distinct phases: the initial YAR contacts which led to US recognition of the YAR on 19 December 1962; the first phase of relations, until diplomatic ties were broken in 1967; and the five-year period ending in the restoration of relations in 1972. The discovery of oil in the YAR by a US company in 1984 brought about a change in the whole nature of the relationship and marked the beginning of a period of greater US interest in the country. The YAR–USA relationship included a key component of any superpower–small state interaction: development assistance. The final chapter covers post-Cold War ROY–US relations, during which the Kuwaiti crisis jeopardized the bilateral relationship and the disappearance of the USSR lessened Yemen's freedom of manoeuvre when determining its foreign priorities.

Themes in Yemeni–US relations

Three arenas or environments affect foreign policy-making in a small state such as Yemen: the global, the regional and the internal. Yemen's foreign relations, and in particular its interactions with the United States, have thus been conducted in the context of the bipolar US–Soviet balance of power for most of the twentieth century, but were deeply affected by the demise of the USSR in the late 1980s. Within this global context, Yemen's foreign policy needs to be seen as a piece of Arab foreign policy, for Yemen's location at the southwestern tip of the Arabian peninsula situates it in a political and strategic position that cannot be separated from other events in the Arab region. Finally, circumstances within Yemen, from resistance to the imamate and the 1962 revolution through to the events leading to unification with the PDRY, play a decisive role in Sana'a's responses to events in the international and regional arenas.

One of the themes examined in this study is that of policy interaction among these different arenas: how Arabian peninsula problems affected US policy, how Yemeni policies affected the region and how relationships in that region affected the superpowers. In particular, the book examines how the YAR's relations with the USA fitted into overall American policy, especially towards Saudi Arabia and South Yemen, which was at first a British protectorate and which was later controlled by the pro-Soviet National Liberation Front (NLF) and the Yemeni Socialist Party (YSP). Relevant to this is an analysis of the extent to which the YAR benefited from relations with the US. Another major theme is that of US policy towards the YAR, seen in the context of US policy towards the rest of the Middle East,[2] in particular the Kingdom of Saudi Arabia (KSA). The Arab–Israeli question and Cold War rivalry with the Soviet bloc, as well as the extent to which the US had a particular interest in the YAR between 1962 and 1990, are also discussed. Related to this is an analysis of the reasons for US interest. A fourth theme is the effect of global strategic rivalries and intersections on Yemen, and how it tried, in varying ways and at different times, to benefit from these rivalries. Also examined are the role played by the Yemeni people in affecting regional and international relations and the effect of regional religious differences on YAR–US relations. A key dimension is the superpower–small state relationship in a highly volatile region and how, within this, a small power maintained a degree of freedom of manoeuvre in deciding its foreign policy. The follow-up to the study shows how the end of the Cold War and disappearance of USSR influence in the area denied the united Yemen part of its limited freedom of manoeuvre when dealing with the only remaining super-power.

These themes recur throughout the US–Yemeni relationship. Between 1918 and 1962 North Yemen's relationship with the US was limited. It was affected negatively by the following factors: US lack of economic interest in the country; the US stance on the Palestinian issue and its role in creating Israel; Zeidi ideology and the imams' fears of exposing their subjects to the modern world; Yemen's dispute with the UK over the southern areas of Yemen (i.e. Aden and the protectorates) and its territorial dispute with Saudi Arabia; and the strong KSA–US relationship. Initially most of these factors were a source of only marginal aggravation to the US, but they were exacerbated after the formation of the YAR in 1962.

Four major issues dominated YAR–US relations in subsequent years: the Cold War, reflected in the Yemeni arena in rivalry between the Western-leaning but technically non-aligned YAR and the Soviet-backed PDRY, known as a 'socialist outpost' in the Arabian peninsula; the triangular relationship of both countries with the Kingdom of Saudi Arabia, whose vast oil wealth the US had sought to protect and which had exercised a hegemonic policy towards Yemen; US policy in the Middle East, vis-à-vis the Europeans, the Soviets, the Israelis, and regional crises including the Iranian revolution and the two Gulf wars; and the nature of the bilateral interaction itself, affected, among other things, by internal Yemeni politics from the fall of the monarchy to unification with South Yemen.

Unification, perhaps the major event in Yemeni history, coincided with the demise of the bipolar global balance of power and with a new crisis in the regional arena. Under these changed circumstances, the major issues in the new Republic of Yemen's relations with the US were their contradictory positions on the Kuwaiti crisis; the grave deterioration of Yemen–Saudi relations, which reached their low point with the latter's claims to petroleum resources and territory within Yemeni boundaries; the end of the Cold War with the collapse of the Soviet bloc and the reduction of Moscow's influence in the Middle East; the discovery of more, though still modest, oil reserves in the ROY and the involvement of more US and Western companies in the republic; and domestic instability, new economic burdens and armed actions followed in April 1993 by Yemen's historic experiment in multi-party elections, the first in the Arabian peninsula.

Evolution of Yemeni foreign policy

Yemen possesses distinguishing, if not unique, features and characteristics: it is a highly populated country, was long supplied with Soviet arms, has a turbulent modern history, controls the southern mouth of the Red Sea and lies adjacent to 60 per cent of the world's oil reserves in what is supposedly an unchallenged sphere of Western influence.

Yemen's policy towards the USA must be seen in the context of its policy towards external powers in general. After the First World War Sana'a sought to counterbalance British pressure in Aden by obtaining territorial integrity and international recognition for its government. The Mutawakkilite Kingdom of Yemen (MKOY), formed in 1948, sought the same objectives, especially when relations with the UK became strained and the inter-Yemeni opposition posed a threat to the Hamid al-Din ruling family. In the 1950s the ruling imam sought a US diplomatic presence to counterbalance the Eastern bloc. He was not concerned with obtaining US assistance, since this would have benefited the Yemeni people rather than himself personally. In the late 1950s the Yemeni monarchy, hoping to counterbalance Soviet and Egyptian influence in the MKOY, appealed to the US to intervene in the border dispute with Aden and to establish a diplomatic legation and a United States Agency for International Development (USAID) office. Washington took the situation seriously and, in the light of the Eisenhower Doctrine,[3] decided to contain Soviet influence in Yemen in order to safeguard Western interests and protect Saudi security.

After the republican revolution, the YAR found itself obliged to follow foreign policies directed by domestic, regional and other external forces. In 1962, in order to survive, it had no choice but to ally itself with the UAR and the USSR. Without Egypt's assistance and protection it was unlikely that the republic would continue to exist. In the late 1960s, without Arab and Soviet military assistance, it was likely to disappear. In the 1970s it was under pressure from both the monarchical pro-US KSA and the radical pro-Soviet PDRY. Although it was destined to become a Saudi client, pressure from the PDRY forced it to adopt a balanced policy. In 1979 the capital, Sana'a, was on the verge of falling to the invading forces of the PDRY and NDF. This was prevented by the assistance and protection of both the KSA and the US. USSR policy towards the YAR from late 1979 gave the YAR room for manoeuvre and allowed it to maintain relations with both the

US and the USSR: economic cooperation with Washington and military cooperation with Moscow. This enabled the YAR to enjoy a period of stability and development throughout the 1980s.

After 1990, unified Yemen saw itself as the pace-setter in inter-Arab cooperation, a contemporary model for the old dream of Arab unification, and as the lone republic in a peninsula of monarchies. This self-perception, coupled with long-standing fears of Saudi hegemony, led the newly founded ROY to call publicly for an 'Arab solution' to the Iraq–Kuwait crisis, and to use its temporary seat on the United Nations Security Council to resist UN resolutions to use force to remove Iraqi forces from Kuwait. This led to a crisis in Yemeni–US relations similar to that of 1967, in that it was caused not so much by bilateral interaction as by differing reactions to events in the Middle East arena. It differed from the earlier breach, however, in that this time Yemen was isolated politically from its immediate neighbours. That Yemen subsequently resorted to concessions designed to restore aid, investment and diplomatic relations with both the West and the monarchies of the peninsula underscores again the limited capacity of small peripheral states to forge an independent foreign policy without suffering intolerable consequences.

US policy and its evolution

Yet another theme of this book is that of US foreign policy and its evolution. After the end of the First World War, American policy in the Arabian peninsula was restricted and hard to implement. When the US became more closely involved in Saudi Arabia and other Gulf states, its interest in Yemen grew.[4] Chapter 1 examines formal and informal North Yemen–US relations before September 1962 at both private and official levels. In addition to its importance in outlining the historical background of YAR–US relations, this establishes a basis for comparison between US policies towards monarchical, conservative Yemen and towards the republic.

After 1945 three aims shaped US foreign policy: to maintain active responsibility for the direction of international affairs; to use all power to combat the spread of the communist 'menace'; and to contain 'Soviet expansionism and influence'.[5] In the Indian Ocean and the Gulf region, this meant the following: a British and a French military presence; US business investment in the region; increased Western demand for oil resources; a Soviet political and military presence; and involvement of the region in Arab–Israeli and Southwest Asian conflicts.

The US emerged from the the Second World War as a superpower at a time when the European countries' dominance over their former colonies, protectorates and allies was declining in the region. Thus the US gradually became the most influential and powerful external force in the Middle East generally and in the Arabian peninsula in particular. The combination of military and economic strength enabled the US to make its presence felt and to influence countries with which it had had no previous relations. After the Second World War, finding that there was no objection from London, the US responded to the imam's demands by deciding not to leave Yemen for other powers to penetrate. Washington also sought stability in the Arabian peninsula in order to safeguard US business interests and world oil reserves. This objective was to be achieved by protecting its KSA ally against any threat that might emerge from MKOY alliances, and by reconciling the imam with the UK. During this period Britain tried but failed tó play a direct role in determining internal Yemeni politics. It finally came to rely heavily on its influence over US officials in order to exert indirect pressure in determining events in Southwest Arabia. This situation made it appropriate for the US and the Kingdom of Yemen to establish formal relations.

Arab nationalism and superpower Cold War rivalries

Nineteen forty-seven witnessed the declaration of the Truman Doctrine, a new principle in America's foreign policy, which aimed to support those 'who are resisting attempted subjugation by armed minorities or by outside pressures'.[6] In this year President Truman announced that his country would assist all countries that opposed Soviet ideology and policies.[7] This led to the creation of economic and military aid packages, mutual defence treaties, regional pacts and alliances and, although the doctrine was initially concluded with Greece and Turkey, to increasing US interest in the Middle East and Southwest Asia. As a result the US came to take its relationship with Yemen more seriously. This doctrine led to a policy of resisting and dislodging the USSR during the subsequent administration. Secretary of State John Dulles visited the area in 1953, one year after the Egyptian revolution, but achieved very little. On his return to Washington, Dulles confirmed that 'many of the Arab League countries were preoccupied with their disputes with Israel, Great Britain and France, a matter which lessened their fear of Communism'.[8] The US secretary's statement indicated clearly that the Arabs were struggling to obtain their independence from the European colonialists and felt that the real threat came from Israel rather than from communism. This prompted a cool response to the US plans.

In 1956 the crisis between Western colonial powers and Arab nationalism came to a head, and the US feared that the Soviet Union would be welcomed into the sphere of influence that the US had inherited from its European predecessors. The Eisenhower administration responded to this situation by pledging the US to exercise a more assertive policy in the Middle East, partly through bilateral relations with most of the local governments in the Arabian peninsula. The USSR reacted by increasing its support to Arab nationalist and anti-colonialist elements in the Arab world and by acquiring a foothold in the Middle East to confront 'colonialism and imperialism'. Their first chance came when President Jamal 'Abdul-Nasser of Egypt nationalized the Suez Canal in 1956. The USSR promptly pledged political and military assistance to Egypt. Under the nationalist movement of the 1950s, Arab countries became hopeful of using possible Soviet support to free themselves from the vestiges of Western colonialism. This, of course, displeased US and West European policy-makers. The Arab nationalist movement faced many difficulties in achieving independence from direct or indirect Western influence, partly because of Middle East dependency upon European economies, and also because of the lingering effects of decades of colonialism. This explains why, by the end of the 1950s, most Arab countries had either traditional or revolutionary foreign policies; the traditional governments placed their fate in the hands of the Western powers, while the revolutionary regimes found that their interests lay in aligning themselves with the Eastern anti-imperialist and anti-colonialist bloc. Thus one of the side-effects of the Cold War was the Arab world's dependence on either the US or the USSR.

In this period, the US continued to maintain in Saudi Arabia military installations that were intended to defend not only the Middle East as a whole but also the oil reserves in the whole Gulf region: these reserves had become essential to the energy supply of the West. Behind this economic and military presence was US concern over Soviet influence in the Yemen. The US was also concerned about Yemen's continuing dispute with the neighbouring KSA. Robert Stookey, the last US chargé d'affaires in monarchical Yemen, pointed out that the ongoing British–Yemen dispute also worried the US more at the outbreak of the Cold War than any other time, since the British military base in Aden was used to underpin the Anglo-American position in the Gulf and the peninsula.[9]

The revolution of 26 September brought the newly formed YAR into the nationalist, Nasserite camp in the Arab world and thus to a position of significant strategic importance for the first time in history. The US became very much alarmed and tried to intervene in Yemen's crisis. Through recognizing the republic and maintaining a presence in both the YAR and the UAR, the US was able to become part of the solution. When the Arab Nationalism Movement faced a defeat by Israel in 1967 and the YAR was forced to become a subsidiary of the KSA, the US showed a lack of interest in the YAR. In 1972, when the British left a vacuum in the Gulf and an 'anti-imperialist' government in South Yemen and other regional concerns, the US sought to break the Arab stand against it and Israel and to restore relations with Sana'a, which had been the first Arab capital to severe its relations with Washington following the Arab–Israeli war.

The sense of real concern in the area was also observed during the 1979 inter-Yemeni war, during which Saudi Arabia felt immediately threatened. What concerned the US more was the fact that this event followed in the wake of the April 1978 revolution in Afghanistan, the signing of an Ethiopian–Soviet treaty in November, the assassination of US Ambassador Adolph Dubs in Kabul in February 1979, and the fall of the Shah (the US 'policeman' in the region). These events created the impression in the area that the US had lost all capacity to control regional events and thus the oil states of the Gulf cultivated relations with the Soviet Union in order to protect themselves. The inter-Yemeni war of 1979 was an opportunity for the US to reassure Saudi Arabia and other US friends in the region and to demonstrate its resolve. In addition to the military measures undertaken to arm Sana'a and warn Aden, and the deployment of AWAC early warning aircraft to bolster Saudi air defences, the secretary of state issued a warning to the Soviets, which Moscow took seriously. The US stand and the YAR's military and political alliance in this period prompted the USSR to re-evaluate its policies in the Yemeni arena. Moscow started to cooperate with Sana'a as of this year, particularly through providing it with the arms it needed. There was no evidence that Washington was greatly alarmed by the new YAR–USSR relations in the military field, perhaps indicating that the two superpowers had agreed on something – probably a kind of strategic intersection, as was the case in 1959 between Washington and London. Sana'a–Washington relations remained at their lowest level after 1979, and were sustained mainly through USAID technical projects.

Change in American foreign policy after 1979 was slow to come, for different reasons, among them the fact that there was no longer any threat from South Yemen. US anxieties were further eased by the fact that the Soviet Union was cooperating with Sana'a and did not encourage a PDRY invasion of the YAR. In 1986, a year after President Gorbachev came to power, the internal power struggle in South Yemen and the discovery of oil in the Yemen by American oil companies led to a change in US policy. In fact US policy towards the Yemen changed periodically because the YAR was neither conservative nor radical. Its attitude towards the YAR was always determined by Washington's concerns in Sana'a – the Soviet role in the Horn of Africa and the Red Sea area, and Saudi security. In 1984, when a US company found oil in the west of the country, the White House showed a tangible interest in the YAR for the first time. The US vice-president's visit in 1986 was evidence of this interest and is considered to mark the beginning of direct YAR–US relations.

The New World Order

The end of the global rivalry between US capitalism and Soviet social-ism removed major external barriers to Yemeni unification and at the same time launched a new phase in US foreign policy. In the 'New World Order' envisaged by President George Bush, Washington would no longer have to compete with another superpower for favour with small states of the Third World, but would be in a position to make a 'take it or leave it' offer of friendship and assistance. Post-Cold War realities have given US forces a freer hand in responding to crises in Kuwait to the north-east and Somalia to the west across the Red Sea from Yemen, as American presidents no longer have to calculate the countermoves of the USSR. Since the fall of the Berlin Wall, the United States has been far more active militarily in the peninsula and the Red Sea region than ever before, and Yemen is thus far more conscious of the role of the US in regional affairs.

The US policy of bolstering the oil-rich monarchies of the Arabian peninsula, long a staple of Washington's global strategy, was under-scored and reinforced by the Gulf Crisis of 1990–91. The strengthening of the US commitment to Saudi Arabia and the Gulf kingdoms in turn reasserted the triangular pattern of US–Yemeni relations via Saudi Arabia. In the wake of Yemen's refusal to support Kuwait and Riyadh against Baghdad, Saudi wrath against its erstwhile client has played a major role in US policy towards Yemen.

But the Saudi-mediated US antipathy towards Yemen was mitigated, at least in part, by US companies' involvement in Yemeni oil and by unified Yemen's progress towards pluralism and parliamentarism. In the case of the latter, in particular, Washington's policy was caught between its strategic and economic interests in Saudi Arabia on the one hand and its rhetorical commitment to democratization on the other. This dilemma was further complicated by the kingdom's open distaste for the multi-party elections in Yemen on 27 April 1993 (it regarded these as a potential threat to its own internal stability) and by two rounds of letters from Riyadh to international oil companies warning them against operations in Yemen. Thus, as always, the relationship between a superpower and a small state proved to be not simply a bilateral relationship but one enmeshed in wider regional politics.

North Yemen–US contacts before 1962

In the period leading up to the 1962 republican revolution Yemen was able to benefit from neither private nor official American contacts, nor, due to its geopolitical location between Saudi Arabia and the Western interests in the British colony of Aden and the surrounding protectorates, was it able to develop cooperative relations with the US government. YAR–US relations were constrained by 1) Yemen's rivalry with the UK over southern Yemen – Aden and the protectorates – and with the Kingdom of Saudi Arabia (KSA); 2) Washington's major interests in the KSA, its Arab and Middle Eastern policy and its fear of communism; 3) internal Yemeni resistance to relations with Washington, which came from Zeidi isolationism and the belief of the Free Yemeni Party (FYP) that the US would provide a lifeline to the country's ruling family. Other important factors affecting US–North Yemeni relations were Italian influence in the Red Sea, British rule in Southern Yemen, and the gradual transition from British to American influence in the Arabian peninsula during the first half of this century. These conditions, in turn affected by internal Yemeni political developments, played off each other during the period between the two world wars, and in different ways in the post-Second World War era.

Private, informal and formal ties

North Yemen's history, its coffee, animal hides and strategic location had attracted the interest of some US businessmen since the late eighteenth century, but the then British and Ottoman dominance delayed the growth of any private American involvement in the country. After the First World War, when Yemen recovered its independence from the Turks, its first choice of ally was the United States of America. Imam Yahya wrote the first official letter in his role as king of Yemen to the government of America, and put his own stamp for the first time on an American passport. Some American entrepreneurs once again showed some interest in Yemen, especially after finding indications of petroleum and minerals there. The US began to give some early technical assistance to Yemen as of the late 1920s, such as connecting the capital, Sana'a, with the port of Hudaidah. For his part, the imam sought Washington's support against the British,˙ support that the US was unwilling to give. This factor, together with the imam's conservatism internally and externally, led to a near failure of efforts aimed at benefiting the country and government through contacts with the outside world and the twentieth century. There was only limited cooperation with the Italians, who were in competition with the British in the Red Sea area.

The retrograde policy of Yemen's rulers, who lacked experience of the outside world, led to cultural isolation and a misguided foreign policy and was ultimately responsible for the collapse of the imamate itself in 1962. Behind the failure of the external policies of Imam Yahya was the Zeidi, or Shi'ite, doctrine. For religious reasons the Imams and the Zeidi ''ulama' (scholars), whose contemporary parallel were the ayatollahs of Iran during the lifetime of Imam al-Khomeini, had never been interested in maintaining any sort of relations with foreigners, unless forced to, simply in order to break a stranglehold by another foreign power. The Yemeni imams largely succeeded in using one superpower against another, but they completely failed to benefit from this policy or to make real friends and allies, either inside or outside the country; this failure led to their demise.

Early Yemeni–US relations were often based on unofficial contacts. American vessels first called at the Yemeni port of Mocha in the late eighteenth century. Trade intensified with Yemen in the early nineteenth century as trade in coffee, gum and hides expanded.[1] By the end of the century American missionaries Dr Samuel Zwemmer and Charles F. Camp and their wives had settled in Yemen. The murder of Camp by the Turks, who were then occupying Yemen, brought the American consul in Aden, Charles K. Moser, to Sana'a in 1910 to investigate the incident.[2]

In 1918 North Yemen gained independence from Ottoman Turkey and the monarch, Imam Yahya, requested US recognition. This resulted in a goodwill visit to the imam by the American consul in British Aden in 1919. His aim was to lay the ground for some American business expeditions the following year.[3] In 1920 the Standard Oil Company made a geological investigation for oil in the kingdom.[4] Amin al-Raihani, an American of Syrian origin, visited the imam in 1921–22, and returned with a letter from the imam to the American consul in Aden which raised the recognition issue once again.[5] In 1926 the

American vice-consul in Aden introduced to the imam the first American businessman, Niton Houlberg, representative of the Houlberg-Kidde Corporation of Aden and New York.[6]

After its independence Yemen sought to establish its authority throughout what it saw as 'historic' Yemen, including the southern areas occupied by the British since 1839. London therefore objected to and resisted all economic and political cooperation between Sana'a and Washington. As an influential power in the region the UK was largely able to contain Yemeni–US relations throughout the period 1918–62.

In 1918, when Imam Yahya requested American recognition, President Wilson took no action[7] because the 'U.S. Department of State followed Great Britain's advice on matters related to the Peninsula'.[8] Despite signing treaties with many countries throughout the 1930s, Imam Yahya continuously sought an American alliance in order to use it against the UK. He understood that his task was difficult because he had been 'a potential enemy of Great Britain, with which country the U.S. is friendly'.[9]

The imam considered the private and informal contacts (i.e. Niton Houlberg, Charles Crane and Karl Twitchell) to be a personal success but thus far none of them had achieved what he really wanted, namely US recognition. The imam encouraged American trade in order to obtain American arms and 'the negotiation of a treaty'; these aims were effectively blocked by the British and by Anglo-American friendship.[10] American businessmen and diplomats insisted that the imam should give up all claims on the British protectorates. This the imam refused to do.[11]

There is some evidence that the US oil companies became interested in oil and mineral exploration in Yemen as early as 1920. A US consular dispatch,[12] commenting on an article by the *Nation Business* of July of the same year about the existence of oil off Yemeni shores, was indicative of this. Further evidence of the American awareness of the existence of Yemen's petroleum and mineral resources can be found in another document[13] which points out that a Standard Oil party, consisting of Mr Fred Ely and Mr R.A. McGovern, guided by a French geologist, Victor L. Cherruau, working under the Paris office of the company, made a geological investigation and exploration of oil in Yahya's kingdom.[14]

In Aden the same party confirmed the existence of manganese and gold but rejected the possibility of the existence of oil.[15] The consul enclosed reports by Cherrau dated 29 April, 5 June and 20 June 1922, concerning the exploration of Yemen between 1 January and 1 April of the same year. In one of the reports he stated: 'the Yemen offers an opening of great commercial and industrial value ... I found that there are veritable riches.'[16] He stressed that petroleum existed in large and commercial quantities and that American petroleum interests would find it greatly to their advantage to cooperate with him, as he assured them that he held the confidence of the Imam of Yemen.[17] At the same time he believed that no great difficulty would be met in securing concessions for the exploration of any petroleum deposits found in that region. The French geologist informed the Americans of evidence of petroleum at different points all through the country: 'it exists at other places near Dhamar de Zebid ... there is one spring whose water is mixed with a blackish substance giving a certain odour, and leaves an oily taste in the mouth ... These regions, situated well above sea level ...'.[18] He also mentioned the existence of petroleum between Taiz and Ibb, in a crude state, at the foot of a mountain between the villages of Madre and Kataba: 'one can get this petroleum by making small holes in the ground at the foot of the mountain as a filtration occurs to about 20 or 30 metres high between the rocks ... the same exists near Dhamar, and near Sana'a Nucum mountain exist several springs.'[19] These reports also gave assurances that minerals such as copper, iron, cerium, manganese, saltpetre, potash, sulphur, mica and phosphate had been discovered during this exploration. A few months later, the US consul in Nantes, France, emphasized in a report to the Department of State the indications of petroleum in Yemen, which he described as a 'considerable quantity'.[20]

It was strange that despite such encouraging reports the American company abandoned its contacts with the imam, a matter which seemed to indicate that a political decision had been made. The silence of Standard Oil angered and disappointed Imam Yahya. In 1925 Sheikh Saleh Hussein, agent of Qadhi Abdulla al-'Arashi, former representative of the imam in Aden, gave a lecture in which he stressed Yemen's relations with European countries. In what could be seen as an oblique message to the Americans, he bitterly criticized Standard Oil's failure to fulfil its promises. Speaking about the imam's policy and the American company, he mentioned that the Imam's policy was to create friendship with all the European powers, particularly with those who had already shown interest in his country. In the context of his elaboration of the Yemen's foreign policy, Sheikh Saleh pointed out clearly that no one government would 'ever be given priority over another under any circumstances. All will be treated alike. Pure business relations and nothing else is sought by the Yemen government. In political matters the assistance of no white government will be invited, nor will the imam's government accept any outside assistance.' The Yemeni lecturer warned on the same occasion that:

interference in any way in its political campaigns will injure the imam's relations with the mediating government and this must be avoided if friendly relations with the imam are to be expected at all. The matter of granting concessions is one of the most important problems occupying the attention of the imam and he is now determined to make concessions to those only who are in a position to handle the situation carefully and agree to his several conditions regarding the actual working of the concessions. Concessions will be granted to several parties and will in no case be confined to one.

Sheikh Saleh ended his lecture by revealing his government's disappointment, but expressed some hope about an American oil company: 'the representatives of an American oil company which passed through Sana'a over two years ago promised then to return to Sana'a once more in order to obtain some sort of concession, and we still hope to hear from them.'[21]

Another American contact was made in 1926, when the American Consulate in Aden introduced the diplomat and entrepreneur Charles Crane to the imam. Crane visited Sana'a several times in 1926 and 1927.[22] When he left Sana'a in 1927 he carried with him an Arabic draft of a proposed treaty with the United States. No treaty was concluded, but the US government approved Crane's activities and instructed its consul in Aden to make an informal trip to the Yemen. Crane introduced to the imam an American engineer, Karl Twitchell, who between 1927 and 1932 studied the geology and infrastructural needs of Yemen. He also provided technical assistance for the construction of roads and bridges and distributed farm and industrial machinery as gifts. Twitchell was responsible for connecting Sana'a with the port of Hudaidah by constructing bridges along approximately 350 kilometres of difficult mountainous country.[23] At the time, it was surprising that the Crane–Yahya relationship was brought to an end,[24] and in 1932 both Crane and Twitchell switched their interest to the KSA.[25]

In 1933 Carleton S. Coon, his wife and Ralph Forbes made a short anthropological expedition into the country, and in 1937 two American oil geologists landed at Hudaidah harbour, but 'they found no oil'.[26] Ford Company representatives arrived in Sana'a in the 1930s offering to construct modern roads all over the country on condition that Yemen committed itself to buy only Ford cars for twenty years. Imam Yahya rejected the offer.[27]

The Yemeni–Italian alliance

North Yemen's attempts to benefit from superpower rivalries first became evident after its independence in 1918, when Sana'a tried to exploit Italian–UK rivalry by attempting to obtain US support for its aims of liberating the southern areas from British colonial rule and reuniting 'historical' Yemen. When Washington refused, Sana'a turned to Italy, a rival of the British in the Red Sea region. In competition with Britain for control of this area, Italy had established a presence on the Asian shores of the sea following its conclusion of a treaty with the Amir of 'Asir, al-Idrissi, in 1911. In Yemen, Rome opened relations by establishing commercial ties with the Yemeni ports of 'Asir, Tihama and Aden. It then established a commercial centre in Sana'a. After three years of diplomacy, Italy signed a treaty with Imam Yahya of Yemen in 1926, guaranteeing freedom of trade between the two states. This was the first treaty the KOY had signed with another state, and Italy was the first European nation to recognize Imam Yahya as king of Yemen. The imam used the treaty to strengthen his position in the talks with the British delegation headed by Sir Gilbert Clayton, which were held in Sana'a in 1926, and broke down just a few days before the treaty with Rome was signed.[28] He also used it to put some pressure on Idrissi to surrender to Sana'a. Yahya gambled all his cards on Italy and challenged his rivals to the north and south – the Saudis and the British – before obtaining the necessary armaments and training. This led directly to the annexation of 'Asir by the KSA and to the weakening of the Imam's position in the south.[29]

While Imam Yahya aimed at gaining international recognition of his rule and obtaining arms to strengthen his position against the rebellious leaders of 'Asir and against the British, Italy sought economic markets and a political position that would secure both its interests in the Red Sea region and its position in its colonies in East Africa. For this reason the treaty with the imam was seen by Italy to be 'the first important step in the history of its penetration in South West Arabia for which it had waited so long'.[30] As well as a five-year gasoline concession this treaty opened up Yemen for Italian arms, goods and doctors, and even allowed Rome to influence the imam's foreign policy. The contrast between Imam Yahya's policies towards the ruler of 'Asir and the British before and after the signing of this treaty indicates that Italian influence lay behind the unexpected decision of the imam in 1927 to terminate the activities of the Twitchell American engineering team, which was attempting to build a harbour and a communication network and to explore for oil.

The Yemeni–Italian alliance must be assessed within the context of British–Italian competition for the control of the Red Sea. Yemen's alliance with Rome was motivated by the wish to counter the British and to liberate the southern areas from their influence. But the flaw in the imam's policy was that he used one colonial power to get rid of another. Instead of strengthening his position against the British, he only stirred up more vigorous British enmity against his rule because London treated the Arabian peninsula in terms of a British equivalent of the Monroe Doctrine.[31] The region of 'Asir, which the imam subsequently lost because of his treaty with the Italians, is a case in point. Italy gained even stronger influence in Yemen following the renewal of the treaty in 1937, especially through the imam's personal Italian physicians. This continued until 1943, when the Axis bloc started to lose the war.[32] In the second half of the 1940s, partly because of growing US interest in the Arabian peninsula, the imam tried to exploit US–UK competition once again in order to enhance his rule and to counterbalance pressure from the British in the south and the Saudis in the north. When this failed in the 1950s, the MKOY sought assistance (mainly military) from the Soviets, who responded positively. This aroused US concern and led to US–UK cooperation in the Yemen resulting in a US offer of development aid. Washington also tried to reconcile the British and the Imam.

Yemen rivalry with the KSA and the UK and Washington's Arab policy

From the early 1920s Imam Yahya competed with King 'Abdul-'Aziz Al-Sa'ud for influence in Arabian peninsula affairs. The dispute between the Zeidi Hamid al-Din royal family in Yemen and the Saudi royal family had a religious basis: the Saudis are Sunni and the Zeidi imams are Shi'ites who believe they are descended from the Prophet Muhammad. Saudi Arabia saw the imams who ruled the most populous country in the area as rivals who might threaten KSA security. Their rivalry was heightened in the 1930s when 'Abdul-'Aziz annexed the disputed border areas claimed by Imam Yahya.

In early 1934 the British defeated the imam in a war on the southern borders; British air power created havoc in the imamate army and alarmed the imam. Weakened and defeated by the British, he engaged in another war with the Saudis, which he also lost. Neither the imam nor the Yemeni people were satisfied with the 1934 peace treaty of Taif, which was concluded at the end of the war to regulate Yemeni–Saudi relations and temporarily define the northern Yemen frontier, because it was negotiated and signed under duress.

Because of this Yemeni–Saudi rivalry and because of an open foreign policy towards the outside world, King 'Abdul-'Aziz welcomed the Crane–Twitchell overtures in the 1930s. He granted the Standard Oil Company of California the first concession to explore and develop his country's oil resources 'in exchange for relatively low payment even in his own terms while his dispute with Imam Yahya reached its climax in the 1934 war between the two neighbours'.[33] Various Yemeni sources suggested to the present writer that King Ibn Sa'ud established stronger relations with the al-Wazir family, rivals to the ruling Hamid al-Din family, and encouraged the al-Wazirs to oppose the policies of Imam Yahya. During the 1934 war, anxious to protect the huge interests of American companies in the KSA, Washington wanted stability and pushed for a peaceful solution. In July of that year Karl Twitchell stated that Charles Crane 'had advised the peaceful settlement between the Imam and Ibn Sa'ud'.[34]

Rising US influence in the post-war era

The years following 1944 witnessed the rise of US influence and interest in the Arabian peninsula. Washington realized that by neglecting Yemen, US long-term interests in Saudi Arabia might be threatened, and established formal relations without British objection because the latter wanted to stabilize the balance of power in the Arabian peninsula.[35] During May 1944, Washington responded to the imam's request to intercede in Yemen's border dispute with the UK and dispatched its newly appointed consul in Aden, Harlan B. Clark, to meet Imam Yahya in March 1945. Meetings between the two resulted in US recognition of Yemen as an independent state on 4 March 1946. A treaty of friendship and commerce was concluded on 4 May 1946, but diplomatic representation with the US was delayed because Imam Yahya, although desirous of obtaining aid and official recognition for his country and for his own position, did not facilitate the exchange of diplomatic representation with countries he had signed treaties with.[36] This was due in part to British obstruction through influential officials inside and outside the palace.[37]

When Imam Yahya established formal relations with the US in 1946, his eldest son, Crown Prince Ahmad, played an effective role in delaying diplomatic representation with Washington for his own purposes. He feared that any further contact with the Americans during the life of his father might deprive him of the throne, since his younger half-brother, 'Abd Allah, had better contacts with both the US and the UK.[38] The numerous opponents of the ruling Hamid al-Din family, displeased by the establishment of formal Yemeni–US relations and by the American medical care of the imam, whose death they had long awaited, also played a role in delaying a diplomatic relationship with the US. The Sayyids and Kadis, the two top tiers of the ruling Zeidi elite, feared that America would manipulate the ruling Hamid al-Din family by military force and played their part in preventing close

Yemeni–US relations. In 1946, after welcoming the American recognition mission headed by Ambassador William Eddy, Kadi 'Abdul-Rahman bin Ahmad al-Sayyaghi, then governor of Hudaidah, 'gave the impression that he thought Yemen was doing all right the way it was and that any changes brought about by Westerners would be for the worse'.[39] Another example of internal obstruction tactics was the implacable opposition from the minister of defence, Prince Ali, and other leading officials, including the foreign minister, Kadi Muhammad Raghib Bey to the supplementary agreement brought to Sana'a by Prince 'Abd Alla in 1947.[40]

In 1947 Saif al-Islam 'Abd Allah, Imam Yahya's son, returned to Sana'a from Washington bringing with him a draft of a supplementary agreement with the US, which proposed that the imam establish some infrastructural projects for roads and water. The British, as the Middle East Office of Great Britain in Cairo indicated,[41] protested, since they considered the supplementary agreement to be contrary to the spirit of the February 1934 Anglo-Yemen treaty whereby Yemen gave preference to the UK in all international dealings. Leading members of the Free Yemeni Movement (FYM) in Sana'a discussed the situation and decided to oust Imam Yahya with Iraqi support, in the hope that this might persuade the UK to support the change.[42] Influenced by Djamal Djamil, the Iraqi military adviser, the FYM believed that Iraq could mediate with Britain to put Anglo-Yemeni relations on a friendly footing, if it agreed to give preference to the UK in international affairs.[43] Yemeni officers, also influenced by Djamil, considered the supplementary agreement to be 'a Jewish plot directed against the Arabs'.[44] Thus relations between Sana'a and Washington once again failed to progress, mainly due to British influence in the Yemen itself. Opposition forces in Yemen began to collaborate, with some seeing the need to depose the imam before an American lifeline enabled him to destroy them.

The official US approach to Yemen exacerbated the hostility of both the internal and external enemies of the ruling family. The establishment of formal relations between Yemen and the United States played on this conflict and was a factor behind the 1948 revolution and the assassination of Imam Yahya on 17 February 1948. An influential Sayyid and the special secretary of Crown Prince Ahmad, al-Shami, maintained that:

> Sayyids, Kadis and Sheikhs plotted against the tradesmen and the peasants; Sayyids and Kadis plotted against the Sheikhs who lost part of their authority; and Sayyids then plotted with the Hamid al-Din family against the Kadis, who lost their high posts in the governing structure of

the country. Because of this background we were sure that Yahya sooner or later would push us out of his way. We were very sure that Imam Yahya, who was the first Imam to violate Zeidism, was going to get rid of all other Sayyids because he wanted to secure the rule of the country for his own sons. That is why we participated in the 1948 revolution and struggled for a constitution that might unite the opposition against the ruling family.[45]

'Although [it] never existed as [a] coherent and organized entity but rather manifested itself through a number of organisations',[46] the FYM was an effective instrument in limiting, if not preventing, cooperation between the imamate regime and the US. The organizations of the FYM that were established between 1935 and 1960 opposed, by all available means, the ruling Hamid al-Din family. They believed the imam had sought American assistance to strengthen his position against his subjects. That object was achieved by warning the imam of the disadvantages of relations with the Americans and by playing on his fear of foreigners. The FYM considered the Yemen–US connection a threat to its existence and its plans for future revolution. It condemned the establishment of formal relations and accused the imam of selling the country and its people to the most powerful country in the world, the USA.[47] For example, Nu'man and Zubairi, the FYM joint leaders, wrote to President Truman asking him not to support the imam against his own people: 'The Yemen population refuses all pacts made by the present Yemen Government which does not represent the nation's will. We request you to remember your statements that you will not make any pacts with governments which do not represent their nations.'[48]

The FYM was the prime mover of the revolution of 17 February 1948, during which Imam Yahya was assassinated and Imam 'Abd Allah al-Wazir was installed as the new imam to lead reform in the country. When the revolution failed, the leaders of the movement were either sentenced to death or jailed. Although secret and suspected members of the FYM were using all their powers to undermine the rule of the Hamid al-Din family, they opposed a later military attempt to replace Imam Ahmad by his brother Prince 'Abd Allah, whom they believed was a pro-US figure, because their objective was to rid the country of the whole family. On 24 March 1955 Prince 'Abd Allah headed a coup against Imam Ahmad in Ta'iz.[49] Although it failed, it provided the FYM with an opportunity to denounce the new imam publicly: 'The Free Yemenis denounced the coup d'état and announced that the new Imam was one of the agents of American imperialism and that he would put Yemen in the US sphere of influence'.[50]

After the failure of the 1948 reformist movement against the Yemeni ruling family, when Imam Ahmad assumed the throne of his assassinated father, the US reconfirmed its recognition of the Yemeni government and a Yemeni consulate was opened in Washington.[51] Yemen, however, denied permission for the Americans to do the same in Sana'a, offsetting this refusal by permitting a number of American scientific missions and expeditions to enter the country. A US Navy medical mission was allowed to survey health conditions and undertake zoological studies, and a major expedition of the American Foundation for the Study of Man, led by Wendell Phillips, visited the Marib area and undertook archaeological and palaeographic investigations of the remains of the pre-Islamic Kingdoms as well as oil explorations.[52] Because of a misunderstanding between Phillips and the Yemeni authorities the expedition was asked to leave the country suddenly in 1952.[53]

When Ahmad became the new imam after the aborted revolution in 1948, he sought to maintain an even-handed policy towards the communist countries and the US in order to secure armaments and to counterbalance the continuous pressure from the British. His initiative to improve his relationship with the US was welcomed by Washington, which extended its recognition to his government. In early 1952, efforts were renewed between the Yemen and American governments to establish closer relations, but these were resisted yet again by the British opposition. Between 1953 and 1954 there were several American efforts to establish a permanent mission in Ta'iz, but the US Department of State thought there was little prospect of achieving this for several reasons, not the least of which was the imam's refusal to allow foreign legations to fly their countries' flags over their buildings in Yemen. Congress would not follow the British example in allowing such a 'derogation of sovereignty'.[54]

Until the early 1950s, Ibn Sa'ud was able to use the leverage of oil, military bases and even the Soviet danger to ward off the Americans from his rival. In May 1949, for example, when Imam Ahmad initiated contacts with the Eastern bloc countries to obtain arms, Ibn Sa'ud warned the American representative in Djiddah, in an audience from which even interpreters were excluded, of the danger of communism, 'stating that he did not fear it at home but was concerned about its taking hold in some neighbouring Arab countries'.[55] He also demanded that the US restrain the Hashimites in Jordan and Yemen and stated that Yemen was flirting with Transjordan and Iraq and that Saudi Arabia might find itself encircled by enemies.[56] Since the major US concerns in the Arab world were the security of Israel, the containment of communism and the securing of oil resources for the industrial world, and since there was no US interest in Yemen, the KSA was able to block any possible US assistance to Yemen.

In 1955 there were signs of improved prospects for Yemeni–US economic cooperation, but this was still strongly resisted by Britain, which suggested 'Britain and America should agree on spheres of influence in the Middle East'.[57] In 1957, the US decided to provide aid to Yemen despite the attitude of King Ibn Sa'ud of the KSA and the British. The Colonial Office in London wrote to its legation in Ta'iz expressing the wish for the US to understand their difficulties with Yemen and therefore to refuse to help a hostile regime. But as 'Yemen was considered a target for Soviet penetration, it had therefore been placed on the list of potential recipients of US economic aid'.[58] Washington assured London that 'Yemen would not receive military aid, and would not be required to cooperate with the US in the military defence sphere'.[59] On this basis the British eventually concluded that they neither could nor should 'attempt to influence the US against continuing their project of economic aid'.[60]

Soviet penetration

Although British interjection succeeded in delaying Yemeni–US economic cooperation, US officials indicated that the lack of such cooperation would promote Yemeni–Soviet cooperation and increasing Soviet penetration in the Arabian peninsula. In late 1956 the US Department of State expressed its concern over the latest Yemeni–Soviet contacts. In a telegram to the US embassy in the KSA, dated 26 March 1956, Secretary Dulles pointed to 'increasingly frequent contact between high-level Yemeni representatives in Cairo and Soviet agents there, coupled with known proliferating arms sales by USSR to Near Eastern countries'; these factors were causing Washington 'considerable concern over real possibility that Yemeni–Soviet trade agreement signed on March 8 may well be a prelude to Yemeni purchases of arms from Soviet bloc'.[61]

Secretary Dulles advised the US ambassador in the KSA to bring the above thoughts to the Saudi monarch's attention: 'you may intimate to King that he may wish in interests of brotherly relations that exist between him and Imam to advise Imam against thus mortgaging his country's resources to Communists and exposing his country to manifold dangers of Communist influence.'[62] Two days later, a departmental memorandum which referred to the American secretary of state by Mr Wilkins, the director of the Office of Near Eastern Affairs, mentioned possible Soviet arms shipments to Yemen and suggested that Washington send a message to the imam through the Yemeni head of mission in Cairo, Abdul-Rahman Abu-Taleb, and also recommended that the department might 'mention generally to George E. Allen, Chairman of the Board of the Yemen Development Corporation, the critical state of our relations with the Yemen and the importance of early action on the part of his company'.[63] Within the context of US concern over tangible Soviet penetration in the Yemen, the US secretary of state advised the embassy in Cairo on the following day to inform Yemen's diplomatic mission that: 'Department likewise aware problems which exist between Yemen and United Kingdom and has, in recent talks with British, emphasized desirably peaceful settlement for all existing disputes in Arabian peninsula.'[64]

Relations between the two countries remained on a low level for nearly another year, but when Yemeni–Soviet cooperation extended to Soviet arms shipments to the Yemen, the US Department of State showed great alarm. Although in early 1957 the Yemeni deputy foreign minister, Sayyid Hassan Ibrahim, implied to British and American journalists that 'the US would not offer help except with strings unacceptable to the Yemen',[65] a memorandum from Mr Wilkins to the assistant secretary of state for Near Eastern, South Asian and African Affairs noted the following concerns with respect to Yemen:

1. At least one major shipment of Soviet arms had been delivered to the Yemen, accompanied by Soviet technicians.
2. Mineral concessions to Western powers had been matched by Soviet trade deals of unknown extent; some of these might have been fronts for arms deals.
3. Yemen appeared to have the desire to increase its ability to raid the Aden protectorate, but the lack of a Yemeni air force would appear to preclude any major Yemeni offensive against the British colony.
4. Moscow and Cairo flattered Yemen and gave it the impression that it was a major Arab power.
5. Yemen desired to gain from both sides in the East–West Cold War.
6. Egypt was training Yemeni officers in the use of Soviet arms, and Yemen accepted Egyptian assistance despite earlier Cairo's support of an anti-monarchical movement.
7. In assisting Yemen both Cairo and Moscow might seek to control the southern entrance of the Red Sea at a time of increased propaganda and reported economic activities by the Soviet bloc and Egypt in Ethiopia, Somalia and Eritreia.
8. Riyadh had granted loans to Yemen that the imam might use to purchase Soviet arms, and despite King Saud's anti-communist feelings there was no evidence that he was concerned about current

developments in Yemen, which he tended to see in an Arab context;

9. Yemen was the only place in the peninsula which had dealings with the Soviet bloc, and while Egypt was active in the Gulf sheikhdoms, its activity had not been matched by active Soviet interest.

10. Washington had not tried in recent months to initiate active efforts to increase its influence in Yemen.

11. Yemen had not asked for any US assistance. An application to the Eximbank for a loan by Yemen had been rejected.

12. The major private US company in Yemen, the Yemen Development Corporation, did not then consider that mineral exploration on its part was commercially viable.[66]

Wilkins recommended that the department ensure that the US government obtain accurate and necessary information about what was going on in Yemen and that it should 'take early steps, either through increasing the staff of the American embassy in Djidda or the Consulate in Aden, to provide personnel to cover Yemen exclusively', as well as undertake 'further reconsideration within Department of approach to government of Yemen on economic assistance through Point Four or a long term development loan for a specific project', and 'on military assistance through an offer of a section 106 reimbursable aid agreement with Yemen'. In addition to the summaries of factual information about Soviet arms in the country which were to be made 'available to King Sa'ud', the department should informally discuss the matter with the British Embassy in Washington 'and counsel the desirability of an early British–Yemeni agreement regarding the border with the Aden protectorate'.[67] Accordingly on 11 January the US Department of State informed US diplomatic missions in Djiddah, Cairo and Aden that the situation on the Yemeni–British border was under 'increasing stress' in Soviet bloc and 'Egyptian directed' propaganda and that there were indications that this might represent a 'coordinated Soviet–Egyptian bloc policy seriously to undermine British position in Aden area'.[68]

Such a diplomatic move by the US Department of State indicates that by the late 1950s the Americans showed sensitivity towards some events in Yemen. The change in the American mood towards Yemen was a response to the 1957 arrival of Soviet arms in Yemen as well as the establishment of a Soviet military mission in Sana'a in the same year. The US broke its silence in this year through fear of its Soviet rivals. CIA Director Allen W. Dulles stated at the 309th meeting of the US National Security Council, which was held on 11 January and chaired by President Eisenhower, that the situation in Yemen had heated up considerably and had been 'worrisome' in the last two weeks due to the fact that Soviet arms were on their way to Yemen, while the British government had removed some of its troops and sent them back home.[69]

This convinced the US that it should offer economic assistance to the country This was rejected. The imam wanted political support against the British, which the Americans could not and would not offer the king.[70] The continuous Yemeni–American efforts to establish cooperation and US diplomatic representation proved useless, mainly because of the lack of vital communication between the two parties, and because of the influence of the British[71] and the internal Yemeni opposition.

Conclusion

American diplomatic representation in Ta'iz began on 16 March 1959. It was followed by economic assistance, not military or political as the imam had proposed. Yemen's permission for the stationing of permanent US representation came out of weakness, resulting from the failure of negotiations with the British that took place in Ethiopia in July 1958, which were followed by the proclamation of the new Federation of South Arabia in February 1959. After these negotiations had failed, Imam Ahmad found it necessary to ask the US to intervene in his dispute with Britain. Washington did not aid him politically but instead used this opportunity to establish an International Cooperation Administration (ICA) mission in Yemen. It also provided 15,000 tons of American foodstuffs, sent as relief after a serious fire in the city of Hudaidah.[72]

Despite the private, informal and formal contacts that occurred before 26 September 1962, North Yemen was unable to develop or benefit greatly from its relations with the US. The failure stemmed in considerable measure from Yemen's rivalry with both the UK and Saudi Arabia, each more central to US strategic thinking and global interests than Yemen itself. But it also demonstrates the lack of diplomatic sophistication on the part of the imams and their family members who formulated government policy, and the limited capacity of a small, resource-poor state to influence the policy of an emerging global superpower.

After the Second World War the US emerged as a superpower, but the British, although greatly weakened, continued to claim great power status and served as a useful ally of the US against the Soviet Union; the US continued generally to defer to British interests in the Red Sea area until the Suez crisis of 1956. At Yemen's request, the US established formal relations with Yemen in 1946 and helped it to enter the UN in 1947, but permanent diplomatic missions were not exchanged between the two countries because of the opposition of the British, the enemies of the Yemen ruling family, and probably also the oppositin of the KSA.

Relations with the US continued to be characterized by frustrations and setbacks until the increasing volume of Eastern-bloc military aid to Yemen in 1957 alarmed the US, Britain and the KSA to the point where all agreed that Washington should step in with serious economic aid to Yemen in accordance with the Eisenhower Doctrine. Imam Ahmad had skilfully played the two powers off against each other to a certain point, but was unable to obtain military or political assistance from the Americans as he wished. Having, as it seemed, no oil, he was also not in a position to play off the Saudis against the Americans. The major interest of the US in Yemen from 1945 until 1962 lay not in the country itself, but rather in its relationship with Saudi Arabia, with its oil supplies, and in the global power struggle with the Soviet Union.

2

Initial YAR–US contacts

The YAR emerged in 1962 out of a complex historical context, the brief highlights of which include the 1918 termination of Turkish occupation, which in varying degrees dated from the sixteenth century; subsequent control by local despotic rulers; territorial disputes with Saudi Arabia; a strong tribal/clan tradition; claims on the British Aden Crown Colony and protectorates which now constitute South Yemen; sometimes strained relations between two different Islamic religious sects; a September 1962 military revolution with Egypt's military support against the harsh rule of the reigning monarch; Saudi assistance to the deposed ruler and direct Egyptian intervention as well as extensive Soviet military assistance on behalf of the new revolutionary republican government, which proclaimed its alliance with the Arab Nationalism Movement founded by the then president of the UAR, Djamal 'Abd al-Nasser.

The revolution in North Yemen, which proclaimed the first republic in the Arabian peninsula, therefore evolved into a regional crisis of significant proportions. It also triggered the involvement of regional and international organizations, and ultimately the superpowers themselves, especially the US. With the 1960s civil war the YAR became part of the 'international scene'. The American ambassador in Cairo said that: 'the civil war in Yemen which broke out in 1962 confronted the United States with a most vexing problem in its recent dealings with Arab affairs'. One of the American interests which were threatened by the Yemeni revolution was the petroleum resources at the head of the Persian Gulf – a resource of abiding interest to the United States. The impact of the Yemeni revolution was not confined to Yemen but spread to embroil Saudi Arabia, Jordan, the UAR and Great Britain.

On the eve of the Yemeni revolution in 1962 Sana'a–Washington relations were no better than those between Sana'a and Moscow; Yemeni–US relations were minimal: US representation in the country simply reflected the desire of Imam Ahmad to achieve a balance between the two superpowers to prevent them from interfering in his kingdom's affairs. Despite the fact that since the Second World War the US has preferred to protect its interests by forming alliances with conservative and monarchical regimes in the area, there were six main factors preventing any real relationship from developing between the two countries: 1) lack of US economic interest in the.country; 2) the opposition of the Yemeni elites to the US policy towards the ruling family; 3) the alliance between Washington and London, which prevented the US from supporting Yemeni demands in the southern areas; 4) Washington's support of Imam 'Abd Allah ibn Yahya Muhammad Hamid al-Din during the 1955 attempted coup; 5) the growing entente between the US and the KSA, which the latter successfully used against its rivals, the ruling Zeidi imams of Yemen; 6) the reactionary religious attitude of the Zeidi imams towards the outside world.

A republic in the monarchical peninsula: 'policy problem' in Washington

On 26 September 1962 North Yemen witnessed a revolution, one which the CIA 'did not forecast'.[1] The revolutionaries in Sana'a declared the first republic in the Arabian peninsula. The birth of the YAR was an outcome of 'the long struggle of the revolutionary element in the country that had been led by the Free Yemeni Movement [FYM] as far back as the 1940s [which had] come [with Iraq and Egypt's support] to a successful ending'.[2] The various forms of persecution, from which the people of Yemen had suffered under the ruling Hamid al-Din family since Yemen independence in 1918, led to the outbreak of the revolution,[3] which opposed 'a corrupt and despotic rule ... against the sloth and indolence of life in Yemen, a sloth that has been responsible for Yemen's failure to emerge from the dark ages. It was to leap forward in the life of the nation, after a long period of stagnation, from the dark ages to the progressive life of the twentieth century.'[4] In his study of the evolution of political awareness in North Yemen, John Peterson, an American specialist on the area, stressed that the roots of the revolution were contained in the pressures for change generated during Imam Yahya's reign, and that its continuing progress 'was marked by the unfinished search for a legitimate replacement for the old Imamate'.[5]

Imam Ahmad died on 19 September 1962 from wounds received from bullets fired by three members of the Free Officers Organization (FOO) who had attempted to assassinate him the previous year in the city of Hudaidah.[6] Muhammad al-Badr, the crown prince, became the new imam of the country. In a speech at the Grand Mosque of Sana'a, al-Badr promised to follow in the footsteps of his father and his grandfather in ruling Yemen. This statement contributed to his overthrow. The revolutionaries realized that they had to depose the new king before he took control of the army and before he executed those whom he suspected were plotting against his monarchy; they decided 'to eat him at lunch before he eats them at dinner', in the words of an Arabic proverb.

Although they opposed Washington's support of the Hamid al-Din family and disliked US policies that favoured both the monarchical and reactionary regimes in the area and in Israel, the leaders of the revolution were not hostile to the US and had no intention of running counter to US policy. The republicans' main concern was to change the political and social structure of their country and to improve the life of the Yemeni people. They announced that the YAR revolution 'believes in Arab reunification and Arab nationalism',[7] but their aim had never been to interfere in external affairs or to threaten the interests of the US in the area.

The idea of a Yemen republic was first discussed during the 1940s when four Zeidi Sayyids were consulted about replacing Imam Yahya. 'Ali al-Wazir, one of the four candidates for successor, failed to fulfil all the fourteen Zeidi conditions[8] for the imamate because he was a one-eyed Sayyid. He therefore suggested to 'make it a republic'.[9] But the idea of a republican Yemen only became serious after the failure of another attempted coup in 1955 and as a result of the developing Arab nationalist movement led by the former UAR president, Djamal 'Abdul-Nasser. Sheikh 'Abd Allah bin Hussein al-Ahmar, the dominant sheikh of the Hashid tribes and the first president of the Republican Consultative Council, stated: 'the idea of the republic sprang up after the failure of the 1955 coup d'etat, when serious thinking in this matter started. It was the 1952 July revolution in Egypt that guided the Freemen Movement towards a better substitute, which is the Republic.'[10]

The Yemeni National Charter pointed out that the 1962 Yemen revolution, although it was encouraged by Egypt, arose from domestic motives and objectives. This charter stressed that 'the revolution was determined to change conditions in Yemen for people of all walks of life. Its aims were set out in the following six objectives:

1. Liberation from despotism and colonial rule and their consequences; the establishment of a just republican government; and the reduction of class distinctions and privileges.

2. The building of a strong national army to protect the country and to safeguard the revolution and its achievements.
3. The elevation of the economic, social, political and cultural standards of the people.
4. The creation of a democratic, co-operative and just society which shall base its laws on the true spirit of Islam.
5. To strive towards the fulfilment of national unity within the framework of an overall Arab unity.
6. To respect the United Nations Charter and to abide by the laws and regulations of International Organizations; to adhere to the principle of neutrality and non-alignment; to strive towards the establishment of world peace and to consolidate the principle of peaceful co-existence among the nations of the world.

Counter-revolution with Saudi support

The new imam's uncle, Prince Hassan bin Yahya Muhammad Hamid al-Din, who was Yemen's ambassador to the US and the UN, left New York on 27 September 1962. Presuming Imam al-Badr dead, he declared himself the successor to the throne and sought British and Saudi support to regain the monarchy. Al-Hassan first contacted Faisal, the Saudi crown prince, who was in Washington when the YAR revolution broke out, and then stopped in London on his way to Saudi Arabia, where he convinced King Saud to help reinstate the royalists because a republic in Yemen 'would be a real threat to Saudi Arabia'.[11] At the same time he initiated diplomatic efforts to win the support of the US government, or at least to delay its recognition of the republic until the counter-revolution was able to bolster its position inside the Yemeni arena.[12]

It was subsequently confirmed that Imam al-Badr had not been killed but had reached Saudi Arabia: there he obtained political and military support for his counter-revolution from King Sa'ud and Crown Prince Faisal, who gave their support to the Hamid al-Din family's claims to the imamate. Yemeni royalist supporters, with their loyalty paid for in Saudi gold pounds, continued attacks on several pro-republican towns. The first diplomatic activity of Imam al-Badr was to contact the President of the United States. On 20 October 1962 'Ameer al-Mumineen al-Mansoor billah Mohammad, King of the Mutawakkilite Kingdom of Yemen' wrote to President Kennedy via the Yemeni Legation in Amman relating the story of his survival, expressing his own willingness to crush the rebels and informing the president that his forces had commenced operations against republican targets.[13]

British support to the royalists

The British decided to support the royalists because they saw that a YAR–UAR alliance would provide a base for political and military activities aimed at undermining the Saudi regime and challenging the British presence in Aden. For London, the YAR revolution took place at the worst possible time, that is, immediately prior to Aden's accession to the Federation of South Arabia, a project Britain was promoting to protect its own interests. Nasser's involvement in Yemen was too deep for Britain to ignore: 'Her Majesty's government would not be happy to see the Aden colony absorbed into a Yemen [which was] Cairo dominated.'[14]

London decided to oppose Yemeni nationalism and counter the increasing Nasserite and anti-colonialist pressures, which were backed by nationalist and communist movements elsewhere.[15] On 31 October 1962 British Foreign Minister Edward Heath stated that no action had been taken on the issue of recognition of the Republic because of 'the doubts we have about the situation in different parts of the Yemen, and about the control of the government over the whole country'.[16]

This argument reflected London's familiarity with internal Yemeni affairs. It thought the Zeidi warriors, if supported by money and arms, would produce 'disastrous' results for Egypt. The British understanding of the situation was that:

> Yemen differs from all the Middle Eastern countries in the degree of preponderance of religion, conservative xenophobic and warlike Zeidi tribesmen ... The Republic and Egyptians will never defeat the Zeidi tribesmen in their mountains. On the other hand, the Zeidi tribesmen might defeat the Republicans and the Egyptians in their towns and strongpoints. They surely can drag the war out at least as long as an Algeria-type war. And if the Egyptians withdraw, the royalist tribesmen will surely win.[17]

This British view was reinforced when Jordan and Saudi Arabia assured the UK they would support Imam al-Badr with arms, ammunition and money for as long and as best as they could. Thus both the British[18] and the Saudis, who held talks on the issue in London on Prince Faisal's way home from Washington in October 1962, made the survival of a republican Yemen dependent upon UAR support.

UAR protection for the YAR

To ensure the survival of the YAR, the revolutionary leaders were forced to turn to Nasserite Egypt for military and political aid. Yemeni revolutionary leaders, 'who feared intervention from Saudi Arabia and the British, informed Egypt of their plans to gain assurances of its support to ensure the success of their attempt'.[19] Nasser and the UAR responded to YAR appeals for help 'under the defence treaty of 1956'.[20] On 1 October 1962 the YAR deputy prime minister, 'Abdul-Rahman al-Baidani, warned the Saudis against making any attempt to cross into Yemeni territories in support of the deposed rulers and stated that any such Saudi hostile action might force the YAR to extend the war into the KSA.[21] Egyptian armed forces immediately started to arrive in Yemen. The first Egyptian ship, the *Sudan*, reached the Yemeni port of Hudaidah on 5 October 1962 carrying arms as well as 100 officers and soldiers.[22] By the end of the third week of October the number of the UAR forces exceeded one thousand. Although this initial military action was limited, it reflected a high degree of UAR political support to act as a deterrent against Saudi aggression.[23] When the counter-revolution commenced its attacks from outside Yemen's borders, Egypt announced its readiness to defend the YAR from any external offensive acts of aggression and dispatched more Egyptian armed soldiers to Yemen. By mid-October 'Nasser was replacing UAR advisors with Soviet-equipped combat troops',[24] whose number exceeded twenty thousand. Nasser defended this intervention on the grounds that the republican government was being threatened with subversion from outside – specifically Saudi Arabia, Jordan and the British. Egypt, which at that time was 'embattled by world imperialism and threatened by Saudi Arabia'[25] considered the revolution in Sana'a to be 'a blow at these forces'[26] and, therefore, lost no time in taking advantage of the opportunity offered. During the following month hundreds of well-armed Egyptian forces, less well-trained and equipped Yemeni fighters and the tribes of Sheikh al-Ahmar[27] became engaged in a battle against the royalist tribes in some northern and western areas of the country; 'this was the start of a bitter Royalist–Republican civil war which ebbed and flowed across the northern and eastern parts of the country'.[28]

UAR–KSA encounter by proxy

The arrival of Egyptian forces in Yemen brought Egyptian–Saudi rivalry, which had begun after the 1952 revolution in Egypt, to a climax. Parker T. Hart, the US ambassador to Saudi Arabia and minister to Yemen at the time of the birth of the YAR, said that the Saudi government was very alarmed and saw the arrival of UAR forces in the Yemen as a threat to its integrity,

because for the first time in a hundred and thirty years or more Egyptian forces were deployed in the peninsula. They have a feeling about the peninsula, similar to our Monroe Doctrine feeling about Latin America, that outside forces don't belong there ... a foreign force coming in (and particularly under these circumstances) to support a republican revolution, with loud propaganda over every medium, Cairo and Sana'a calling for the overthrow of the Saudi clan and the overthrow of the monarchy in Saudi Arabia, it couldn't be regarded as other than a hostile act toward Saudi Arabia.[29]

What the US minister did not mention was that the Saudi monarchy was afraid that the Yemenis, if they gained the necessary strength and opportunity, would want to liberate their three northern provinces, which King 'Abdul-'Aziz had annexed by force following the Yemeni–Saudi war in 1934. More important was the fact that a revolutionary and republican Yemen at Riyadh's doors was a serious threat to the rule of the Saudi royal family and the sheikhdoms of the area. The YAR revolution and the advent of UAR forces on KSA territory shook the political foundations of the Saudi regime. Edgar O'Ballance observed that at the time the Saudi military appeared to be more loyal to Nasser than to the Saudi family, and that between 2 and 8 October 1962, 'four Saudi aircraft crews defected to Egypt with planeloads of arms intended for the royalists'.[30] Some days later many high-ranking Saudi officials signed a memorandum urging the king to recognize the YAR.[31] A few days after that, it was reported in Cairo that four Saudi princes, Talal, Badr, Fawaz 'Abdul-'Aziz and Sa'd bin Fahd, had arrived in the UAR capital and formed the Committee of Free Princes, which called for reform and change in their country. To save the Saudi monarchy from collapse, the Saudi family quickly appointed Crown Prince Faisal prime minister; he agreed to form his government without any interference from the king.[32]

As the Yemeni revolution brought Cairo's presence closer to the KSA and other sheikhdoms of the peninsula, US anxiety was aroused concerning its interests and strategic position in the area. Washington was particularly fearful lest the Saudi–Egyptian encounter expand outside the Yemeni stage,[33] and perceived the situation in the context of 'this business of the so-called progressive Arabs versus the reactionaries with a strong socialist overture'.[34] In an attempt to interdict the flow of money and military 'surplus' to the royalists in the British colony of Aden and in Saudi Arabia, President Nasser ordered air strikes against towns that were serving as Saudi points of supply for the royalists as from 3 November 1062.

US response

The US response to the YAR revolution was cautious. Initially there were contradictory statements made by senior US officials and ambassadors within the Kennedy administration. Chester L. Cooper, a liaison officer to the National Security Staff with the CIA from 1961 to 1962, claimed that there was a tendency on the part of some in the White House to come out very strongly and very quickly in support of recognizing the revolutionary Yemen regime. Others, however, felt that 'either it wasn't necessary to do it quite that fast, or maybe we didn't need to do it at all'.[35] Parker T. Hart maintained that the question of recognition of the new YAR government 'did not arise immediately' in Washington, because 'the biggest concern was, what has happened to our own people[36] and what are the status of those people?' He added:

> Our earliest report made it quite clear that there should be no recognition until they treated us like a legation, gave us our security of communication, pouch, telegraph, protection to our personnel, diplomatic privilege. They were not giving them at first. They were trying to pressure us in to recognize as the price of giving us these. We said, 'Nothing doing. You will give us those privileges, and then we'll think about it.' And we held firm on that.[37]

On the same point Robert Stookey, the US chargé d'affaires in Ta'iz[38] in 1962, has stated that since there were about a hundred American engineers and technicians building the road from Mocha to Ta'iz and Sana'a, his concern was the security of this American community for which he was responsible. He also revealed the real source of his concern for this community:

> Since we were foreigners allied with the British, we were not on good terms with the new revolutionary government. There were no violent incidents but sort of incidents where Americans felt under threat from some force of some sort. So, that was a preoccupation of mind throughout this uncertain period before our government decided to set up normal relations.[39]

It was evident at the time that although US interests were not directly threatened by the civil war in Yemen, Washington was concerned about the possibility of a more overt confrontation between the UAR and Saudi Arabia. The US 'had a clear interest in the maintenance of a pro-American regime in Saudi Arabia'.[40] Confirming this, the US ambassador to Saudi Arabia, Parker T. Hart, minister to the Yemen in 1962, stated:

When the Egyptians came in with these troops and began supporting a Republic that was stridently anti-Saudi, frequently anti-American in its pronouncements, anti-British, calling for the expulsion of them from Aden, really beating the war drum, it began to be a changed picture.[41]

US concern was related to the presence of UAR troops in this strategically important part of the world. A study based largely on the official record and the personal papers of Ambassador Ellsworth Bunker, and supported by interviews with Ambassador Parker T. Hart, John S. Badeau, ambassador to the UAR and the YAR after the Yemeni revolution, and Ambassador Talcott W. Seelye, then in charge of the Arabian peninsula affairs in the State Department, who later assisted Bunker during the mediation mission of 1963, states:

> While it was recognized that the presence of the UAR troops in the strategic southern tip of the Arabian Peninsula was not a direct extension of Soviet power to that area, it was felt, nevertheless, that given the close relationship between the U.A.R. and the USSR, it offered dangerous opportunities to the Soviets. [42]

Ignoring the obvious need of the Yemeni people to overthrow the repressive imamate, Washington judged the revolution only by its effect on its own economic, political and strategic interests in the area and the YAR's connections with the UAR and the USSR. Ambassador Hart stated that:

> [the] Hamid al-Din family had thoroughly discredited itself in the Yemen. And God knows, they had. That was a regime which belonged to the Middle Ages, and there was no basis for supporting the return of that regime. Of course the Saudis claimed al-Badr would have been different. Well, maybe he would, but he had done very little before as Crown Prince to recommend him.[43]

The US was not specifically interested in the YAR as it made little difference to their position whether Yemen was ruled by a monarchical government or a republican one. Robert Stookey noted that 'the revolution of 1962 and the ensuing civil war greatly stimulated interest in Yemen's politics',[44] especially since the political outlook of the government and people of Yemen 'has important implications for the security and prosperity of the region'.[45] He concluded that 'the anxiety to promote stability in the region, rather than any direct stake in the country itself, has shaped US policies toward Yemen'.[46]

The encounter between the KSA and the UAR was, in effect, one between US and Soviet interests. It happened while Washington was involved in the Cuban missile crisis and in the Vietnam war, and when the Cold War was at its peak. The US considered the revolution in Sana'a an integral part of the Cold War and it became 'important that South Arabia ... should be neither occupied nor dominated by unfriendly countries'.[47] This assessment of the YAR revolution by the US is revealed in a then secret memorandum to President Kennedy from his adviser for national security, R.W. Komer, dated 4 October, 1962:

> the Yemen revolt has brought to a boil all Saudi fears of Nasserism (the house of Saud well knows it might be next). Faisal wants US backing for the UK/Saudi counter-effort in Yemen ... Our current Yemen policy is one of non-involvement. We can't do much anyway, and the Imam's regime was one of the most backward. However, Nasser clearly backed the revolt and his radio has been telling Saud he'll be next. So the Saudis are compelled to react ... Here the important thing is to reassure Faisal as to our firm backing of the House of Saud ... our policy toward Nasser is designed (a) to turn him inward; (b) to increase US leverage on him so that we can encourage policies less antagonistic to our interests and those of our friends. We do not think US aid (mostly food) is keeping Nasser in power. If we didn't help, he'd turn more to the Soviets, which would be emphatically against [the] US ... We think the Saudis themselves must press forward with modernization and development. Deliberate, controlled internal reform is the best antidote to Nasserism.[48]

As this memorandum reveals, the issue of the revolution in Yemen was complex for the US administration: 'the first thing to realise about the Yemen war, is that, like so many crises in the Middle East, it came with practically no warning'.[49] This is why it took the policy-makers in Washington as long as eighty-four days, which was 'a quite long time',[50] to study the novel situation of the first republic in the Arabian peninsula and to decide what official stance to take.[51]

As the Yemeni revolution generated new tensions between important Arab states, especially the UAR and the KSA, Washington was in a dilemma over whether it should withhold recognition of the new government, as the British had been advocating, or recognize the republic in the hope of curtailing the spread of Egyptian and Soviet influence there. It is important to note that at that time US diplomatic policy was aimed at moderating President Nasser's anti-American feelings. The dilemma was heightened because the Kennedy administration had been trying to improve relations with Nasser in order to draw the UAR out of the Soviet embrace. To this end, Kennedy appointed a Middle Eastern expert and director of the American University in Alexandria, John S. Badeau, as American ambassador to Cairo.[52] Badeau revealed that in respect to President Kennedy's wish to mend fences with the Egyptian president, who was seen as a 'progressive, non-

Communist local counterweight to Soviet expansion',[53] he personally prepared the ground for Nasser's visit to the US. The Yemeni revolution and subsequent UAR involvement meant that US efforts to win Nasser's understanding of the West were spoiled.[54]

In order to protect its access to cheap oil the Kennedy administration was interested in maintaining a stable situation in the Gulf–Arabian peninsula region and in forestalling any future revolutionary wave which might supplant the ruling families in the region.[55] It aimed to prevent the war in Yemen from spreading to Saudi Arabia, to counter a stronger communist presence in the area, to maintain stability in Jordan against the spread of a pro-Nasser element, and to protect Israel. The US took the view that the new 'situation in Yemen threatened the uneasy equilibrium between radical and monarchical forces in the area', and that if this collapsed 'it could have led to either a move for union, or domination by the UAR', which would create a serious threat to Israel and to Western oil interests in the Arabian peninsula.[56]

As a result, the US decided to 'stoop to conquer' by trying to remain on speaking terms with all parties involved in the dispute. However, the revolution, the counter-revolution and the KSA–UAR–UK–USSR involvement created a 'policy problem' in Washington: the Kennedy administration had to determine how to get the Egyptians to agree 'to pull their troops out in return for the Saudis stopping aid to the royalists' as well as getting President al-Sallal 'to quiet down his imprecations and his threats against the Saudis in return for recognition by us of the regime'.[57]

Initial YAR–US contacts

When the Yemen Arab Republic was proclaimed on 26 September 1962, the leader of the revolution, 'Abd Allah al-Sallal, sent President Kennedy a telegram that informed Washington of what had happened in Sana'a. Due to the poor communications system in the Yemeni capital, it was not cabled from Sana'a until the 30th of the month. Sallal's message, which was in Arabic but badly transcribed into a Roman script, read as follows:

BAAEWNAH TAELI KED NAFZNA RAGHAMT ALSHAB FI TAGHIR ALAWDAEA
ALBALIAH FI ALIMEN WKMNA BTATER NDAM ALHKM ALBAEID ALI NDM
JAMHWRI DAIMW KRATI AESSRAY IHAFAD ALI KRAMATH ALANSAN
WHKAWKAH WALI ALAEDLAH WALAJTMAEIAH WALMSAWAH BIN ABNA
ALSHAIB WAELNA KIAM ALJAMHWRAIH ALAERABIAH ALIMNIAH ABTDAN
MN IWMNA 27 RBAIAA ALTANI SAH 82 ALMWFAK 26 SEPTEMBER SANAH
62 WKDFAWDNA ALMAMTHLOUN ALHKIWIN LLSHAB BAN TSAR

ALAMWR WNSATLM ZMAM ALHKAM RITHMA ITM WDAA ALJAZAT ALJDID
MWADAA ALTANAFIZ NRJWA SIAD TKOUN TAKHZWA ALMAN BHDA
BANNA SNHFAD ALI JAMIAASSLAT ALSADAKAH WALTAAEAWN ALKAEIMAH
BIN SHABNA WDWALTNA MAA ALRAGABAH FI ZIADAT TWATHAIK ALSSLAE
ALWDAHAH WTKBLWA AKHLASS TAMNIATNA WAWAMR ALHTRAM.[58]

Ungarbled, Sallal's cable stated that the revolutionaries in Sana'a had
ousted the imamate in response to the wishes of the Yemeni people
and proclaimed a republic on the same day, and that al-Sallal had been
chosen to head the revolutionary cabinet until matters become settled;
it was hoped that the US president would be helpful to the Yemenis.

The first mission of the YAR foreign minister, Muhsin al-'Aini,
who was appointed to this post while in Baghdad, was to meet President Jamal 'Abdul-Nasser of the UAR and to contact the UK, Italian
and US ambassadors in Cairo. He met the US ambassador on 1
October 1962. According to Ambassador Badeau, al-'Aini stated that
past attempts by tribal sheikhs and military leaders to depose the
imamate had failed because they were based on factional support. The
revolution, therefore, had been delayed until widespread suprafactional
support was assured. He informed Badeau that the new republic was
expecting 'some trouble' from the border 'tribes with Saudi connections', but expressed his belief that the YAR was strong enough to
handle the problem. The YAR foreign minister also stated that the
objective of the new government was to bring about progress in Yemen;
it did not intend to 'dabble' in foreign affairs, but hoped to maintain
and continue friendly relations with Western countries.[59] Al-'Aini
specifically requested that the interview be reported to Washington.[60]
Twenty-seven years later, al'Aini told the present author:

> I explained to him [Badeau] the story of the revolution, its motives, its
> objectives and our hopes in Yemen that the superpowers would welcome
> the change and hence recognize the republican regime. Ambassador John
> Badeau's reply was 'we are looking into the matter and we will inform
> our government of your wish'.[61]

The American ambassador's response was that Washington's position
would be one of mediation, but he stressed US concern for stability in
the Gulf region and its desire to provide continued support for the
British presence in Aden.[62] This early contact with the US administration through the al-Sallal telegram and the YAR foreign minister's
meeting with US Ambassador Badeau, preceded meetings between the
Ministry of Foreign Affairs with the US chargé d'affaires in Sana'a.
They all indicated the naïve hope that the republican United States
would be of assistance to the republican Yemen in achieving its
objectives for the welfare of the Yemeni people and for the mutual

well-being of the two nations. But while waiting for a positive reply from the Kennedy administration to the Sallal appeal, the Yemeni leaders were disappointed to learn that it was an American citizen who first revealed that Imam al-Badr was still alive. Some of the revolutionary leaders considered this a bad sign despite the fact that this American who went by the name of 'Abdul-Rahman Conde[63] was no more than an American adventurer and a friend of the Yemeni royal family, especially Imam al-Badr.

According to the vice-president of the Revolutionary Commanding Council, Dr al-Baidani, the Yemeni leadership was aware that the Cuban crisis affected the superpowers' response to the Yemeni revolution and that the US might not favour a new involvement on another front against the Soviets for the sake of al-Badr, as long as the YAR demonstrated good intentions towards US interests in the area, and an awareness that Moscow was 'interested in seizing a great opportunity to counter imperialism in a very sensitive arena such as the oil-rich Arabian peninsula'.[64] To avoid an East–West crisis or encounter in the Yemen, the Yemeni leadership decided to make contact with the US. Thus, in the first few days of the YAR revolution, the new government rejected Egyptian advice to close the US and UK diplomatic legations. The Yemeni vice-president stated:

> I received advice from Djamal Abdul-Nasser to close the American and British missions because their governments did not recognise the Yemeni Republican regime, but I apologised, arguing that their existence in our country during war time is more important than in peace and that through these missions we can convey to Washington and London our intentions directly ... President Nasser asked me if I had ever heard of a similar event in the history of international relations, but I replied: why can't this policy, if it succeeds, be a contribution to international law by the Yemeni revolutionists?[65]

In Sana'a, the Yemeni government conveyed the same message to the US administration in Washington through the US chargé d'affaires, Robert Stookey. Recalling the content of these contacts, Stookey told the present author that the YAR leaders were urging his government to recognize the YAR:

> This took a long time, many trips by myself from Ta'iz where the legation was to Sana'a where the government headquarters was, before some formula was worked out that was formally satisfactory to us so that we could go ahead and recognize. Our government was concerned about the attitude of the government of North Yemen towards Saudi Arabia, what course had to be taken because the Egyptians were really in substantial

control of the Yemeni government, because the Egyptians were not at all friendly with Saudi Arabia.[66]

Stookey recalled that these contacts took place very soon after the declaration of the Republic: 'immediately after they took control of Sana'a, very early, within the first week', but that 'it took a quite long time for formal relations to be established between the US and the new government', because 'the principal preoccupations in Washington were the positions and status of the British in the Arabian peninsula at least generally, as well as the security of Saudi Arabia. And one principal issue was the claim of North Yemen to sovereignty over all South Yemen.'[67]

According to Stookey direct contacts between the YAR government and Washington were difficult at the time:

> This ... involved my travelling between Ta'iz and Sana'a every time to exchange telegrams between me and Washington on the subject of recognition. It was not a very comfortable situation for me because I had no faith in the ancient Yemeni planes that flew between Ta'iz and Sana'a, so I travelled back and forth by jeep every time and I was always received by the new leaders very cordially and the negotiations were very pleasant on both sides but it was an impediment to full cooperation on both sides.[68]

Stookey also mentioned that telegrams were the only way to contact Washington:

> There was no aeroplane service into Yemen at that time. The department was worried, of course, about the safety of my legation and the American community and they kept urging me to report every day by telegram. But at that time, telegrams sent from Yemen were the most expensive in the world. A two- or three-page telegram cost $1,500 for just one message, and of course I was not paying by a cheque or paper money. Only the Maria Theresa dollars. A bag of one thousand weighed 65 lbs. A three- or four-page telegram cost two thousand of these dollars.[69]

His important meetings were normally with President al-Sallal himself, but there was little privacy:

> I usually saw al-Sallal, and my conversations with him took place either in his headquarters, which were swarming with Egyptian advisers, or at the hotel at night, where we could talk with very few other people around. And it was very apparent to me how resentful al-Sallal was at the close control the Egyptians were attempting to maintain over him. At the end of one of our conversations in Sana'a, he accompanied me from his office to the front door, and one of the Egyptians was designated

to interpret ... Of course I was talking with him in Arabic and during
our walk down to the door the Egyptian soldier attempted to interpret
some remarks, so al-Sallal said to him 'yetkallam 'Arabi ahsan minnak'
[he speaks Arabic better than you do].

Although Stookey reported that the YAR was not in control of
some bordering areas, he assumed that it was in full control of the
country, and urged for recognition.[70] Some officials of the US Department of State in Washington, however, questioned his advice, pointing
out that all communication was being channelled through the Yemeni-
controlled cable system and therefore could not be trusted, and that
the British government was insisting on the strength of tribal support
for the imam's opposition to the republic.[71] Despite this situation the
Yemeni government pursued its contacts with the Kennedy administration. In October 1962 the YAR government sent two letters to
President Kennedy in an attempt to persuade him to recognise the
new republic. Several meetings between the Yemeni vice-president and
foreign minister, Dr al-Baidani, and Robert Stookey were held in Sana'a
to promote the Republican argument for recognition.

While diplomatic efforts seemed likely to succeed, Washington used
economic aid to induce apparently hostile regimes to create situations
more favourable to US interests. To this end, on 18 October Stookey
informed the YAR Foreign Ministry of Kennedy's decision to present
Sana'a with 20,000 tons of wheat.[72] Stookey told an interesting story
about the US present of wheat to the YAR:

> The food supply was in a very crucial state at this particular time. Our
> bags [of wheat] arrived one month earlier than the Chinese food supply
> which arrived in one of their bulk ships. Yemeni officials in the port of
> Hudaidah filled our bags all stamped with the US AID emblem with the
> Chinese flour, so a lot of the Yemeni people thought it was still American
> wheat. The Chinese were a little put out by this. This was symbolic. It
> was ironical rather than amusing for me.[73]

There was another indication of the improvement in the relations
between Washington and Sana'a. During a meeting held on 18 November 1962, Stookey delivered to the Yemeni foreign minister a list of
seventeen Yemeni communists who held key posts in the republican
government, and requested their removal. Stookey stated the list was
delivered because 'we see Communists behind every bush and so
forth'.[74] The Yemeni foreign minister assured the American diplomat
that there were more than forty-three communists in different positions
in the government, but that the government was not under their
influence.[75]

Muhsin al-'Aini,[76] by now YAR ambassador to the United Nations, was in New York to urge friendly nations to recognize both his government and the Republican delegation in the UN and found the official US attitude less than forthcoming. He travelled to Washington to try to arrange talks with Talcott Seelye, the director of Arabian peninsula affairs in the US Department of State. Al-'Aini told me that it had not been easy to contact the Department of State, and that when he finally succeeded in meeting Seelye he was only granted informal talks (in a restaurant located where the Watergate complex – incidently housing the ROY Embassy – now stands) 'because they wouldn't meet officially before recognition'. He added:

> I used the opportunity of being in the UN to take this initiative. At this unofficial meeting, I tried to convince him, arguing: 'If the US wants stability in the Arabian peninsula, it would be achieved by recognizing the Yemen Arab Republic and that Saudi Arabia and Great Britain should do the same thing. That's the only way avoid the escalation of struggle, dispute and the Egyptian presence.' I also told Seelye: 'If the objection is to the Egyptian troops in the Yemen, which is surrounded by enemies from south and north, it is only natural to expect the YAR to do anything to protect itself and seek help from any source.' That's why the Americans found that by withholding recognition Sana'a was forced to seek the help of another power.[77]

As understanding of the Yemeni people's cause slowly developed in Washington, the talks between al-'Aini and Seelye concentrated on the conditions of US recognition for the YAR. Seelye told me:

> I had informal talks with al-Aini about the condtions for recognition in November which were later outlined in the statement, and again in December when Ahmad Zabarah, the head of Yemen Legation in Washington, refused to give up the legation offices. We tried to disengage but the Saudis were not happy because they thought we were helping Nasser.[78]

In addition to the effective diplomatic efforts in Sana'a, Washington and Cairo, the Yemeni official statements were studied carefully by American policy-makers, particularly the threat by President 'Abd Allah al-Sallal in November that 'our massed forces have orders from the Yemeni Supreme Command Council to march into Djizan and Nadjran to regain Yemen's stolen territory'[79] and his declaration a week later concerning the foundation of an Arabian peninsula republic.[80]

The UAR aerial bombardment that began on 3 November 1962, in retaliation for the arms and money that the Saudis gave to a number of northern tribes that had entered the conflict when al-Badr returned to Yemen, had caused acute intensification of the tension between Cairo and Riyadh.[81] By 6 November, when Faisal broke diplomatic relations with Cairo, the situation had reached the brink of open war. This immediately caused concern in Washington. In reaction to these developments the US administration decided to bolster Saudi Arabia, which was threatened by internal and external forces stemming from the Yemen conflict. On 14 November Washington ordered some of its jet fighters to make a display of air power over the Saudi cities of Jiddah and Riyadh.[82] The military implications were clear to both the UAR and the YAR. At the same time, while the US declared its commitment to protect the Saudi Kingdom by all means, it tried to solve the problem by contacting the other parties of the conflict, in order to try to bring about a peaceful resolution to the crisis. It also continued to implement its diplomatic policy.

On 17 November, President Kennedy wrote to President Nasser proposing a peace plan and sent identical letters to King Hussein, Prince Faisal and President 'Abd Allah al-Sallal. Robert Stookey delivered Kennedy's proposal on 18 November to the YAR Foreign Minister. The main points of the proposal were as follows:

1. Saudi and Jordanian troops concentrated on the Yemeni border would 'gradually but promptly' withdraw;
2. the UAR troops would 'gradually but promptly' withdraw from Yemen;
3. some neutral body or third party would be brought in to guarantee that these measures were carried out – the United Nations might play a role;
4. the YAR would recognize its international obligations and would negotiate with other elements in Yemen to stabilize the situation in the country; and
5. the United States would recognize the YAR government and extend aid to it.[83]

Kennedy also proposed direct contact between all the parties concerned, and a possible observation or supervision of the disengagement process by the United Nations.[84]

The Yemeni royalists, whom President Kennedy had neglected, protested against this US proposal. Al-Badr wrote to Kennedy:

I am surprised to learn that you have sent letters concerning my country to the governments of Egypt, Saudi Arabia and Jordan, and also to the rebel Colonel Sallal, without consulting or even informing me or my government which is the legitimate government of the Kingdom of Yemen as recognized by the United States and eighty other nations. I must protest with utmost vigour against this unprecedented treatment of a friendly sovereign state, and can only suppose that you have been misinformed about the true situation in my country ... I ask you as a matter of urgency to send a mission of enquiry to the Yemen to ascertain for yourself the true facts as outlined above, before any irrevocable decision is taken by your government which might prejudice the future of my country.[85]

In London the *Guardian* quoted US sources as saying that as President Kennedy had not written to the imam, 'presumably he would have to accept exile, or battle on in the mountains without the support of foreign money or arms'.[86]

In Washington there were fears that President Nasser might 'have plunged into an all-out war against Saudi Arabia and presented the White House with a painful dilemma, whether to turn against Nasser or to betray the United States commitments to Riyadh'.[87] The essential American concerns in Yemen were outlined by US Secretary of State Philip Talbot in a letter to Senator Bourke Hickenlooper:

1. To keep the Yemeni conflict and its repercussions from spreading and endangering vital US and Western interests in the Middle East, outside of Yemen, particularly in Saudi Arabia and Jordan.
2. To prevent the development by the Soviet bloc of a predominant position in Yemen.
3. To encourage the prospects for a relatively stable and independent Yemen.[88]

'Only by recognizing the regime could we play a useful role in preventing an escalation of the Yemen conflict, causing even more foreign interference,' Talbot stated.[89]

The YAR government, which insisted upon a complete halt to every form of hostile activity on the part of Saudi Arabia and Jordan, and the withdrawal of Egyptian troops in stages,[90] stated that it welcomed the US administration's offer of mediation, especially if Washington was prepared to use its influence to prevent aggression on the Yemeni northern borders. To encourage a friendly US stance, al-Sallal, emphasized that Yemen had 'no aggressive intentions against the Arab people in Hidjaz'.[91] It is noteworthy, however, that al-Sallal used the term 'Hidjaz' rather than the official title of the country, Saudi Arabia.

Because of the UAR bombardments, the diplomatic efforts in Cairo, Sana'a and Washington did not succeed in achieving US recognition for the republic. On 14 December, the YAR warned that it would close the embassies and diplomatic missions of all countries that had not as yet officially recognized the republic.[92] The result was that the US administration decided to act without delay. The American ambassador in Cairo, John Badeau, met President Nasser to seek his assurances that Yemen would not be used to export revolution to the rest of the Arabian peninsula, nor to harass British positions in South Yemen. On 16 December the American chargé d'affaires in Sana'a met the Yemeni foreign minister to assure him that Washington was going to recognize the republic.

Nasser accepted the plan but said that clashes were inevitable unless Saudi Arabia abandoned its attempt to invade the Yemen. Nasser also said that King Sa'ud 'imagined the revolution in Yemen to be a battle between the monarchical and republican regimes', and 'with that erroneous impression, he launched himself with all his power and resources into an attempt to invade Yemen'. This was when the UAR had placed 'some of our forces' at the YAR's disposal, 'to help it face the fierce assaults'.[93]

The Saudis accepted the US peace plan only because they did not wish to appear to be swimming against the tide. This became quickly evident, because only two days before American recognition, reports reached Nasser of KSA preparations for further attacks on the YAR. In a letter dated 17 December to Field Marshal 'Abdul-Hakim 'Amer, the commander of UAR forces, who was then visiting Sana'a, Nasser stated that a plane loaded with arms and ammunitions had arrived in Nadjran on 16 December from Belgium, that a second would arrive on 28 December while a third and a fourth would arrive on the 30th[94]. On 18 December, one day before US recognition Nasser wrote:

> 'Ali Sabri met the American Ambassador at noon and it was agreed that we announce our statement at 11 p.m. tonight and that the American communiqué should be issued tomorrow ... 'Ali Sabri had informed the American Ambassador of the developments in the Saudi territories near the Yemeni borders, especially in Nadjran, which showed that Saudi Arabia would not commit itself to the Kennedy disengagement plan, because they were still storing arms and ammunitions and pushing in infiltrators and paying money to the royalists. The American answer was that they would use their pressure to ease Saudi support to the Hamid al-Din family. However, after the American recognition ... In my opinion, we ought to re-try to stop the Saudi activity politically.[95]

President Nasser's letter implied that the Saudis never intended to stop their support of the royalists and that their official acceptance of the plan was 'for political expediency only'.[96] The US minister to Yemen, then residing in the KSA, stated:

> This was cooked up as a formula between Washington and Cairo and agreed to, and then I was told to sell it to King Faisal. Well, he was absolutely furious; I've never seen the man so angry in my life. Here

we'd been a close friend of Saudi Arabia, and he was handed a *fait accompli*. He said, 'You know what the Egyptians are going to do? They're just not going to withdraw. They'll take advantage of the stopping of aid to the royalists and liquidate the royalists.' He said, 'I won't agree to it.' And he refused to.[97]

It was evident that US recognition was part of a deal with Egypt, which agreed to withdraw its forces from Yemen if the Saudis and the Jordanians ceased their aid to the royalists, US recognition was a means of containing both the UAR and the YAR from within. A statement by the US ambassador in Saudi Arabia concerning the British diplomacy at that time revealed the true US intentions:

> We're not so worried about the East Aden protectorate or, heaven knows, with the West Aden protectorate. And they would be supporting forces of radical change that they thought would affect adversely their interests in South Arabia. So they never could bring themselves to go along with our formula for disengagement. We tried very hard to get them aboard ... I question their judgement of the problem itself, whether it would have made any difference if they'd recognized the republic or not.[98]

US recognition and implications

As demanded by Washington, the republic declared it would honour Yemen's international obligations, including all treaties concluded by previous governments. The communiqué which was issued in Sana'a on 18 December 1962 stated:

> Since the first day of the Yemeni revolution, we have announced our sincere willingness to concentrate our efforts on improving the life of the Yemeni people and developing friendly relations with all countries. Yet, during the last few weeks we have found ourselves obliged to defend our republic against foreign invasion and against those persons who continued their contact with this foreign invasion and are obtaining its assistance and encouragement. These tragic events might have been due to the fact that some powers did not realize the factual principles of the Yemeni people and their objectives. Again, we announce that the YAR is still committed to this policy, which includes its respect of its international obligations including all the treaties signed by the late government. We are hoping to live in peace and harmony with our neighbours as far as they cherish this hope with us. Also, we call upon all our Yemeni brothers in the neighbouring areas to preserve law and order.[99]

Cairo responded by issuing a communiqué on the same day, stating:

The UAR confirms and supports the full contents of the communiqué released by the government of the Yemen Arab Republic. The UAR is proud of having extended full support to the Yemen revolution since the early hours of its outbreak, a support in consonance with existing agreements. Now that the Yemen Arab Republic has firmly established itself as the government of Yemen and inasmuch as we deplore the continuation of the bloodshed, the UAR hereby signifies its willingness to undertake a reciprocal expeditious disengagement and phased removal of its troops from Yemen, as soon as the Saudi and Jordanian forces' support of the Yemen royalists is terminated, whenever the government of the YAR should make such a request. To this we pledge ourselves provided the foregoing conditions are met.[100]

The following day the US formally recognized the YAR, not because of any American intentions to cooperate with or aid the new regime, but 'as a part of its political and strategic policies toward the events of the Yemeni arena'.[101] Chester L. Cooper subsequently revealed that there had been mixed feelings in Washington:

On the very day that recognition was to be announced, I had gotten some intelligence to the effect that the fighting was not going along as well for the revolutionaries as we had thus far been led to believe. And I made a fairly strong pitch to at least postpone the announcement of our recognition of the revolutionary regime at least for a couple of weeks until we could assess the significance of some of the stuff that was coming in that indicated that for one reason or another – either because we didn't really have a good feel for the situation up to then or because there had been significant changes in the capabilities of the loyalists – the royalists – that might indicate that it wasn't a cut and dried affair that would be over in a month or so. Unfortunately we had gone pretty far down the line by them. It was one of these unfinished problems. I got this stuff in time for the 9 o'clock staff meeting, and the recognition was to be announced at noon. And I just wasn't able to turn this thing off, or turn it around. And I am sorry I wasn't. As it turned out, two or three years later the thing was still going on unresolved.[102]

However, Washington recognized the YAR on condition that the latter honour its international obligations including the treaties with the US, the UK and the KSA and that Egypt withdraw its forces as soon as external support to the royalists ceased. The US Department of State issued the following statement:

In view of confusing and contradictory statements which have cast doubt upon the intentions of the new regime in Yemen, the United States government welcomes the reaffirmation by the Yemen Arab Republic government of its intention to honour its international obligations, of its desire for normalization and establishment of friendly relations with its neighbours, and its intention to concentrate on internal affairs to raise the living standards of the Yemeni people. The United States is also gratified by the statesmanlike appeal of the Yemen Arab Republic to the Yemenis in adjacent areas to be law-abiding citizens and notes its undertaking to honour all treaties concluded by previous governments. This, of course, includes the Treaty of Sana'a concluded with the British government in 1934, which provides reciprocal guarantees that neither party should intervene in the affairs of the other across the existing international frontier dividing the Yemen from territory under British protection. Further, the United States government welcomes the declaration of the United Arab Republic, signifying its willingness to undertake a reciprocal disengagement and expeditious phased removal of troops from Yemen as external forces engaged in support of the Yemen Republicans are removed from the frontier, and as external support of the Royalists is stopped. In believing that these declarations provide a basis for terminating the conflict over Yemen and in expressing the hope that all parties involved in the conflict will cooperate to the end that the Yemeni people themselves be permitted to decide their own future, the United States has today decided to recognize the government of the Yemen Arab Republic, and to extend to that government its best wishes for success and prosperity. The United States has instructed its Chargé d'Affaires in Yemen to confirm this decision in writing to the Ministry of Foreign Affairs of the Yemen Arab Republic.[103]

Washington observed that most of the Arab and communist countries, including China, recognized the republic very quickly and that the Soviet Union had gained a considerable foothold in the area through the Yemeni revolution. The US could not neglect its allies in the area who were supporting the counter-revolution but the Kennedy administration was anxious to change world opinion about its associations with reactionary regimes for the sake of its interests.[104] By recognizing the YAR, the US adopted a policy that would enable it to participate in shaping the future of the new republic.

Dana Adams Schmidt, the author of *Yemen: The Unknown War*, argues that the revolution of 26 September took place at 'a time when the "new frontiersmen" were anxious to escape from the stigma of American association with reactionary, feudalistic and sometimes anachronistic regimes in various parts of the world' and that recognition of the new republic was probably 'an easy way to help restore mobility of American policy in the Middle East and identify the US with progressive and popular forces' since 'if the US did not recognise the regime, there would be no major Western presence to offset the activities of the Communist bloc'.[105]

Patrick Seale, a British reporter in the Middle East, stated at the

time that the Kennedy administration was trying to associate itself
with President Nasser, hoping to win his friendship because of his
popularity and progressive reputation in both Asia and Africa. Recognizing the YAR, therefore, was meant to satisfy Nasser and form a
kind of association with the nationalist and anti-communist element in
the Arab world.[106]

Thus US policy after the Yemeni revolution was aimed at preventing
the Yemeni conflict from spreading outside the country and endangering vital US and Western interests in the peninsula, particularly in
Saudi Arabia and Jordan. It also sought to prevent the Soviet Union
from taking a strong position in the region.[107]

Stookey, emphasizing that the Saudi monarchy was 'under no threat,
no matter how shaky some people imagine it to be', commented that
Washington chose to mediate because of 'the communist element, the
British factor and the general impulse to be helpful to less fortunate
peoples'. He elaborated: 'We didn't want to see the British kicked out
of South Yemen at that time, even though the British were having
second thoughts about their position in east of Suez generally, we still
wanted to encourage them to stay on to defend Western interests in
that part of the world.'[108] He added:

> By recognizing the new regime and conducting normal relations with it
> we had a better chance of furthering our own interests ... as well as the
> British position. We could influence the new YAR government to main-
> tain decent relations with the British across the border in South Yemen.
> Normal relations would make it possible for any official to plead their
> case in Yemen. Without recognition we would have no influence at all.
> The British ... refused to follow our example and therefore the YAR
> forced them to close their diplomatic office.[109]

In London the *Guardian* expressed its belief that what made the
US recognize the YAR at that particular time were the reports from
Yemen that 'in the last few weeks Russia has been sending by air
equipment to Yemen that can be used in guerrilla warfare, and the
amount which has already arrived is three times greater than the
supplies sent by Egypt'.[110]

Cortada also reasoned that: 'In view of the United States government objective of peace in the Middle East, and policies designed to
deny the area to Soviet control, it became apparent that if American
influence was to be exerted on behalf of peace, it was important for
the United States to remain on talking terms with all parties to the
dispute.'[111] He concluded:

> An alternative to the recognition policy would have been continued
> support for the Royalist regime, the United States thus becoming a direct

partisan in the conflict, with unforeseeable consequences in view of the danger of an armed conflict between the Saudis and the Egyptians. The United States could also have backed away from the situation entirely and allowed events to develop without an American attempt to influence their course. The latter decision would, in effect, have been a signal to the Soviets that no obstacle was to be placed before them. Since a basic American consideration in the Middle East is to help keep the area free of Soviet domination, it would have been unrealistic, in the light of this objective, to remain aloof from trying to help solve the conflict ... When the United States recognized the Republic, it had become quite evident that the United Arab Republic had the capability of maintaining itself indefinitely in Yemen.[112]

Another reason for recognition, according to Cortada, was that 'tensions were developing in Saudi Arabia, in whose welfare the United States had considerable interest'. He pointed out that any KSA involvement in the conflict in support of the royalists, coupled with the general effects in Saudi Arabia of the Yemen revolution, was straining the fabric of stability in the kingdom. He stated:

In fact, there was evidence that even before the United Arab Republic bombed Saudi depots in November 1962, there was considerable opposition within Saudi Arabia to any kind of Saudi military venture. Saudi nationalists opposed the return of the Imamate, and many economy-minded Saudis saw financing of the Imam's counterrevolution as a serious strain on the country's financial resources at a time when economic and social development plans were about to be strongly supported by the government. Furthermore, Saudi army officers, aware of the country's military limitations, were concerned over the possible military confrontation with a relatively powerful United Arab Republic army. It seemed to many Saudis that since Saudi Arabia could not hope to cope militarily with the United Arab Republic, and since royalist forces were quite small in numbers and poorly trained, it was only a question of time before Egyptian aerial attacks would increase and Egyptian subversive attempts to destroy the Saudi Arabia regime would be intensified.[113]

Thus, according to the first US chargé d'affaires in Sana'a after US recognition, Washington's policy was a means of countering the UAR and communist influence from within the YAR itself rather than from outside it.

According to Cortada there were four specific reasons for US recognition: 1) the YAR's control over most of Yemen; 2) the YAR's undertaking to adhere to previous international agreements, among which was the Treaty of Sana'a of 1934 between the British and the imam; 3) the USAID mission, which afforded a means for the US to exert its influence in Yemen and which would have had to be withdrawn if recognition had not been forthcoming; and 4) the acquisition of a position of influence inside Yemen with a government which had evidenced a desire to work with the Western world, thus enabling the US to work more effectively for a negotiated agreement designed to reduce the tensions flowing from the conflict.[114]

There were also four narrower US objectives: 1) development of a situation which would lead to the safeguarding of American private and national interests in the Arabian peninsula; 2) prevention of the conflict's escalation; 3) termination of outside intervention in Yemen; 4) avoidance of further enhancement of Soviet influence in Yemen.[115]

International recognition of the YAR

Many other countries followed the US example and the next day, the 1202nd Plenary Meeting of the Seventeenth Session of the General Assembly discussed the draft resolution of the Credentials Committee of the UN. The meeting witnessed an acrimonious encounter between the representatives of the UAR and the KSA. The Egyptian foreign minister, Mahmoud Riyadh, pointed out that the General Assembly had before it the report of the Credentials Committee, which unanimously recommended the YAR to be accepted as the only valid Yemeni credentials, in accordance with the Rules of Procedure. He expressed his confidence that the General Assembly would uphold the recommendation of the Credentials Committee and that the Secretariat would be instructed to see that the delegation of the YAR occupied its rightful seat in the General Assembly. He asked the members of the General Assembly to support the lawful representation of the YAR in the UN. He went on to say that 'since the emergence of the new progressive revolution of the people of Yemen against the reactionary feudalist regime, the Yemeni people have been subjected to a brutal combination of the reactionary forces in the Arab world', and stated that 'all means of slander and terror have been mobilized against the peaceful people of Yemen and its new progressive revolution'. To explain the UAR role in the Yemeni arena, he stated that the UAR was duty bound to come to the assistance of the Republic to defend its sovereignty and its territorial integrity, and that his government 'could not conceivably be indifferent to the reactionary aggressive conspiracies designed to re-impose the monarchy which isolated the Yemeni people from the world and from civilization for generations'. Riyadh ended his speech by saying:

> In the Arab world, as in other parts of the world, there exists a decisive battle between the forces of reaction and the forces of progress, between

the will of the people and the reactionary regimes. It is the determined desire of the people to liberate themselves from poverty, injustice and exploitation. The victory of the forces of progress will be an accomplished fact in the foreseeable future. No effort to stifle the people and challenge the power of these new forces will be successful. This is what happened in Yemen, and any honest and objective observer could not but welcome the great achievements of the people of Yemen.[116]

The Saudi representative (in fact, a Palestinian), Djamil Baroudy, opposed the YAR delegation occupying the Yemen seat in the General Assembly. Quoting part of a memorandum that the Saudi delegation had received from its government and which he considered presented the facts as they actually obtained in Yemen, Baroudy argued that: 'ever since the rebellion of a small group of Yemeni citizens occurred on 27 September 1962 against their lawful government by resorting to armed force for the attainment of their objectives, the Saudi Arabian government has been watching closely and with deep concern the development of events in Yemen – and naturally so, because Yemen is on our frontiers.' He stated that: 'the main interest of the government of Saudi Arabia has been motivated by its genuine desire to safeguard a neighbouring sister state from becoming the victim of evil strife and civil war.' He also said that: 'the interventionist government seems to have forgotten or tried to ignore the fact that no sooner had His Majesty Mohammed al-Badr ascended the throne after the death of his father, the late Imam Ahmad, then he declared a new policy introducing various reforms.' The Saudi report denied any Saudi intervention in the Yemen affairs and declared that 'there is not a single Saudi soldier on Yemeni territory, nor has the government of Saudi Arabia at any time interfered by the dispatch of troops in the internal affairs of Yemen.'[117]

The Saudi representative also said that: 'The persistent foreign interference in the internal affairs of Yemen is likely to worsen the situation and cause the present conflict to spread into other countries.' He warned: 'Recognition or no recognition, the fight will go on in Yemen because the Yemeni people are fighting in their homeland.'[118]

The UN General Assembly adopted the resolution of the Credentials Committee by seventy-three votes to four, with twenty-three abstentions. It was clear from the debate that the US position led to the welcoming of the first YAR delegation to the United Nations. After the vote was taken, Muhsin Ahmad al-'Aini, who headed the Yemeni delegation, mounted the rostrum and expressed 'the gratitude of the people of Yemen and their progressive government to all the countries which have recognized us and supported our people's aspirations' and proclaimed that 'those countries have thus demonstrated their friendship and their desire to promote the well-being, development and progress of our people and our country'.[119] Al-'Aini also reaffirmed the YAR's adherence and dedication to the United Nations.[120]

On 26 December 1962 the YAR representative to the UN presented his credentials to the UN secretary-general, U Thant. On that important day in the history of the YAR, the old flag was replaced by the flag of the republic in the United Nations.[121] Al-'Aini, the first YAR ambassador to the UN and ambassador to the US, considered US recognition and support in the UN to be a very symbolic moment in the history of YAR–US relations:

> As you know, the annual meeting of the UN starts in the second week of September and the royalist delegation was occupying Yemen's seat as of the 17th of the month. It was necessary, therefore, to move quickly to represent the people's Republic. I arrived there to face this problem,' especially since the Committee of Credentials discusses the papers on the last few days of the session to deliver its report recommendations to the General Assembly in the last session. That's why everything continued to be the same until the end of the session. So we used the time to present our cause outside the hall, where we succeeded in getting recognition from many countries. President Ahmad bin Billah of Algeria helped us. And at the end of the session the US who recognized us on 19 December helped us to regain the seat of Yemen. There were many Latin American countries who were not for or against recognition, but when the US recognized the republic they followed its path. During the last session we took over the Yemen seats. Despite its strong connection with Saudi Arabia, the US stand was unforgettable in comparison to France or Britain, who recognized us only in 1970.[122]

Conclusion

The US response to the initial Yemeni contacts during the first three months of the birth of the YAR indicates the following: the emergence of a US policy towards Yemen independent from that of the British; the US foreign policy priority given to the KSA, where huge US interests existed (more than in Aden); and US concern over likely Soviet and UAR influence in the Arabian peninsula, which gave Washington a motive to participate in the Yemeni arena.

Independent US policy towards Yemen showed that its chief concern was the protection of its basic interests by diplomacy and by providing political and military support to its allies. According to an American source seven months later, in reply to the inquiry from Senator Bourke Hickenlooper in a letter of 16 July 1963 as to whether in view of 'the growing discredit of the republican government' American recognition should be withdrawn, US Assistant Secretary of State Philip Talbot revealed that Washington had never insisted upon the withdrawal of Egyptian troops once Saudi Arabia had begun to observe the terms of the disengagement agreement, but merely expected the Egyptians to 'withdraw in a phased and expeditious fashion'. He said that US recognition of the republican government was based on 'its control of the apparatus of government and most of the country, apparent popular support and ability to honour international obligations'.[123] However, such a statement was clearly not a full account of US thinking, because the US denied recognition to the People's Republic of China for many years while the latter was in total control of its territory.[124]

3

Relations breached and
restored, 1962–72

When the Yemen civil war began, as a consequence of the revolution and the counter-revolution, US policy towards Yemen was greatly influenced by the Soviet, Egyptian, British and Saudi positions. The Americans saw that the Yemeni revolution could provide the communist bloc, mainly the USSR, with an opportunity to penetrate deeply into the oil-rich Arabian peninsula. In 1962 the US administration therefore realized that it should work in cooperation with all parties involved in the ensuing Yemeni crisis. It even, in this context, decided to talk with the Soviets themselves. Unlike the Truman and Eisenhower Administrations, which maintained a consistent policy in the Middle East that gave little consideration to the Arab causes, the Kennedy administration worked closely with the main Arab states, especially the UAR, in order to limit Soviet influence in the YAR – a common US–UAR objective. President Kennedy realized that President Eisenhower and Secretary of State Dulles, in one way or another, were, in the mid-1950s, responsible for pushing President Nasser into the arms of the Soviets when they refused to provide Egypt with a loan to finance the Aswan Dam. In this respect Kennedy took an understanding and friendly approach towards both the UAR and the YAR. The Johnson administration swerved back to a more hard-line policy, but also encouraged contacts between the UAR and KSA. When these failed to produce results, Washington assumed a more distant, but not necessarily hostile, attitude (although YAR support for the resistance movement in the Aden protectorate did not draw the two together). Relations continued to deteriorate until they were broken off, only partially due to the Arab–Israeli war of 1967.

To achieve its objectives, the US recognized the republic and became part of the solution, working actively towards getting the UAR out of Yemen; preventing the USSR from having any real influence; curtailing Nasser's nationalist expansionist aims; and taming the

Yemeni revolution so that it would not affect American allies and interests in Saudi Arabia, Aden and the protectorates and Jordan. The American ambassador in Cairo, John Badeau, justified this stance:

> the object of American diplomacy was to create a situation in which the integrity and stability of Saudi Arabia and Jordan would be protected from the shock waves of civil war in Yemen. By entering the fray on behalf of the royalist cause, the two countries were committing their resources to a prolonged and uncertain struggle, and inviting an even sharper Egyptian response. Given this involvement, the question the United States faced was how civil war in Yemen could be confined to Yemen and defused as a threat to neighbouring countries.[1]

The benefits of the YAR–US relations during their first phase were very limited for Yemen because Washington's policy, throughout 1963–67, in Yemen was subordinated to its general policy in the Middle East as a whole. As David Ransom subsequently commented:

> What we were trying to do in the Middle East as a whole was to prevent a split between the conservative Arab countries and the progressive Arab countries, a split between the Soviet Union on one side and us on the other. It was called at that time a pluralization, which means that any dispute could become a broader, very serious, dispute. And in Yemen, we tried with recognition, to stand with one foot in both camps. And in fact what happened was that neither the Saudis nor the Egyptians were happy. Each kept pulling us. The situation was difficult for the US. Yes, because the situation was difficult in the Arab world. You have to remember the attacks from Egypt on Saudi Arabia and on Jordan ... Anyway the policy failed, because, we think, the government of Egypt went too far. Although to my mind, this is all speculation. After we were thrown out of Yemen, the British had already announced that they were leaving South Yemen, and the Egyptians were very confident and decided to stay. They also felt that they were coming into a new era where they have the backing of the Soviet Union, where no Arab could oppose them, and where they would be able to expand their influence in the Arab world.[2]

The break in diplomatic relations was relatively short-lived, for by 1972 both sides had an interest in their restoration. Sana'a, in particular, was anxious to reestablish ties with Washington for both political and economic reasons. The emergence of a radical Marxist regime in South Yemen, the YAR's sense of political isolation, and Washington's wider strategic interests in the area led to Secretary of State Rogers' visit to Sana'a in 1972 and a new agreement between the two countries even before the better-publicized US–Egyptian rapprochement.

Bilateral and regional relations

The US position towards the YAR, the KSA and the UAR immediately after the revolution is evidence that Washington was mainly concerned with protecting Western interests in the KSA and Aden. The US realized that the KSA's best interests would be served by leaving Yemen to the Yemenis, by convincing the UAR to withdraw its troops from the Yemen, and by convincing the Saudis to end their support for the counter-revolution. This was overtly expressed in a telegram from the US Embassy in Ta'iz to the State Department on 14 September 1964: 'US is willing to guarantee support of SAG [South Arabian government] territorial integrity if SAG cooperates in the proposed positive program. Conversely, if SAG chooses to intervene directly in Yemen, the YAR and its ally, the UAR, would be justified in retaliating and the USG could not make a commitment to defend SAG in these circumstances.' In another telegram to Washington, the US Legation in the YAR revealed the American position on the southern areas of Yemen:

> Considerable importance we attach to base dependent on wise UK handling of complex situation in Aden's hinterland, which UK sees as buffer zone for Aden and base. Conceivably ill considered UK measures toward SAF on Yemen could make continued USG support for UK position so impracticable as to lead USG reconsider importance of base itself. Above all we must not allow Aden develop into another Cyprus or Algeria.[3]

Once American and international recognition had been achieved, Sana'a was hopeful that this diplomatic victory would mean that both the UK and the Saudi Kingdom would withdraw their opposition to the republic.

But US recognition of the YAR angered Washington's allies in the area. The royalists, supported by Saudi Arabia and Jordan, launched offensive attacks on many northern areas. This led to the resumption of UAR aerial bombardment (which had been halted before the US recognition of the YAR) of many Saudi targets, including Djizan and Nadjran. On 1 January 1963 the KSA reported the UAR air attacks on 'its territory'; two days later the KSA ordered a general mobilization. Washington 'was concerned lest a situation develop in which the Saudis might ask [them] to come to their aid militarily'.[4] On 3 January the US Department of State publicly deplored the UAR air attacks and emphasized US interest in the preservation of Saudi Arabian integrity. On 7 January President al-Sallal summoned the American chargé d'affaires and warned him that Yemen would not hesitate to defend its territories.[5] In a reaction to the American and Saudi stances al-Sallal announced a general mobilization on 11 January 'to launch a last effective attack against the reactionary regimes in the area', which he called 'the dregs of the Saud, Faisal, and Hussein Houses'.[6] On 17 January the YAR president announced he was going to seek the support of Arab volunteers and claimed 'the Arab people and our friends the Soviet Union and the Eastern bloc are all backing the Yemeni people'.[7]

These developments coincided with greater pressure from the US allies in the area, who called for a US policy review towards the UAR and the YAR. In an effort to influence the US, the prime minister of the KSA restored diplomatic relations with Britain, which supported the royalists with arms and military advisers.[8] Even the royalists tried to influence decision-making in the White House. Royalist appeals did not change US policy towards Yemen because the US was aware when it recognized the YAR that 'the royalists had scored considerable successes but did not seem to have the weapons or the organization for a really decisive push'.[9] Royalist attempts to put pressure on Washington may, however, have influenced the US decision to encourage the UN to send a fact-finding mission to the YAR.

The Kennedy Administration not only supported the Saudi government's commitment to the preservation of the KSA's integrity, but also dispatched a number of jet fighters, a destroyer, and American paratroopers to express US determination to defend Saudi Arabia.[10] In early February 1990 the YAR ambassador in Washington said that Kennedy had supplied the KSA with arms only after the bombing raids of the Egyptian air force on Saudi supplies and when Riyadh was 'under real threat'.[11] US anger was also expressed through a show of force – an aerial demonstration over Djiddah in mid-January. In an interview on 25 February 1967, Ambassador John Badeau revealed that US Advisor for National Security R.W. Komer had urged 'much stronger tactics: possibly, letting American planes patrol the border and shooting any Egyptian plane that got out of line. By this time Yemen was called "Komer's war." I set myself very strongly in opposition to that course of policy.'[12] At the time the State Department declared: 'The United States, as an impartial friend of all governments involved, remains convinced that the best interests of the Yemeni people will be served by the disengagement of foreign military forces and termination of external intervention.'[13]

Vice-President and Foreign Minister 'Abdul-Rahman al-Baidani threatened: 'if the despatch of the American naval forces endangers the Yemeni revolution there is another military force which is no less mighty that will come to help us.'[14] Following this statement, which illustrates the deterioration in bilateral relations, the US tried to assure the Yemen government that it was doing its best to stop Saudi aid to the royalists. American diplomatic efforts succeeded in calming Yemeni anger during the following week. On 28 January 1963 it was announced that Sana'a and Washington had signed a new agreement concerning the construction of the Ta'iz-Sana'a road and the Ta'iz water project in addition to the study of other projects that might be implemented with US assistance.[15] On 2 February, the Yemeni Foreign Ministry welcomed the upgrading of the US legation to the level of embassy.[16] Five days later, William Polk, a personal envoy of President Kennedy, arrived in Sana'a, where he stated that his mission was not political but merely 'a regional tour of reconnaissance'.[17] Within the same year the US Department of State assigned to Sana'a a first secretary, a third secretary, an administrative officer, a public affairs officer and an army attaché with the rank of lieutenant-colonel.[18] A suitable building for the first American embassy in Sana'a was found in the spring of that year.[19]

Following the upgrading of its diplomatic representation, the US government tried to create a close relationship with the Yemeni government through development assistance, trade and cultural cooperation.[20] Despite this improvement in YAR–US contacts during the end of January and in early February 1963, the bilateral talks did not achieve a great deal. The upgrading of American representation in Yemen was not in itself enough to cement YAR–US relations completely.

As a result of this situation, which provided US diplomacy in the Middle East with 'its greatest challenge since Suez',[21] the US continued to play what was seen as 'an ambiguous role'.[22] The US ambassador to Saudi Arabia and minister to Yemen, Parker Hart, who indicated that Washington expected Egyptian withdrawal from Sana'a in return for recognition, later explained his government's stance:

> Nasser didn't repay our recognition of the YAR very well ... in February of '63, in the middle of the night – believing, with false intelligence, that there was a big resistance group on his side that could be helped – he dropped by parachute force a hundred and eight bundles of ready-to-go weapons and ammunition on the Saudi coast north of [D]jidda where they were spotted in the early hours of the morning by an American special forces mission flying with Saudis on a training flight ... this deepened, of course, the feeling of distrust in Washington of Nasser's intentions.[23]

According to the US chargé d'affaires, Robert Stookey, another factor that contributed to the uneasy YAR–US relations 'was that when the British were expelled we were in charge of their interests and there were incursions from the territory of Sherif Beihan across the border into the Yemen and things of that sort'.[24] Muhsin Al-'Aini doubted that Sana'a benefited from US recognition because of the very high tension in the area during that period.[25]

US concern over the effects of the Yemen conflict on the KSA increased further when a military coup on 8 February 1963 deposed the Kassim regime in Iraq. The leader of the coup, 'Abdul-Salam 'Arif, announced his support for Nasserism. This seriously threatened the existence of the sheikhdoms and the Saudi and Jordanian monarchical governments. Thirty days later another pro-UAR coup occurred in Syria. Although the Syrian revolution did not directly threaten the KSA, it was clear that pro-Nasser governments in countries close to Israel and the Gulf sheikhdoms – at a time when Nasser was trying to provoke revolution in Riyadh – did not fit in with US foreign policy in the region. As a US study of the Yemeni crisis stated:

> Nasser was a popular, charismatic figure whose doctrine of Arab unity had great appeal to many Arabs who looked upon the Egyptian leader as a twentieth-century Muhammad or Saladin ... In view of these perceived threats from the outside, the US urged Faisal not only to disengage from Yemen but to concentrate on internal reforms which would bolster his own political position within Saudi Arabia.[26]

On 8 February 1963 Washington again stressed the importance it attached to Saudi Arabia by releasing a letter that President Kennedy had sent on 25 October 1962 to Saudi Crown Prince Faisal, who as Viceroy was the *de facto* ruler of the monarchy while King Saud was in Europe. This letter pledged full American support for the maintenance of Saudi territorial integrity.[27] This was followed by repeated private assurances that the US was making the greatest efforts to get Nasser to end his air attacks on Saudi territory. However, it had to be recognized that 'not only the UAR but also Saudi Arabia was intervening in Yemen'.[28]

On 9 February it was announced in Sana'a that USSR representation had been upgraded to the level of embassy.[29] On 22 February President al-Sallal warned that he would support any popular revolution in the Arabian Peninsula against Saud and his brother Faisal.[30]

On 27 February, in a reaction to developments in Yemen, Iraq and Syria, Kennedy approved the sending of a special emissary to Prince Faisal to reassure him of US interest in Saudi Arabia and to convince him of the importance of disengaging from Yemen. The memorandum authorized the emissary to inform the king that the US would consider stationing a temporary air defence squadron in Saudi Arabia to deter UAR air operations.[31]

Meanwhile, correspondence between Kennedy and Nasser continued. This indicated that Saudi Arabia did not accept the American disengagement plan and that the US could not force it to do so. The US president urged Nasser to withdraw his forces from Yemen. Nasser refused on the grounds that the KSA was continuing to give aid to the royalists. He stressed that the basic aim behind the dispatch of Egyptian forces to Yemen was to stop any invasion of the YAR. Defending his policy toward Yemen, Nasser wrote a letter to Kennedy on 3 March 1963 in which hesaid he trusted the sincere efforts of the US president regarding the conflict between the KSA and the YAR, but he could not tie his hands and just watch Saud invade Yemen, or the fierce assaults of the British on the Yemeni people.[32] But he declared his interest in achieving peace and avoiding an armed clash with the KSA through American mediation:

> The UAR certainly seeks no war with Saudi Arabia along the Yemeni borders. The historic difference between [the KSA and the UAR] is not the kind to be settled by armed clash. The difference is much deeper: its roots are well imbedded in the depths of the social conditions prevailing in the Arab world, with hopes in the future striving to break away from the remnants and residue of the past to forge an honourable future for the Arab human being, owner and master of his land.[33]

The Kennedy administration believed it was possible to persuade the governments of the UAR and the KSA to disengage from the Yemeni conflict because it was very much in their interests to do so. The only problem was 'how to find a formula which would prove face-saving for both parties?'[34] Washington felt that the best approach was 'to persuade the UN to become concerned with the Yemen question as a threat to peace, and to use its influence in helping to calm down the situation'.[35] The US succeeded in getting the UN to send Dr Ralph Bunche, the United Nations under-secretary for special political affairs, to the area in early March on a fact-finding mission on behalf of the UN secretary-general. George McGhee, former US under-secretary for political affairs, explained Washington's reasons: 'The Department and the President had become concerned about the Yemeni affair largely because of the introduction of large number of UAR troops. We feared that if this build-up continued there might ultimately be war between the UAR troops in the Yemen, and Saudi Arabia, who was supplying the Royalist forces.'[36]

Washington was convinced that the royalists could not win and that the UAR could not be driven out of the YAR except by direct full-scale military intervention by the UK or other Western powers. In addition, the US administration was unable to assess reactions to the Yemen republic in other parts of the Arab world, and was particularly ignorant of internal political developments in the UAR. Washington believed that further instability and bloodshed in Yemen, which was not in the interest of the KSA or the UK, might well spread across borders. The longer the massive UAR military presence was required because of the security threat to the YAR, 'the more firmly entrenched Nasser becomes and the less authoritative become the voices of the Yemeni moderates, such as al-Iryani, Zubairi, Nu'man and 'Uthman'.[37] Nasser could not be bled to death but had to be allowed to withdraw with honour; if war was prolonged it was al-Badr and his supporters who were more likely to bleed to death. It was realized that there was a little chance of a compromise Yemeni government that would include the Hamid al-Din family and that the moderate YAR leaders, who were more Yemeni than Arab nationalist, had no designs on Saudi territory nor any basic antipathy towards the Saudi monarchy, but wanted cordial relations with the South Arabian Federation (SAF) government and friendly relations as well as help from the UK. Washington felt that the moderate Yemeni leaders would agree to establish a 'Dawlat al-Yaman' (State of Yemen) instead of the YAR that would exclude both al-Sallal and al-Badr. It was also expected that, if the Yemenis were left alone, 'a strong Zeidi leader might sooner or later restore [a] reconstituted monarchy or at least [a] spiritual Imamate, applicable to tribal society'.[38]

To prepare the way for a US mediation mission to be led by the diplomat Ellsworth Bunker, the US ambassador in Cairo, John Badeau, wrote to Nasser on 4 March requesting that the UAR suspend its air attacks on Saudi Arabia during the Bunker–Bunche efforts. Badeau told the UAR president that President Kennedy considered the Yemen dilemma a test case for Cairo–Washington cooperation in the Middle East and that Washington did not object to Nasser's commitment to protect the YAR revolution as long as the affair was contained within Yemen.[39] Nasser replied that Cairo's involvement was 'more costly than had been envisioned and that he was anxious to remove his troops from the YAR' provided the US persuaded the KSA to accept the disengagement plan. He agreed to suspend air attacks on Saudi supplies to the royalists during 'the course of the American-sponsored mediation exercise'.[40]

The UN mission under Ralph Bunche, known as 'an American-instigated mediation effort by the UN',[41] began to alleviate the crisis. It was clear that US recognition had paved the way for the UN to take a role in resolving the conflict and for reducing the chances of the struggle endangering world peace. Bunchearrived in Ta'iz on 1 March. He visited many parts of the country, including the Aden colony, and was disheartened by the conditions of the Yemeni people but moved by the warm welcome he received. In Sana'a he met President al-Sallal and 'Abdul-Hakim 'Amir, the deputy supreme commander of the UAR armed forces.

After this visit Bunche announced that the republic was in effective control of the country and persuaded the UN fact-finding Mission of this. He even asserted that the YAR had a right to call in Egyptian troops to help deal with the Saudi-backed royalists, and that the Egyptians had not tried to interfere in Yemeni affairs.[42] Bunche's findings were not accepted by the royalists or the Saudis and the latter refused to accept that either the US or the UN could play the role of neutral mediator.

Bunker mission, 1963

With the approval of the US president, the US Department of State decided to play a more direct role. First, it dispatched Terry Duce, an ex-vice-president of the Arabian–American Oil Company (ARAMCO), 'who was highly respected by the Saudis', to talk with Prince Faisal and 'to see what he could do to try to find a bridge with Faisal and with the Saudis that could be useful in bringing about a disengagement on the Saudi side if there were a disengagement on the Egyptian side'.[43] But his efforts failed.

US efforts continued when Ellsworth Bunker,[44] a former American ambassador, was sent to the area in March 1963 to reduce the pace of hostilities and to prepare the way for a UN peace-observing mission. US planes and warships were sent to bolster the Saudi position in an operation called 'Hard Surface', while Bunker flew to Riyadh to assure the Saudi government of US support. This threatened to turn Yemen into a stage for a full-scale civil war with republicans supported by Egypt and the Soviet Union, and the royalists supported by the KSA, Britain, Jordan, Morocco and the US. On 6 March 1963, Bunker initiated talks with Prince Faisal of Saudi Arabia to persuade him to support the UN mediation effort. Bunker returned to the region three weeks later to negotiate with Faisal the cessation of Saudi assistance to the Yemeni royalists while, at the same time, seeking from Nasser a phased withdrawal of UAR troops. Bunker's presence was part of Kennedy's general policy of using high-ranking Americans to inject US influence and prestige.[45] On 1 April 1963 Bunker initiated talks with President Nasser. On 5 April he returned to Riyadh, and four days later he returned to Cairo where he successfully obtained a dis-engagement agreement which he delivered to the UN secretary-general on 13 April.[46] Bunker obtained the agreement of all parties concerned on a withdrawal of most UAR troops and a cessation of Saudi assistance to the royalists. Both sides also agreed on the stationing of neutral troops on the Saudi side of the border, at Yemeni airports and at the port of Hudaidah.[47] Though successful on reaching an agreement, the former US ambassador did not use straightforward mediation methods in either Djiddah or Cairo. From examining the personal papers of the US emissary, Christopher McMullen observed an extraordinary feature of Bunker's *modus operandi* regarding:

> his use of papers detailing the points to be agreed, which in each case left out – to be covered in oral pleadings – a point that was most sensitive to his interlocutors: In the case of Nasser, the proposal that he handed him did not include the element of simultaneity (which was resolved eventually by Nasser's agreement to an initial token withdrawal), and in the case of Faisal the proposal handed to him on 5 April did not include the element of restrictions on the activities of the Yemeni royal family (which was resolved by a carefully worded clause in the agreement).[48]

The terms of the agreement announced by the UN secretary-general in his report to the Security Council, dated 29 April 1963, were as follows:

1. A demilitarized zone was to be established and extended twenty kilometres on either side of the demarcated Saudi Arabian-Yemeni border from which all military and para military forces and military equipment were to be excluded.
2. An agreement was to take place over the stationing of United Nations observers within this zone on both sides of the border to observe, report on and prevent any continued attempt by the Saudi Arabians to supply Royalist forces with arms and supplies.
3. Simultaneously, the United Arab Republic would begin a phased withdrawal of all its troops from Yemen to take place as soon as possible. The United Arab Republic would also abstain from taking punitive action against the royalists for any assistance prior to the disengagement and would likewise put an end to any actions on Saudi Arabian territory.[49]

Washington's assessment of the YAR's military strength without UAR backing was accurate. In their interventionist policy, they emphasized that the Yemenis should be isolated because they knew that this would enable the Saudis, Great Britain and Jordan to defeat the Nasserite element in Yemen. The US Embassy in Cairo stated some time later in 1964 that though the Bunker agreement did not succeed 'in bringing about withdrawal of the UAR troops,' it had 'given Faisal breathing room to strengthen his internal position and had averted a KSA–UAR confrontation.'[50]

UN Observation Mission, 1963

These US and UN mediation efforts resulted in the UN–Yemen Observation Mission, whose task was to supervise the disengagement plan which had been proposed originally by the Kennedy Administration. On 30 April 1963 the UN appointed Major-General Von Horn, chief of staff of the UN Truce Supervision Organization, to consult with the relevant governments on the details of setting up a UN Observation Mission.[51] He arrived in the area in late May to observe whether the disengagement agreement was being complied with.[52] An observation group of about two hundred personnel was initially agreed upon; this was later reduced for security reasons. The units were furnished mainly by Canada, Sweden and Yugoslavia. The UAR and the KSA agreed to finance the mission.

In reaction to the US and UN efforts to bring about peace in the peninsula, the royalists, backed by the Saudis, tried to gain control of some northern areas of Yemen to demonstrate their existence and to demand that they should be part of the solution. Sana'a confirmed that the UAR and YAR air forces had bombed Saudi targets, where the rebels were gathering to cross the border.[53] As a result, American military units engaged in joint manoeuvres with Saudi military personnel in May 1963: however, in the words of one authority, 'no decisive American reaction occurred, in part due to Saudi refusal to permit the stationing of Jewish personnel among the American military forces there due to its open opposition to Israel, and partially because the UAR operations did not threaten the survival of the Saudi monarchy'.[54]

In June 1963 the UN observation units arrived, and on 4 July the mission was officially established and commenced operations. On 15 July 1963 the US sent an air defence squadron of eight F-100s to the KSA, where it remained until 1 January 1964: 'its orders were to conduct a training exercise with the Saudi air force as part of our overall effort to improve Saudi defense forces and as evidence of continuing US interest in the security of the country. The squadron was also to provide a limited air defense capability.'[55] The most important role to be played by the UN group was to prevent any direct clash between the UAR and the KSA forces. At the same time the US government urged the two countries to cooperate with the UN efforts. The UN Mission continued its work until 4 September 1964, but due to difficulties, such as Saudi Arabia withholding instalments of the mission expenses, it ultimately failed.

To implement the Bunker agreement Washington instructed its embassies in Djiddah, Cairo, Ta'iz and London to persuade the UK to maintain the 'moratorium on assistance to Yemeni royalists' and to 'dissuade' the KSA 'from any action to renew aid which it might be tempted to take in view [of] reports [on] royalists suffering serious military reverses' while pressing on the UAR the need to withdraw its forces from Yemen.[56]

On 22 November President John F. Kennedy was assassinated; under Lyndon Johnson, Washington's policy towards President Nasser, and towards the Arab world in general, changed. The Johnson administration gave the Israelis and the Saudis a free hand in the area as well as stronger American commitment to protect their security. The Saudi prime minister and ruler *de facto*, Faisal, adopted a tough strategy towards both the YAR and the UAR and received all the necessary political, economic and military support from Washington:

> Faisal was favored by a rapid increase in revenues during the first two years of his reign, which rose at about double the 11 percent annual rate of the previous two years. It was clear that the increase, which [was] derived mainly from greater oil production, was the result of a deliberate move by ARAMCO and its parent companies to help Faisal. It was clear then that the American government [had] adopted a more cooperative attitude toward Faisal's strategy. Disappointed by Kennedy's attempt to woo Nasser, the United States under President Johnson was more willing to support Faisal's plan to build up the Saudi armed forces.[57]

To counter Nasser's Arab Nationalist Movement, Faisal, backed by Iran and Jordan, called for and sponsored what became known as 'the Islamic Conference Organization' in an attempt 'to widen the scope of regional politics to include non-Arab Muslim states, such as Iran and Pakistan, and thus to dilute Egypt's dominance of Arab politics.' In the case of the neighbouring republic, Faisal encouraged some traditional Yemeni tribes to counter the YAR and the UAR from within.[58]

The outbreak of guerrilla warfare against the British in the southern areas of Yemen on 14 October 1963 encouraged Cairo to extend the presence of its forces in the YAR, and the subsequent YAR and UAR support to the guerrillas caused concern in Washington. On 28 May 1964, Washington instructed its chargé d'affaires in Ta'iz to:

> reiterate that the US was motivated by the desire that Yemen be fully independent and able to control its own destiny. The Chargé was to urge the Yemenis to meet with British representatives under United Nations auspices for the purpose of considering [the] creation of a demilitarized zone. He was also instructed to urge the Yemeni government to make known directly to the Saudis its desires for peaceful relations.[59]

The American Embassy in Cairo revealed that Washington instructed the UN representative in Yemen, assisted by the US and probably by others, to prepare for talks with the KSA, the UAR, the UK and the YAR concerning the normalization of relations between the republic and the UK.[60]

In January 1964 an Arab summit meeting was held in Cairo; President Nasser and King Saud met and discussed a reconciliation. This resulted in the resumption of diplomatic relations between Cairo and Riyadh on 3 March 1964. The YAR president met King Saud at the same summit but nothing concrete in Riyadh–Sana'a relations resulted. The restoration of diplomatic relations between Cairo and Riyadh was not welcomed by the crown prince and resulted in an inter-Saudi conflict between King Saud and Prince Faisal, which showed Faisal's greater influence. This undermined the UAR–KSA reconciliation and thus fighting in Yemen continued.

On 14 April 1964 President al-Sallal returned from his tour to the Eastern bloc, where he had sought military assistance.[61] His tour had not been approved by Cairo and this led to President Nasser's visit to Sana'a. During Nasser's visit it was announced that the YAR president had decided to delay a second official trip to the Eastern bloc, scheduled for the following month, in order to attend the Aswan Dam celebrations in Egypt on 14 May 1964.[62] In Cairo, President al-Sallal succeeded in persuading Egypt that a further tour of the Eastern bloc would be fruitful and he left for Warsaw on 20 May and for Budapest on 26 May. It was reported later that he had arrived in Beijing on 9 June.[63] This is evidence that the UAR, which had until now preferred to keep the Eastern bloc as far as possible from peninsula affairs, now chose to engage it more directly in the Yemeni conflict in order to secure additional support for republican Sana'a.

On 25 May 1964, Washington instructed its embassy in Cairo[64] to express concern over the failure of the UAR to make even a token withdrawal and to urge it to do so.[65] But the situation on the ground continued unaltered. The American Embassy in Ta'iz noted that unless the second Nasser–Faisal summit resolved the Yemen question, the prospects for escalation of the Yemen conflict in the south as well as in the north were 'more alarming than at any time since before the disengagement agreement'.[66] The US government supported a Faisal–Nasser reconciliation because this would mean a containment of the Nasserite threat and of the Soviet threat of greater involvement in the Arabian peninsula.[67]

During an Arab summit in Alexandria on 14 September 1964, President Nasser and Crown Prince Faisal jointly pledged cooperation to settle the Yemen dispute. The communiqué they issued called for a seven-month armistice during which the UAR would begin to withdraw its troops; the KSA would cease support for the royalists, who would meet with the republicans to discuss a reconciliation. Yemen republicans and royalists met under Egyptian and Saudi auspices without any concrete results, but with indications that a formula for national reconciliation would be found.[68]

Following the Nasser–Faisal communiqué, the Yemen government clarified to the US government its aims for a peaceful solution. During a visit by Ambassador al-'Aini to the US assistant secretary of state, the former outlined the following points: Washington should use its influence on both parties to promote a settlement in Yemen; the settlement should involve the elimination of the Hamid al-Din family, and as a necessary *quid pro quo*, the YAR would expel al-Sallal; a conference of up to 300 representatives of various Yemeni factions would be held outside Yemen to determine the new government; UAR troops would withdraw from the YAR, and the KSA would cease its interference in Yemeni affairs; a joint Arab force from countries not involved in the dispute might be required in Yemen for a limited period of time; the UAR and the KSA would divert a percentage of their military budgets to economic and developmental assistance for the YAR; the solution was not to be imposed by outsiders; and the fact that republican moderates interpreted the Nasser–Faisal communiqué which had divided Yemen into spheres of influence – as an indication of an intent to play off the YAR government against the wishes of its people. As far as the south was concerned, al-'Aini repeated his government's willingness to accept a demilitarized zone, UN observers and even demarcation, provided these were part of an overall settlement in which Britain recognized the YAR and conceded to the people in the south the right to choose their own government. In the name of the YAR foreign minister, Muhammad Sirri, al-'Aini conveyed Yemen's assurances that it would not exacerbate the situation on the border, even though it was being pushed unwillingly in this direction by the UAR.[69]

On 3 November 1964 Yemeni royalists and republicans met at Erkwit in Sudan to discuss the means for convening a reconciliation conference and forming an all-Yemen government. Washington showed its goodwill towards the Yemeni people by sending, on 7 November, another shipment of American wheat, which arrived in the port of Hudaidah (3,000 tons as part of a 20,000-ton gift). But it became clear that the events in Washington, Riyadh and Aden did not serve to improve YAR–US relations.[70] On 1 December the Erkwit conference broke down in disagreement over use of the term 'republic' and the future status of the royal family.

Following the failure of the reconciliation attempt in Sudan, the Yemeni republican opposition leaders continued to make unofficial contact with the US government. In order to obtain US support to solve the Yemeni crisis by political means, they even promised to withdraw support to the southerners if the US succeeded in getting the UAR troops to withdraw. On 13 December, the US Embassy in Ta'iz reported that Ahmad Nu'man, president of Madjlis al-Shura [parliament], had summoned the US chargé d'affairs to his residence in Sana'a where Kadi al-Iryani, the leader of the moderate republicans and a member of the cabinet, joined them. Both confirmed their resignation from the government

> because it was [the] powerless puppet of the UAR, and made [a] renewed impassioned plea for western and particularly [for] US help to save Yemen from Egyptian bondage; they asserted [that] all responsible Yemen leaders wanted to stop the fighting and effect [a] UAR withdrawal, which would bring [an] immediate end [to] interference in [the] SAF over which they now have no control.

Nu'man and al-Iryani also stressed that the key to the solution was that the US should persuade the UK and the KSA to deal with the national Yemen government.[71]

There was no concrete cooperation between Sana'a and Washington for a long period following the assassination of President Kennedy, mainly due to the YAR–UAR alliance. Dana Adams Schmidt, an American writer, claims that during October 1964, Egypt asked the US for assistance to help solve its foreign exchange problems, but the State Department refused, and pointed out that the war in Yemen was draining Egyptian finances; there was clearly a paradox in Egypt opposing the policies and interests of a superpower and, at the same time, seeking its help.[72] On 26 November Egyptian demonstrators attacked the US Embassy in Cairo protesting against Washington's role in helping to rescue white hostages in the Congo.[73] In December a private American aircraft was shot down over Egypt for intruding into its airspace; the US retaliated by postponing shipments of food assistance to the UAR.[74] In January 1965 the Johnson administration revealed that it had secretly approved the sale of West German tanks to Israel, a fact which outraged the UAR.[75]

In early February 1965 the US chargé d'affaires, Clark, met President al-Sallal and his foreign minister, A. Hamim, to discuss US efforts to 'promote peace and progress in Yemen and emphasize recent US steps toward resumption of PL-480 shipments and construction of [the] Rahidah spur road'.[76] Clark expressed Washington's concern 'at rumours reported to US that in face of this dramatic support for Yemeni independence, peace and progress, some YAR officials still questioned US good faith and friendship.'[77] The chargé d'affaires also expressed his concern at the arrest of a local employee, Yahya al-

Dailami, who had assisted the embassy in talks regarding US assistance and friendship.[78]

Al-Sallal took the opportunity to express Yemen's appreciation of US assistance and Yemen's trust that the US was helping Yemen 'out of sincere friendship'.[79] Al-Sallal also stated that he had given up hope of an improvement in relations with the UK because the new Labour government had failed to heed his foreign minister's pleas for cooperation with the YAR. Al-Sallal believed that Britain was still 'following 19th century imperialist policies', and was committing in his country a 'crime of supporting discredited forces of reaction and oppression' whereas the 'US had demonstrated its support of popular movements by recognizing the YARG'. The YAR president thought the UK was a 'great power but had misused its power and thereby had lost the world'.[80] Clark's reply was that 'it should be easy for Yemen to settle its problems with the UK if it was willing to take meaningful steps to relax tensions'.[81]

Clark raised the issue of Vietnam and the Yemen media's anti-US coverage. Al-Sallal expressed neutrality, and from that day the Yemeni media either ignored or treated temperately all reports about US action in the Vietnam war. This was an indication that al-Sallal was willing to come to an understanding with the US as long as it supported the political status quo in his country. Clark reported al-Sallal's comments as being 'noteworthy and more in keeping with traditional cautious Yemeni attitude than might be expected', and hoped that the 'YARG neutral stance continues [and] since it [is] probably [the] best we can hope for in view [of] considerable and growing Soviet and CHICOM presence and massive bloc aid programs' in Yemen.[82]

Following the failure of the republican–royalist negotiations, fighting in the Yemen intensified and, in early March 1965, UAR planes bombed Saudi depots inside Saudi territory.[83] Washington instructed its embassy in Cairo to express its disappointment over the breakdown of the ceasefire, and to stress US support for the integrity and independence of Saudi Arabia. Riyadh and Cairo were urged to continue discussions. On 2 April 1965, having been informed by the Saudis of another air strike, the US administration asked the embassy in Cairo to 'express our concern over these reports of violation of Saudi integrity and to note our commitment to Saudi security'.[84]

On 25 April 1965 Sheikh Ahmad Muhammad Nu'man was appointed prime minister. Nu'man informed the US administration that he aimed to improve the YAR's relations with the KSA and the UK.[85] Some observers saw his abolishing of the ministry for the Occupied South as a gesture towards London.[86] He initiated his premiership by sending 'a peace delegation' on a tour of Arab countries. On 10 May he sent a telegram directly to the Saudi crown prince and prime minister, Faisal, publicly offering to hold informal talks with the Saudis and asking Faisal's assistance in establishing peace in Yemen.[87] His proposal was rejected even though he asked Kuwait, Jordan and Syria to mediate.[88]

On 1 May 1965 the US chargé d'affaires paid his first visit to the newly reappointed YAR foreign minister, Muhsin al-'Aini. During this visit, the YAR foreign minister expressed friendship for the US and urged the US government to stand by the YAR. He said that the Nu'man government represented what the Yemeni people had hoped for when the 1962 revolution broke out, but that they had been prevented from realizing it by the Egyptians. The new government, he claimed, had the backing of the entire Yemeni nation but lacked an army and was beset by many obstacles. It was believed in Sana'a that the UAR wanted to discredit the group of politicians under Nu'man and the proposed republican–royalist conference in Khamir, which al-'Aini believed would succeed and which would lead to some changes in the government and in the powers of the Presidential Council where President al-Sallal was trying to thwart Nu'man's policies. According to al-'Aini the YAR really wanted peace with the KSA and the UK and that if only they would adopt more understanding attitudes, peace would come and UAR troops would be withdrawn. Furthermore, although the YAR wanted good relations with the UAR, it did not want to follow Nasserite policies. He pointed out that Nu'man had taken a brave step in dropping the post of minister of the occupied South Yemen. Nu'man was under pressure from the UAR to restore it and the new prime minister, despite al-Sallal's objections to ending criticism of other Arabs, was trying to control the media in an effort to stop criticism of the KSA and the SAF. However, because he was accused of being an imperialist tool, he was obliged to move cautiously. Al-'Aini urged King Faisal to be understanding and patient until Nu'man won this battle, but he could not do so if Riyadh continued its support of the Hamid al-Din family, who had no chance of returning to power. The US, therefore, could help best by convincing Britain and, more importantly, Prince Faisal, of this fact because otherwise the Nu'man government would fall and UAR policies would triumph. Al-'Aini advised Clark not to call on the YAR prime minister because such a meeting would endorse Egyptian propaganda that Nu'man was a US stooge.[89]

After this meeting Clark informed Washington: 'we earnestly hope that SAG and UKG would realize that the present opportunity is a golden one and that if lost is not likely ever to recur.' He concluded: 'I recommend US do its best in Riyadh and London to enlist the "understanding attitude" al-'Aini seeks.'[90]

The course of YAR–US relations continued to be affected by fears that Washington was trying to undermine the republic through diplomatic means. On 2 May 1965 the US Embassy in Ta'iz reported to Washington that a 'sizeable' 'UAR intelligence type' pro-NLF and anti-Nu'man demonstration was taking place in Ta'iz and had passed in front of the USAID and American Embassy offices. The demonstrators opposed the Khamir conference on Yemeni reconciliation which was due to start the next day, as well as Nu'man's policy of seeking reconciliation with the UK and the SAF. The report also mentioned that several Aden leaders: A. al-Asnadj, H. Kadi and A. Badhib, were in Ta'iz to attend a counter-Khamir conference.[91] According to a Ta'iz US Embassy note, Ahmad Dahmash, who had been appointed director-general of YAR Broadcasting in early May 1965, was later the first anti-Egyptian Yemeni official to criticize the Nasser–Faisal agreement at Djiddah on the grounds that Yemenis had not been part of it.[92]

At the request of Prime Minister Nu'man, in May 1965 the Yemeni republican forces held a conference in the town of Khamir, the capital of the Hashid tribal confederation, in order to agree on a peaceful settlement with the Yemeni royalists. But Nu'man's efforts failed when he was forced to resign a month later on 1 July 1965. Three days earlier, Nu'man and many of his supporters had flown to Cairo in an attempt to persuade Nasser of their point of view, but they had been put under house arrest; the Egyptian leadership knew it could not depend on Nu'man to achieve its policies in Yemen.[93]

The replacing of Nu'man did not solve the Yemeni dispute and the UAR found itself more involved in the military encounter in the Yemeni arena where the number of its troops reached nearly 70,000. After Nu'man's arrest in Cairo, Sheikh 'Abd Allah bin Hussein al-Ahmar and around 250 of the main pro-republican tribal leaders were forced on 20 July to leave Yemen via Beihan, a border British protectorate, where they announced they would travel to the KSA to meet Crown Prince Faisal.[94]

In March 1965 Faisal had attempted to ease internal Saudi resentment about corruption within the KSA by reducing Saud's status to that of a figurehead and by taking virtual control of the government; in November he acceded to the throne and pressed Washington to approve the sale of an air defence system to his country.[95] The US supported the Saudi purchase of modern British aircraft worth over $100 million, with Washington supplying related missiles and communications equipment. In June 1966 Faisal visited Washington and was rewarded with a contract to buy some $100 million worth of military vehicles.[96]

Following reports that Saudi Arabia had received the first large shipment of aircraft and other modern military equipment from both the US and the UK[97], President Nasser visited Djiddah in Saudi Arabia on 21 August and signed the Djiddah agreement with Prince Faisal on 23 August. This was welcomed by the Johnson administration:

> In the Middle East, we are happy to see the statesmanlike agreement between King Faisal (of Saudi Arabia) and President Nasser (of the United Arab Republic) which seems to offer great promise of a peaceful settlement in Yemen.[98]

This agreement called for: an immediate ceasefire in Yemen under the auspices of a KSA–UAR peace committee; a plebiscite to be held in Yemen by November 1966; a republican–royalist conference to be held in the town of Harad in Yemen to agree on a provisional government; the departure of UAR troops over a ten-month period beginning on 23 November 1965; the cessation of KSA military assistance to royalists, and prohibition on the use of Saudi soil against Yemen.[99]

On 23 November, a third republican-royalist conference convened in Harad with UAR and KSA observers in attendance. This conference lasted until 24 December when it was announced that it had failed. This put an end to further political efforts to solve royalist–republican differences. It had become clear during the last two weeks of the conference that neither side was prepared to reconcile its beliefs and objectives without a fight. Meanwhile there were indications that the Egyptian–Saudi agreement on the Yemeni dispute had not actually solved the Yemeni problem and that the UAR and the KSA were willing to support their allies by all means. On 21 December, Riyadh announced it had signed letters of intent (subsequently implemented), with US and UK companies for a $400 million air defence project which would include British interceptors, US Hawk missiles, ground radar and communications equipment.[100]

The war worsened as a direct result of the support given to the counter-revolution by the KSA; Egyptian casualties were greater than at any previous time. This appeared to be part of a tougher American policy toward Nasser's Egypt:

> The Johnson administration didn't display as much patience toward Arab affairs as President Kennedy had, and President Johnson's identification, in Arab eyes, with a pro-Israel position made it difficult to continue the same openness of dialogue in Cairo that had emerged during the negotiations on Yemen.[101]

Despite the failure of the Djiddah agreement, which had only been reached under US pressure on both Cairo and Riyadh, the US administration tried to revive it. US Secretary of State Dean Rusk told the UAR parliamentary speaker, Anwar al-Sadat, who was then in Washington, that he felt the agreement was not dead, and urged further Egyptian–Saudi efforts to implement it. The same views were expressed in an exchange of letters between the king of the KSA and the US president, who considered the Djiddah agreement 'an act of statesmanship which still affords the best approach for peaceful resolution of the Yemen conflict'.[102]

In late February 1966, press sources linked the simultaneous visit of both Prince Sultan bin 'Abdul-'Aziz of Saudi Arabia and Anwar al-Sadat to Washington, indicating that the US was mediating in the Yemeni conflict.[103] The same sources added that Dean Rusk was on his way to Cairo and Riyadh. The earlier US mediation efforts in the Yemeni conflict seemed to have paved the way for a reconciliation during 1966.[104]

While the Yemeni conflict was moving toward a solution, London announced on 22 February that it would withdraw from the southern areas of Yemen in 1969. This encouraged Egypt to strengthen its forces in the YAR at the cost of Cairo's 'readiness against the Israelis.'[105] On the same day, Nasser announced that he would keep his forces in the YAR for a few years more to protect the Yemeni revolution against 'imperialist and reactionary conspiracies'.[106]

On 15 March 1966 the US informed the UAR that the KSA sincerely wanted a settlement and Washington 'wished to avoid becoming a party to negotiations and did not espouse any particular formula for implementing the agreement'.[107] In the spring of 1966, Kuwait began to mediate. The US administration instructed its embassies in Cairo, Riyadh and Kuwait to encourage the UAR and the KSA to make some concessions in order to reach a fruitful and peaceful settlement.[108]

At the same time the Johnson administration continued to pursue a tough policy towards Egypt. Ambassador Hart justified this policy saying that the Egyptian president, who

followed the policy of maintaining a kind of equilibrium between the Soviet bloc on the one side and the Western bloc on the other ... gave encouragement to the formation of the Afro-Asian Solidarity Conference, which had a very pronounced left-wing anti-Western, anti-U.S. flavour, really was almost Communist-dominated from the beginning. This puzzled Washington. And he did things of that kind.[109]

The US wheat shipments[110] to Cairo were reduced while more military and political support was given to Saudi Arabia and Israel. This situation, as was revealed later, was a result of misunderstanding on the part of, or exaggeration by, some members of the Egyptian government. 'Ali Sabri,[111] for example distorted facts to Nasser, and then attacked the US in one of his speeches. The deterioration of relations between Cairo and Washington at that time led to a more rigid US stance against both the UAR and the YAR and greater support to both Israel and the KSA.[112]

On 22 June 1966 King Faisal arrived in Washington, where President Johnson reaffirmed US interest in Saudi Arabia 'and Faisal's personal security'.[113] Both sides determined 'to guard the free nations against the threat of international Communism'.[114] Johnson also told Faisal that 'though we had difficulties with President Nasser, we believed it was prudent to leave room for dialogue and not force Nasser further toward the Communist countries'. On the Yemeni issue, Johnson urged Faisal to maintain self-restraint and expressed his conviction that 'he doubted Nasser would dare attack Saudi Arabia without provocation'.[115]

This appeared to coincide with some improvement in YAR–US relations. On 2 July 1966, the US chargé d'affaires visited the acting YAR president, Muhammad 'Ali 'Uthman (al-Sallal was summoned by Cairo), and the former presented an explanation and justification for the US bombardment of storage depots in North Vietnam. The chargé d'affaires noted in a telegram to the US department that though the Yemeni media had become once again influenced by Cairo and which 'was sharply critical of US bombing and other actions in Vietnam, 'Uthman seemed understanding of US goals and action, and receptive to our position'. The YAR acting president also passed on to the chargé what he believed to be secret information: that Soviet Prime Minister Kosygin, during his recent visit to Egypt, had advised Cairo to improve its relations with the US as well as to seek wheat aid from it.[116]

During the second half of 1966, the US Embassy in the YAR maintained contact with the anti-Egyptian Yemeni republican leaders. Records of meetings show cautious US sympathy for politicians such as Muhammad 'Ali 'Uthman, the acting president, who 'desire to free themselves from UAR embrace'. The US Embassy official dealings with the republican leaders were cautious, expressing moral support and advising them to contact the Saudis, without giving any political or financial support because 'among other major considerations would be [the] effect on overall US–UAR relations of our backing [an] openly anti-UAR coup in Yemen'.[117] The instructions of the US secretary of state to the US Embassy in Ta'iz in August stressed the following points to be communicated to the republican leaders:

1. the US sympathized with those Yemenis who desired to be their own masters;

2. it was not US policy to become involved in Yemeni internal politics;
3. Kuwaiti mediation efforts offered the best hope for the withdrawal
   of UAR forces from Yemen and for the overall settlement of the
   conflict, and the US therefore hoped the YAR would cooperate
   with the KSA and the UAR; and
4. as the US secretary had promised the YAR foreign minister, Dr
   Hassan Makki, in 1965, the US would help the Yemenis to any
   extent possible once the settlement was achieved and a broad-based
   regime was set up.[118]

US Secretary of State Dean Rusk also informed the American
Embassy in Ta'iz of the following:

> American involvement in 'Uthman scheme[119] would entail major US
> political and financial commitment to group we have little fundamental
> reason to trust and whose chances success on surface at least seem
> extremely slim. Expect $700 thousand monthly figure would be only
> beginning Yemeni financial needs. Political consequences our involvement
> would far exceed limits Near East ... While we do not wish push 'Uth-
> man back into UAR arms, they should be given clearly to understand
> USG unprepared become involved in factional Yemeni politics.[120]

The cautious US sympathy with the republican opposition shows that
Washington was also continuing its efforts to establish better communication with the pro-UAR republicans. President al-Sallal, who,
on 12 August returned from a semi-exile in Cairo, also made a new
move towards Washington. A few days before his return to Sana'a
from Cairo, the Yemeni president stated publicly: 'We do not plan to
implement Socialism here. We have no capitalism. All are poor here.'
In the same statement he expressed his appreciation of the Eastern
bloc as well of the United States for their unconditional assistance.[121]

US assistance: first phase

US economic assistance to the YAR was resumed in 1963 as a continuation of the programme that had started in 1959. It was conceived
politically within the context of Washington's effort to counter the
Soviet and communist presence in the Middle East, to protect its
interests in Saudi Arabia and to confront therising nationalist, and
what the US saw as 'radical', forces in the region.[122]

From 1959 to 1967, US economic assistance to Yemen dealt prin-
cipally with infrastructure, training and humanitarian assistance via
Public Law 480, Title II (Food for Peace). During this period the
USAID programme accomplished or assisted in the following projects:

1. 400 km of the major 'stabilized earth, gravel-topped highway'[123] from Mocha on the Red Sea through Ta'iz and to Sana'a was completed in 1965.
2. Wheat was provided under the Food for Peace Program.
3. Yemen's first modern water system, the Kennedy Memorial Water System, was completed in Ta'iz in 1965.
4. The establishment of the National Department of Public Water Supply and Sanitation; nearly 250 personnel were trained to manage, operate and maintain the system in all phases of water systems management, from basic chemistry and sanitation to warehousing and administration.
5. Scholarship funds were provided for approximately one hundred Yemenis to be trained and educated at the American University in Beirut in engineering, agriculture, business administration, education and communications.
6. Eighty-five self-help projects relating to potable water and feeder road development were completed.[124]

Thus pre-1967 US aid to Yemen, costing nearly $42.7 million, focused primarily on the development of basic infrastructure, training and education. A Ta'iz US Embassy memorandum dated 1965 (when al-Sallal was president) stressed political concern about the Yemeni students, pointing out that some of the nine who had been sent to the USA for college education in the mid-1950s became members of the radical republican 'famous forty'.[125] The memorandum also expressed concern about the possible future activities of many Yemeni students who were in the Soviet Union at that time. It gave detailed information about thirteen of forty-seven graduates in the YAR at the time who were from the 'famous forty'.[126] US and Western European graduates at that time represented about 40 per cent of the total. Of the forty-seven graduates, twelve were diplomats posted abroad but expected to return. It maintained that the current group was 'not as cohesive as the famous forty' but was generally nationalistic, interested more in Yemen than in other Arab causes ('they are not as emotional as other Arabs on, say, the Arab–Israeli question'), and that a number of them were anti-Egyptian, a feeling generated mainly by the UAR 'occupation' of Yemen. It further commented that, like the famous forty, 'they provide a desperately-needed reservoir of skills but their number is small ... the small size of this group is also disturbing when considering the number of students' who were 'in training in the Communist bloc. It would appear that they will eventually be submerged as most of these students come back to Yemen.'[127]

Perhaps because it was politically motivated, and intended to win influence, US assistance to the YAR and the provision of educational opportunities during this first phase, was what the Yemenis wanted. According to US documents the US Administration represented by its embassy in Ta'iz, was keen during this period to play a constructive role in Yemen by providing the country with projects that would help to stabilize the country in favour of the Republic, especially in the northern areas. The US Embassy in Ta'iz suggested to the department in Washington that the improvement of agricultural techniques and development water resources, particularly in northern areas, would redirect the Zeidis from fighting towards the pursuit of traditional soil-tilling occupations.[128] It was also mentioned that the US government could play a useful role by stepping up famine relief shipments of surplus agricultural products. The US Embassy in Ta'iz went on to say: 'Most feasible and promising in our view is possibility of marshalling world opinion, including Arab states, for a settlement which safeguards legitimate interests and security of parties.'[129]

During this phase, the Yemenis were impressed by the USAID projects, such as the Mocha–Ta'iz–Sana'a road[130] and the Kennedy Water System since they were a source of new jobs and an effective training for their people. Dr 'Abdul-Karim al-Iryani, later deputy prime minister and foreign minister of the YAR, described the projects of 1963–67 as 'development projects'[131] and stated that the Yemeni people were introduced to development assistance only through the Americans when they undertook the Kennedy Water Project and the Mocha–Ta'iz–Sana'a road. He added that these projects were simple 'but in the eyes of the Yemeni people they were great. Many Yemenis were trained and worked and got salaries from the projects and that was reflected on the standard of living of many families.'[132] It can be concluded that the substance of USAID to the YAR in this period reflected US concern over the communist and Nasserite presence in the country. It was, therefore, intended to compete with the other rival powers in the Yemen. Other US officials took a different view and considered assistance to the YAR at that time to be:

> incompatible both with US interests and free world security for the US government to continue to provide political and economic support to a state which is used as: (a) a base for subversion in SAF, in which the Western alliance has important interests; and (b) a base for subversion of, or military attack against, SAG.[133]

Severance of diplomatic relations, 1967

Al-Sallal's return led to a dispute with Prime Minister Hassan al-'Amri, his cabinet, and other high-ranking officers. The dispute reached its climax in mid-September when the Egyptian army captured the opponents of the Egyptian policy, among them forty officers, the prime minister and his cabinet, and sent them all into exile and detention in the UAR capital. Sana'a Radio announced on 16 September that Premier al-'Amri had resigned. President al-Sallal formed a new cabinet whose members were mostly supporters of the UAR.[134]

These internal developments, which showed enormous UAR influence in the YAR, had a negative effect on the YAR's foreign relations, which had been initiated during the Nu'man and the 'Amri governments. As the relationship between Nasser's UAR and the Johnson administration was deteriorating at this time, YAR–US relations were also badly affected. Evidence of the deteriorating relations between Sana'a and Washington appeared on 28 September 1966, when the YAR government declared a USAID employee who was an American citizen *persona non grata*, and the US Embassy failed to have the decision reversed.[135]

Another encounter between the Yemeni opponents of UAR policies in Yemen and al-Sallal's government took place in October 1966, when the Egyptian forces executed the minister of tribal affairs, Muhammad al-Ru'aini, and four other high-ranking officers, on fabricated charges of having 'plotted against the Republican and progressive orientation of the YAR'.[136] The executions were followed by anti-US demonstrations and strong anti-US campaigns in the YAR and UAR media.

On 11 October 1966, the YAR foreign minister, Muhammad 'Abdul-'Aziz Sallam, who was attending the UN General Assembly in New York, visited Washington, where he met US Assistant Secretary of State Raymond Hare, and USAID Assistant Administrator William B. Macomber. During this meeting Hare denied his country's involvement 'in any attempts to manipulate the internal affairs'[137] of the YAR. Following Sallam's talks in Washington, the US administration informed its embassy in Sana'a of the 'firm intent to continue to maintain the US presence in Yemen in order not to leave the field open to Russian and Chinese Communist penetration, and to continue to provide a major Western alternative to Arab reliance on Communist powers'.[138]

Meanwhile, in November 1966, the first Hawk battery arrived in Saudi Arabia. Following UAR air attacks on Saudi depots in Nadjran, the US deployed a supply unit to the town of Djizan in mid-February 1967. It also instructed the US military training mission to assist the Saudi air defence units on the border with the YAR, and confirmed, in principle, the Saudi commitment to a US agreement to provide Riyadh with air-to-air missiles.[139]

Despite these setbacks to its relations with the YAR and the UAR, in early April 1967 the US proposed a US mission of mediation to meet all the parties involved in the Yemeni issue. Cairo and Riyadh 'agreed to accept Ambassador Hare, but final agreement on terms of reference were never reached'.[140]

On 25 April 1967 the crisis between Sana'a and Washington reached a climax. The YAR announced on this day that two USAID employees, Liapis and Hartman, had been arrested while allegedly entering a military warehouse in Ta'iz, events that had resulted in the killing of a Yemeni and an Egyptian soldier.[141] The US Embassy asked the Yemeni authorities to allow an embassy officer to remain with the detained men. The YAR media claimed a US plot to destroy the city. Demonstrations followed the announcement of the so-called offensive and Yemeni students attacked the American Embassy in Ta'iz with stones 'and AID offices were broken into and ransacked'.[142] The anti-US propaganda arising from the case of the USAID employees in Ta'iz worried the US. The Ta'iz Embassy suggested that a US presidential letter, and Arab and Eastern European mediation on a humanitarian basis, might solve the problem. The chargé expressed sorrow that in the light of UAR influence at that time: '[As] far as we know not one Arab government has put in [a] sympathetic word for us in [the] right places.'[143]

David Ransom, then a junior officer in the US Embassy in Ta'iz, remembered:

> I was sitting in my house at night. Knocks. 'Beit al-Halali.' I went to the door and it was a messenger of the Ministry of Foreign Affairs and 10 o'clock at night. I took the note. I had only had a little Arabic, and he said I had to deliver it at night. It was a very dark night, dark in the streets. No lights outside. No traffic. I opened the note and I couldn't understand it ... It was a long list of names and there was one phrase which I couldn't translate: 'ashkhas gheir marghoobeen' [*personae non grata*]. I didn't know what it meant. My wife and I had the dictionary out and we were looking it up. Suddenly we realized that this was a long list of names, 26 names of people who were being asked to leave ... then I walked over to the Charge's house, at midnight, knocked at the door and gave him the note ... and the result was that the American government withdrew most of the American mission.[144]

The YAR foreign minister at the time, Muhammad 'Abdul-'Aziz Sallam, subsequently suggested that the whole story had been fabricated.[145]

Sallam also revealed he had attended part of the interrogation of the two USAID employees, who complained to him that they had been mistreated and beaten by the Egyptians. He continued: 'the Egyptian intelligence had arranged the burning of the American Embassy, a decision which was not sanctioned by the Yemeni government.' He maintained that what happened was a reflection of the US–Egyptian relations at that time, and did not serve Yemen interests. 'The UAR wanted to wreak revenge on the Americans in Yemen.' To justify his position and that of his government, Sallam made it clear that 'at that time there were 70,000 Egyptian troops in the country and if any objected to Tala't Hassan's decisions' they would 'manufacture an accusation and execute us as traitors of God and Yemen.'[146] He also said there was little he could do to express goodwill towards US employees serving in Yemen, apart from going to their homes to personally help with departure arrangements. The expulsion, in his view, threatened future mutual relations, and were based on Egyptian policies not serving Yemen's interests.[147]

The US secretary of state immediately ordered all USAID personnel and dependents of other US government personnel to leave the YAR, and announced that there was to be an immediate reduction to a skeleton staff in the US Embassy. By 1 May all Americans, except nine diplomats who were ordered to remain, had been flown to Ethiopia.[148] According to Sallam, US Secretary of State Dean Rusk wrote a warning letter to the UAR foreign minister saying that he would take retaliatory action 'against the forgery of the incident and the mistreatment and beating of the two USAID employees', and he ended his letter by saying that 'what happened would not pass without retaliation'.[149]

The release of the two USAID employees on 16 May 1967, and their departure the next day, calmed the crisis, preventing further deterioration in the relationship between the YAR and the US. According to a well-informed Yemeni security source the crisis had been created by both Yemeni and Egyptian intelligence, in reaction to US policies towards the UAR and YAR;[150] it was meant to halt any further contact between Sana'a and Washington. It succeeded in that relations between the two nations were virtually frozen for a period.

The breach

Although relations had thus deteriorated, it was on account of pan-Arab politics and the US policy towards Israel that formal diplomatic relations between Washington and Sana'a were severed. On 5 June 1967 the Arab–Israeli Six Day War broke out. Cairo saw it as 'a US–Israeli war against the anti-Western movement in the area'.[151] The US, which had supplied Israel with tanks, bombers and fighters for the first time just a few months before, succeeded in striking at the Arab nationalist movement from Tel Aviv and in reducing the Nasserite influence in the region.

By involving itself in the YAR, the UAR acted upon its national obligation to support liberation movements against colonialism and imperialism but it did not calculate that its military involvement would last for long. Nasser stated later: 'I sent a squadron to the Yemen, then I needed to consolidate it with 70,000 men.'[152] The Six Day War came at a time when Egyptian resources and forces were nearly drained by their long involvement in the Yemeni arena.

On 6 June 1967 Sana'a, along with several other Arab states, officially severed its diplomatic relations with Washington and with all other pro-US countries ostensibly because of 'Washington's blind support to Israel against the Arab cause in Palestine'. According to the US Department of State:

> following the lead of the UAR, the Yemeni government called in our Chargé d'Affaires and delivered a memorandum charging US participation with Israel in attacks against the UAR, and severing Yemen's diplomatic relations with us. The Yemenis asked the remaining staff of our Embassy to depart. By June 9, the last person had left, and the Italian Embassy in Yemen accepted responsibility for US affairs.[153]

The total dependence of the YAR on the UAR had led to Egyptian interference in domestic Yemeni affairs to the extent that the Revolutionary Commanding Council and Yemeni Cabinet meetings were attended by an Egyptian secretary who reported every detail to Cairo. According to a former US ambassador to Yemen 'the trouble with the Republic was it was in the wrong hands at that time.' He expressed his belief that 'if it had been in the hands of Ahmad Nu'man or Muhammad Zubairi it would have been in good hands, and it would have been very much easier for the British to recognize it'.[154] This judgement ignores the fact that without UAR support during the first two years of the revolution it was unlikely that the republic would have survived. On the other hand, without UAR influence, Sana'a–Washington relations might have not deteriorated to the point of complete severance of relations which was not in the YAR's interests.

Up to June 1967 the US achieved its objectives in the region, 'for the Yemeni revolution was prevented from bringing about either the instability of Saudi Arabia or a direct UAR–KSA military clash, and the oil resources of the Gulf were not jeopardized'.[155] On this issue Ambassador Hart commented:

> It didn't gain us very much to stay either because we really never accomplished anything in the Yemen during that period. ['Abd Allah al-Sallal]

was a man you couldn't accomplish any business with ... They finally threw us out in '67. We'd put our money in and we hated to give it up. We had a position there; the Russians were trying to move in; the Chinese, the Red Chinese were there; the Egyptians were there. What we would have missed by being thrown out was intelligence take and the informational take that we were able to get over that occupational period. And that was useful for us to have it.[156]

Yemen's dissatisfaction with the US during 1967 was mainly a result of Washington's policies towards republican Yemen. Although Yemen's decision to break relations with the US was consistent with Arab policies at that time, as a result of the US attitude towards the Palestinian cause, it was mostly the outcome of the deterioration in bilateral relations.

Despite the fact that the change of the US administration, following the assassination of President Kennedy in 1963, completely changed the US approach towards the UAR and the YAR, it was clear that Cairo's involvement and policies implemented in the YAR by the Egyptians' officers and politicians without the approval of President Nasser himself were detrimental to both the YAR as well as the YAR–US bilateral relations.

Interlude

The severance of relations between Sana'a and Washington in June 1967 isolated the YAR more than ever before. Many Yemeni leaders were aware that cutting off direct communications with the US did not serve the best interests of their country, especially since the decision had been taken under UAR influence. They decided that one of their major tasks, after achieving an internal reconciliation, would be to repair relations with the rich and developed West, as events within Yemen and the region after severance demonstrate.

A month after the 1967 Arab–Israeli war, an Arab summit took place in Khartum, the capital of Sudan. At the end of this summit, President Nasser and King Faisal agreed to the formation of a tripartite committee on Yemen to prepare plans to guarantee UAR troop withdrawal and the suspension of Saudi support for the counter-revolution. Nasser and Faisal reached a *modus vivendi* by which Cairo decided to come to terms with Riyadh and withdraw its forces from the YAR, paving the way for Saudi Arabia and Washington to give more assistance and backing to the royalists. This happened because Egypt had become financially dependent on Saudi Arabia, Kuwait and Libya in its struggle to overcome the consequences of the Six Day War.[157] Kuwait, the KSA and Libya pledged an annual sum, totalling £135 million, to help the UAR and Jordan recover from their economic losses of the war. Riyadh's share in this pledge was equivalent to $98 million[158] every year in return for Nasser's assurances of complete withdrawal.

The YAR dependence on the UAR between 1962 and 1967 left Sana'a alone to deal with its own internal and external problems. The republican leaders, who had been detained in Cairo since 15 September 1966, returned to Sana'a where, on 5 November, they deposed the president and his government. By early December 1967 all Egyptian troops had withdrawn. This was followed by increased royalist military activity around Sana'a in preparation for a planned final assault on the capital. The royalists, backed by the Saudis and British directly and by the US indirectly, launched the strongest attack of the civil war and layed seige to Sana'a for seventy days between 28 November 1967 and 8 February 1968. The YAR prime minister and commander-general of the armed forces officially accused the US of continuing its supply of arms to the royalists, stating that 'the Republican forces had captured some American arms which were different from those supplied by the Kingdom of Saudi Arabia'.[159] During the siege the YAR government also issued a communiqué stating that mercenaries from Great Britain, France, Belgium, Holland and the US were the real organizers of the strong offensive against Sana'a. The communiqué also accused Washington of supervising the siege.[160] In fact there is no evidence that the US was providing the royalists with arms to counteract the republican government; it was the KSA that financed American arms from various sources as well as arms from its own stocks and made them available for the counter-revolution.

Some US military advisers participated in the civil war as individuals, not as representatives of official US government policy. Among them was Bushrod Howard who, through contacting the royalist prime minister, Hassan bin Yahya Hamid al-Din, offered his services in propaganda and political work in the US, and who succeeded in campaigning against Egyptian intervention inside the Senate and in cutting US aid to Nasser. These American individuals may have had contact with US intelligence agencies. Thus the US sought to contain the Yemeni conflict, but avoided any military Vietnam-like involvement. The US minister to Yemen in 1962 later stated:

> Some boxes bearing the AID handclasp symbol and some weapons or pieces of military equipment were found or captured from the Royalists by the Republicans ... [but] basically the weaponry did not come from our sources. It came from other places, old miscellaneous this and that they'd picked up all over the place (there was a great deal of help given

by Iran, eventually), but it was small arms weaponry of miscellaneous kinds.[161]

Based on an agreement signed by President al-Sallal and the Soviets in September of 1967, Moscow provided Sana'a with aircraft and other military supplies.[162] On 1 December the royalists announced that they had shot down a Soviet-piloted MiG, and evidence was published in the British press to prove direct Soviet military participation.[163] The US Department of State confirmed on 13 December 1967 that in addition to the participation of Soviet pilots the USSR had supplied arms to the republic.[164] The Yemeni revolutionary forces, supported by republican Sayyids, some tribal leaders and army officers sympathetic to the republican front, eventually defeated the siege.[165] Soviet support of the YAR was severely criticized by Washington, and the US Department of State warned the Soviet Union that it would not permit the continuation of Soviet interference in the Yemeni conflict.[166]

Two contacts between the YAR and the US government occurred between June 1967 and March 1968. While no details were released about the first meeting, the US Department of State revealed that during the second meeting the YAR had 'suggested to the Department's Arabian Peninsula Country Director that the United States assign an officer to the Italian Embassy in Yemen, and asked us to communicate to the Saudi Arabian government the interest of the Yemeni government in ending the war'.[167] The Yemeni representative, 'Ali Lutf al-Thawr,[168] told the US officials that 'Yemeni Republican leaders were worried over the threat from leftist-radicals'.[169] The US representative 'assured the Minister of our basic friendly intentions and noted that our recognition of the YAR had not been withdrawn', but pointed out that 'the continuing civil war created a serious problem for the United States in considering any resumption of diplomatic ties.' 'We did not', he affirmed, 'wish to become involved on either side of the Yemen conflict.'[170]

Kadi 'Abdul-Rahman al-Iryani stated clearly in late July 1968 that the two revolutions in the south and the north of Yemen were 'being exposed to aggression perpetrated by the same enemy'[171] and that both revolutions were 'facing the same imperialist and reactionary forces'.[172] While in early 1968 the YAR continued to accuse the United States of being a 'colonialist and imperialist' country, these accusations were toned down after the internal crisis of August 1968, which witnessed the military defeat of the Yemen left by the 'moderate Republicans'. However, no US response was forthcoming during 1968, possibly because the US wanted to ensure that the Yemeni left was completely defeated. In early 1969 some official statements expressed the YAR's wish to restore relations with the US, and in an official statement the Yemeni foreign minister unveiled an initiative to restore relations with Washington. He justified this step by saying that 'Yemen was compelled by other forces when it severed its ties with the US in 1967'[173] and that these 'foreign partners were to blame for the decline of the relations in the past'.[174] In September 1969, under pressure from the growing strength of the People's Republic of South Yemen (PRSY), which was getting aid from the Soviet Union, and due to the need for the American aid, Prime Minister 'Abd Allah al-Kurshmi announced that Yemen would welcome the restoration of relations with the US if the latter showed good intentions.[175] Two months after the prime minister's widely quoted statement, an official meeting between foreign ministers of the two countries was held in the UN after which the Yemeni foreign minister said they had 'discussed the issue of restoring relations'.[176]

The seventy-day seige of Sana'a in 1967–68 was the basis for a reconciliation with the forces opposing Egyptian involvement in Yemeni affairs. The civil war came to an end in April 1970 and a compromise was reached that retained the republic and brought back some former royalist leaders, with the exception of members of the Hamid al-Din family. In early 1970 while a Sana'a–Riyadh reconciliation was being negotiated, it was reported that on a YAR initiative an American diplomatic office was to be permitted to open within the Italian Embassy in Sana'a. The US reciprocated by permitting a Yemeni political office to open within the Somali Embassy in Washington.[177] When Sana'a and Riyadh reached a compromise in 1970, it was expected that Sana'a–Washington relations would be quickly restored. But there seemed to be no pressure from the US to do so; this was perhaps because Washington had no reason to feel any threat from the YAR since the general situation in the Middle East was already dominated by the US presence. The US department director of the Arabian peninsula country desk stated other reasons for US caution towards the YAR after 1967: the possible influence of many other nations and the unstable political situation in Sana'a and the rest of the country.[178]

The same attitude towards Sana'a prevailed in Riyadh. YAR–KSA reconciliation was greatly affected by the poor relations between Aden and Riyadh, which had resulted in a limited military encounter during the last few days of 1969. This confrontation did not seem to affect US policies towards North Yemen during this period. The US administration left the KSA to tackle the republican regime in Sana'a. Faisal continued to use tribal leverage against the republican forces, but after the proclamation of the PRSY and the royalist failure of the seige of Sana'a, he recognized the YAR and became reconciled with its leaders. However, Faisal continued to use his influence on the tribal and traditional forces in North Yemen in order to address the more radical forces in Aden, which started to threaten the sheikhdoms of the peninsula.[179]

Political developments within the two Yemens in 1970, it seemed, started to attract some US political interest in the YAR. On 29 April 1970 it was reported that Robert McClintock, the second secretary at the US Embassy in Sana'a before the severing of relations in 1967, had returned to work in the American interests section of the Italian Embassy.[180] The famine that affected some two million people in many North Yemeni provinces in the summer of 1970 caused more problems for the Yemeni economy. The famine was caused by three consecutive years of drought which dried up the country's complex irrigation and well system. The low-lying Tihama region along the Red Sea was the worst affected. The US was the most active country in the international relief operation, which lasted for more than a year.[181]

On 25 May 1971, the YAR's economic plight was highlighted by Prime Minister Ahmad Muhammad Nu'man, who told the Yemeni Parliament, the Consultative Assembly, that a deficit of 90 million riyals (£8 million) was foreseen for that year's budget, which estimated an expenditure of 170 million riyals while exports would cover only 10 per cent of the annual import bill. He also said that 'appropriations needed for schools, hospitals, development and the maintenance of roads have been excluded from the budget'. Premier Nu'man warned that the government had to repay a debt of £78 million that had been accumulated since 1956, of which £51 million had come from the Soviet Union and China.[182] Nu'man made it clear that he was in favour of restoring relations with the US in the hope of receiving economic aid.

By 1972, several factors affecting the balance of power and oil interests in the region had aroused US interest in restoring relations with the YAR. In 1971 the British withdrew from the Gulf two years after the intention of withdrawal had been announced by Labour Prime Minister Harold Wilson, leaving a political vacuum threatened by the growing Soviet presence in the Indian Ocean–Persian Gulf area, South Yemen and the Horn of Africa. Another factor was the Arab boycott of the US following the 1967 Six Day War. David Ransom, whose 'recommendations brought Secretary Rogers to Sana'a in 1972',[183] told the present author that a major incentive for the US to restore relations was 'to break the front of the Arab world against the US'; thus relations with Sana'a were 'the first step by an Arab country after the 1967 rupture … at that time that was important'. He also said that the

US had contacted the governments of Sudan and Algeria recommending that they follow the path of the YAR in restoring relations with the US. Both agreed to do this but ultimately only Khartum did so.[184] The US was also concerned about the attempted 1969 coup in Saudi Arabia which, although it had been crushed, had aimed to replace the monarchical regime by a republican one.[185] In Libya, a successful revolution in 1969 had overthrown the monarch; President Kadhafi's anti-Western attitude led to the evacuation of the US air force base at Wheelus Field and the nationalization of the marketing facilities of four North American oil companies, as well as the cutback of the production operations of three others. Developments in the oil market were another factor. In December 1970, a decision had been taken in Caracas to raise oil prices and there was talk in Riyadh of nationalizing ARAMCO. There was pressure on the Nixon administration from a number of US oil companies, which assured the US government that there existed a real need for Arab oil to supplement declining domestic resources. The drift of the YAR towards Saudi Arabia, resulting from its rivalry with South Yemen, had led to a deterioration in relations with the USSR, making it a suitable buffer zone between the KSA (for Washington, the most important country in terms of oil interests), and the most anti-US Arab country, the PRSY.[186]

Also of considerable importance was the rise of a radical South Yemen, which severed relations with Washington on 24 October 1969. Aden started to enjoy increasing Soviet military and economic assistance, and began to incite the YAR opposition based in Aden to launch guerrilla attacks to overthrow the YAR government. Washington saw that the Soviet Union had gained a military foothold in South Yemen, and, therefore, decided not to see another YAR challenge to Saudi Arabia, or to other friends in the peninsula.[187]

The rise of a radical pro-Soviet South Yemen in 1969, the beginnings of a leftist opposition guerrilla war on YAR territory in an encounter with the strong Saudi influence in Sana'a, and the YAR's support of the PRSY opposition can be seen as the most important factors behind renewed US interest in the YAR. In a reaction to some anti-PRSY activities by neighbouring states inside its borders, and as a result of its ideological orientation, the 1969 South Yemen government decided to give full support to national liberation movements in neighbouring states and sheikhdoms, mainly in Oman, which borders on the Persian Gulf and the Straits of Hormuz. The Western powers, especially the US, recognized this to be a destabilizing factor in the area. The Western media reported that the Soviets were using Aden as a military base and the British-built airfield outside the city as a base for their reconnaissance. It was alleged that Moscow had constructed a naval radio station and ammunition depot on the Island of Socotra. Soviet and Cuban military advisers and East German police advisers were reported to be at work in the PRSY. In November 1969, limited border clashes between Saudi Arabia and the PRSY demonstrated KSA military superiority. From 1968, the Revolutionary Democratic Party (RDP) of Yemen, based in Aden, launched a guerrilla war in 'al-manatikal-wusta' or the central areas of the YAR in order 'to restore the revolution in Sana'a'[188] which had been undermined by the KSA. This ended a phase of cordial relations between the two Yemeni states which had characterized the period following the independence of South Yemen on 30 November 1967. The RDP guerrilla operations that escalated throughout 1971 and 1972 with the Southern Yemeni armed forces were, reportedly, supplied with modern Soviet equipment. This situation in Aden, which gave Moscow a strong foothold in the PDRY, heightened once again the concern and alarm of the KSA and the US, both of which sought to tie Sana'a closely to them in order to use it as a 'buffer zone' and as a weapon against the radical PDRY. Following the Saudi recognition of the moderate YAR in 1970, Riyadh gradually became able to affect the political outcome in Sana'a. In an effective move against radicalism and revolution in Yemen, a Saudi military delegation visited Sana'a in May 1972 to prepare for direct military cooperation to accompany the financial aid and tribal subsidies which tied the YAR tightly to Saudi Arabia. This Saudi initiative, which widened the political gap between Sana'a and Aden and Sana'a and Moscow, two months later brought the YAR closer to the US.

Renewal of diplomatic relations

On 1 July 1972 diplomatic relations were restored between Sana'a and Washington, ostensibly following a Yemeni initiative. This was a significant move by the YAR, which had been the first Arab country to sever its ties with Washington. The YAR government sought to restore its relations with the US for political and economic reasons. Sana'a calculated that good relations with Washington would lessen the threat and pressure from the post-1969 radical PDRY government, as well as compensating for the rapidly deteriorating relations with its old ally, the Soviet Union, which curtailed its economic aid and arms supplies to the country in 1970 and 1971. Kadi 'Abdul-Rahman ibn Yahya al-Iryani, Chairman of the YAR Republican Council 1967–74, emphasized that his country, 'which suffered a lot during the civil war, found itself in need of aid from any source ... therefore it restored its relations with the US'.[189] The YAR prime minister at the time later affirmed that the other reason was political: some of his government colleagues believed that such a step would help Sana'a counter the Marxist threat from the South.[190]

The prompt, positive US response to the Yemeni initiative indicates that renewed US interest in the YAR reflected Washington's wider concerns in the area. The US objective at that time was to break the anti-US front in the Arab world. There is some evidence to suggest that the US indirectly pushed Sana'a to seek a restoration in relations, as the YAR prime minister and foreign minister in 1972, Muhsin Ahmad al-'Aini, revealed.[191]

The importance to the US of good relations with the Arab world was also indicated by America's decision to approach Egypt in July 1972. Cairo made a sudden move towards the West later in the same month when President Muhammad Anwar Al-Sadat ordered all Soviet advisers out of Egypt. The US had clearly decided to take a firmer stand in the Middle East against the Soviet Union and the anti-US element because it perceived its economic and political interests to be seriously threatened.

Between 1967 and 1972 there were many indicators of the growth in influence of the USSR, and the nationalist and radical elements in the Middle East, especially in the Gulf and the Arabian peninsula. It was this that caused the US to renew its interest in the YAR in early 1970s. US policy was also affected by Washington's concern to protect American oil interests in the KSA and the Sultanate of Oman and its determination to counter the USSR in the PDRY. As David Ransom later recalled:

> We were interested from the beginning as soon as it was clear that the Republic was going to survive as an independent government from attacks from both the south and the north – we were interested. The Yemeni government moved slowly, step by step, and in the end, Yemen took the step on its own initiative – the first step by an Arab country to renew relations with the US after the 1967 rupture. I think it was in the interest of Yemen to do that.[192]

Secretary of State William Rogers in Sana'a

On 1 July 1972, US Secretary of State William Rogers arrived in Sana'a to restore relations between the two countries. Rogers, who described the occasion as 'historic ... marking a new beginning of mutually beneficial ties', revealed his hope it would 'contribute in a modest way to stability and tranquillity in the Arabian peninsula', and said his discussions with the YAR prime minister and other Yemeni officials would concentrate on 'the prospects for cooperation among neighbouring countries of the peninsula'.[193] Rogers stressed that his country's response to the YAR initiative 'reflects a US policy ... in the area' and that Washington 'looks forward to the day when the few remaining states in the Arab world will take a similar step'.[194]

At a dinner in his honour on the night of his arrival, Rogers said that his country intended 'to continue its efforts to promote a peaceful settlement of the Arab–Israeli dispute, based on full implementation of the UN Security Council resolution of November 1967, number 242.'[195] In his speech of reply, Prime Minister Muhsin al-'Aini announced the resumption of diplomatic relations, and stressed that his country had never forgotten that the US was one of the first countries to have recognized the first republic in the Arabian peninsula, and it had been due to this recognition that 'we were able to occupy our seat in the United Nations, in spite of the fact that the General Assembly session was nearing its end'.[196] After mentioning what he described as 'useful' US-initiated projects in parts of Yemen, he pleaded the Arab cause in Palestine.[197]

The YAR government's enthusiasm for the restoration of relations with the US reflected several factors:

1. It doubted the justice of the severance decision because it had been dictated by the UAR. This was stated clearly by President al-Iryani three months after Rogers' visit when he told foreign correspondents that severance had not been a Yemeni decision.[198]
2. The YAR was convinced that any substantial development aid could be better obtained from the Western powers.[199]
3. The YAR, situated between the closest friends of both superpowers in the Arab world, needed to break the seige.
4. The UAR's plea for the Arab cause in Palestine reflected Sana'a's earlier belief that the Arab–Israeli conflict could not be solved without the participation of the US government, which had the greatest influence in the area.

The YAR government did not expect or ask for prompt aid in return for the restoration of the relations. Al-'Aini later said that the US government did not promise any aid: 'Promises came from others, on my part I was aware that to get paid for restoring relations with a big country is degrading and an insult to the small country – as if they had paid for these relations.' But he stressed that the important thing was that mutual relations had returned to normal, as they should be.[200]

A leading article in the *Washington Post* on 11 July 1972 welcomed the decision of the YAR to become the first Arab League member to resume formal diplomatic relations with the US since the Six Day War, but pointed out that: 'Yemen being the small, poor, strife-plagued country it is, of no particular strategic importance with the Suez Canal closed, the step is no coup for the US.' It added that the restoration decision was of greater importance for Yemen, which 'presumably welcomes the extra political propping against neighbouring South Yemen'. It stressed that a symbolic measure of balance was being restored to a part of the world, which had seemed to be tipping against the US and towards Soviet interests: 'If only psychologically, it is good to see an American Ambassador headed back to Sana'a', and pointed out that the most interesting aspect of the development was 'its evidence of the increased irrelevance of the Arab–Israeli dispute to those Arab countries not directly involved in it'. It concluded by expressing the belief that the resumption of relations between Sana'a and Washington, and the expected restoration of relations with Khartoum, was a blow against Egyptian policy, which wanted to isolate Washington and Tel Aviv, but which actually resulted in Egypt being isolated and penalized.[201]

On 14 July 1972 Secretary of State William Rogers announced that the decision had been taken following appropriate consultations with Congress and that his government intended 'to resume economic assistance programs patterned on our previous programs in Yemen'.[202] Before the end of 1972, Prime Minister al-'Aini expressed the belief that Secretary Rogers' recommendation of the YAR to the International Monetary Fund, the International Food Program and other international economic institutions for which the US provided most of the finance, paved the way for the flow of international aid to the country.[203]

On 29 January 1973 the Yemeni government approved an agreement proposed by the US Embassy in Sana'a in September 1972 concerning an invitation to US Peace Corps volunteers to work in the country.[204] The first US volunteers arrived in 1973 to serve in health, education and rural and urban development programmes.

The full US economic assistance programme to the YAR was resumed on 20 April 1974 upon the signing of the Economic, Technical, and Related Assistance Agreement by the YAR's first minister of development, Dr 'Abdul-Karim al-Iryani and the first US ambassador to the YAR, William R. Crawford. Washington agreed to furnish such economic, technical and related assistance as might be requested by Sana'a and approved by the US government. The YAR agreed to the agreement's terms.[205] The restoration of relations between Sana'a and Washington also opened the YAR to US scholars, journalists and politicians who furthered American understanding of the country.

Inter-Yemeni war follows restoration
of relations

After the restoration of YAR–US diplomatic relations, a point of high tension was reached in Sana'a's relations with the PDRY. These had been deteriorating since July 1968, when South Yemen claimed that Washington was providing the southern opposition with arms and training inside Saudi Arabia and the YAR for the overthrow of the 'Revolutionary regime in the Yemeni arena.'[206] The Northern opposition forces stationed in the PRSY[207] reacted by launching attacks in the central areas of the YAR. In early December 1970, the secretary-general of the ruling NLF announced the PDRY's support for all 'liberation movements' in the Arabian peninsula.[208] This drove an even greater wedge between the YAR and the Soviet-backed South and provided the US with the opportunity to challenge Soviet influence in the PDRY. The NLF perceived the renewal of YAR–US relations as an aggressive act and a threat to its 'revolutionary' orientation from 'reactionary and imperialist forces.'[209] The resumption of YAR–US diplomatic relations was responsible for this heightened tension and distrust between the two Yemeni states.

The first inter-Yemeni war broke out on 26 September 1972, and continued until 13 October as a direct result of the tension and the border clashes which had been escalating since the assassination on 21 February that year of Sheikh 'Ali Bin Nadji al-Ghadir, a leading sheikh of the northern Bakil tribes,[210] and more than sixty of his followers. According to an official YAR statement the South Yemenis had invited the sheikh to a banquet where he and his party had been killed. Rumours in Sana'a at the time claimed that mines had been planted beneath the tents of the Khawlan[211] guests before the feast and that they had been killed while asleep that night. The immediate cause of the outbreak of war on 26 September was an attack on southern areas by the southern armed opposition forces stationed in the YAR. According to Prime Minister al-'Aini, the KSA persuaded the Southern opposition in the YAR to attack Southern areas while he was out of the country.[212] But according to a statement by Sheikh 'Abd Allah al-Ahmar, the paramount sheikh of the Hashid confederation tribes and adviser to the president and the chairman of the parliament 'Madjlis Al-Shoura' (The Consultative Assembly), the YAR parliament had decided, even before the eruption of war, to reunite Yemen by use of force.[213]

In part, this inter-Yemeni war can be seen as a consequence of superpower rivalry. Riyadh feared that stable and strong regimes in the more populous YAR and PDRY could exert a serious threat to its

monarchy and security; the Libyan support to the Front for the Liberation of Occupied South Yemen (FLOSY) forces in the YAR was also
a contributory factor. Yet another factor was that the armed groups
opposed to the two Yemeni republics were stationed under supervision
in both capitals. The restoration of YAR–US relations exacerbated the
situation: the US was judged, by its willingness to counter radicalism
in the Arabian peninsula, to be safeguarding its own interests in such
a highly volatile region.

The military government of Ibrahim al-Hamdi, which took power
in 1974, found itself subjected to increasing Saudi influence and confronted by deteriorating relations with both the PDRY and the Soviet
Union. In this year the hundred Soviet advisers employed to train the
Yemeni army became isolated. The expulsion of the Soviet advisers
from Egypt by President Sadat pushed Moscow to send more arms to
Aden to defend and help its 'people's revolution' and strengthen its
foothold in this strategic part of the Western sphere of influence. All
this occurred in the wake of the October 1973 Arab–Israeli war, which
created an oil boom and gave Saudi Arabia a greater opportunity to
exert influence in the Middle East. It was evident that the wealthier
Saudis, encouraged by the US, became more influential in the YAR
and more dependent on it for their labour force and, consequently,
more able and more willing to attempt to contain the USSR in the
PDRY and the Red Sea region.

YAR–US relations were affected by the Saudi policy of offering aid
to Sana'a, a policy that promoted and utilized the political instability
in the YAR for its own ends. Lieutenant-Colonel Ibrahim al-Hamdi,
who assumed power in Sana'a on 13 June 1974, was considered pro-
Riyadh. Yet he tried to lessen the heavy Saudi hand on his country by
seeking US arms and economic assistance, as had his predecessor. In
August 1975 al-Hamdi confirmed that his country was negotiating with
the US for a package of arms, including several F-5 fighters worth
nearly $100 million. In 1977 the deal was increased to a total of $138
million of arms, to be financed by and channelled through Saudi
Arabia.[214]

Riyadh vetoes direct YAR–US dealings

Despite a united Riyadh–Sana'a stand against a radical threat from the
PDRY, there were many long-term political, territorial and religious
differences, dating back to the 1920s[215] between the YAR and the KSA
which inhibited any amelioration in their relationship. Sana'a's efforts
to have direct dealings with Washington were intercepted by the KSA,
which did not want to weaken its own influence in the internal affairs

of the YAR. KSA leaders calculated that if the Yemenis were to gain political stability, economic independence and military strength, there would be an attempt to recapture the three bordering provinces which had been annexed by King 'Abdul-'Aziz in 1934.

On the other hand, Saudi Arabia could not forget the insecurity it had experienced during the five years following the outbreak of the YAR revolution, in 1962. It became alarmed by the prospect of a stronger, more radical PDRY, which might gain control of the YAR. An anti-Saudi government in North Yemen had always been the main fear of the government in Riyadh and it therefore concerned itself with all developments in Sana'a. On this, the London *Financial Times*[216] wrote: 'The Saudis fear Yemen's political volatility, which is made important for them by the fact that the Yemeni population of some [10][217] million is ... bigger than their population. One specific fear is that there might be a left wing coup d'etat in Sana'a. Even more alarming is the thought of a union of the two Yemens, with a combined population of some 13 million, under a left wing government.' In the words of a Saudi senior intelligence official, 'Saudi Arabia views events in North Yemen as having a major influence on Saudi internal security, whether positively or negatively.'[218]

Direct relations between the YAR and the US commenced in 1974 through some small-scale military dealings. But against the YAR's wishes, these military dealings soon became indirect as they were channelled through Saudi Arabia. This Saudi policy towards the YAR was approved by Washington when in this year the KSA forwarded to the United States the YAR's list of new weapon requirements. This eventually led to the dispatch of an American military team to study the republic's military needs, although negotiations for a long-term US arms deal with Sana'a did not start until near the end of 1975.[219] Early in 1975, the YAR's president, al-Hamdi, asserted his government's willingness to accept arms without conditions from any source.[220] He also showed eagerness to ease military ties with the USSR and to expel the Soviet experts if the US would provide the necessary arms. His efforts were ignored because, according to Yemeni sources, the Saudis continued 'to delay in making a firm commitment on which arms will be purchased for Yemen despite warnings that delay could be disastrous for Colonel Hamdi's still weak central government'.[221] Due to this complex situation, the US Embassy in Djiddah prodded the Saudis 'to be swift and generous in helping bolster Colonel al-Hamdi's position with arms'.[222] In early 1975, to overcome this problem, President al-Hamdi expressed his hope that 'a new friendship with the US will exist', and sought to consolidate relations with Riyadh at the cost of further deteriorating relations with the PDRY. Relations with Washington improved as a result. In the same year the US prepared a plan to provide the YAR with arms to be financed by Saudi Arabia; a trilateral agreement to provide Sana'a with a package of modern US arms was signed in 1976.

This agreement with Saudi Arabia to modernize the YAR's armed forces indicated that the US had 'approved and encouraged Saudi Arabia's desire to become a leading force in the region of the Persian Gulf to tackle radicalism'.[223] At this time it was reported that South Yemen had begun to receive modern tanks, planes and naval vessels from the Soviet Union to counter the Saudi–US supply of arms to the YAR. On 11 February 1976, the leftist northern opposition in the YAR formed the National Democratic Front (NDF) with Sultan Ahmad 'Umar as its secretary-general, indicating that the opposition, supported by the PDRY, was willing to escalate its military operations in the YAR. The US consequently put strong pressure on Saudi Arabia to finance the arms deal since it perceived the YAR to be 'a useful Western-orientated buffer state between the traditionally ruled oil-producing states of the Gulf and South Yemen'.[224] But the idea of providing the YAR with free arms was not acceptable to Saudi Arabia which continued to depend on the belligerent northern tribes to imple-ment its policies towards Sana'a. In the words of the American military attaché in Sana'a: Saudi Arabia had caught itself in the impossible bind of wanting a North Yemen that was 'strong enough but not too strong'.[225] In the words of US Ambassador George Lane: 'the Saudis wanted the North Yemenis to have guns that will only point South.'[226]

Because Riyadh was not convinced it should provide Sana'a with modern arms, it tried to contain the threat from South Yemen by other means. The Saudi government responded to a two-year-old PDRY initiative to establish relations based on mutual respect and non-interference in each other's affairs. Saudi Arabia and the PDRY established diplomatic relations just one month after the formation of the NDF. A joint communiqué was broadcast in both Aden and Riyadh on 10 March 1976, in which the two Arab and Islamic states expressed their 'desire to create an atmosphere of mutual understanding to serve their causes and those of the Arabian Peninsula ... in affirmation of the importance of safeguarding and consolidating relations among all the states of the region in an atmosphere of mutual respect for the sovereignty of every state over its territory.'[227] It confirmed that both states had reviewed their relations 'in present circumstances' and con-cluded that Riyadh and Aden 'declare their intention to establish normal relations between them on the basis of Arab fraternity, good-neighbourliness, unity of destiny and non-interference in internal affairs, in a manner that realises the security and stability of the Arab peninsula and the interest of the Arab nation, away from foreign influence.'[228] PDRY internal political and economic problems, its need to obtain some Saudi assistance, its plans to activate the strategic Aden harbour after the reopening of the Suez Canal, and the mutual KSA–PDRY concern over the growing Iranian military presence in Oman, pushed the two countries towardscooperation for the first time. The Saudi response had a calming effect on the NDF and the People's Front for the Liberation of Oman (PFLO) guerrilla war that was taking place in the YAR and in Dhofar, a southern province of Oman. This development gave Saudi Arabia an excuse to argue with both Washington and Sana'a that arms were not needed in Sana'a. Riyadh also convinced the US of the feasibility of initiating some contacts with the PDRY instead of providing the YAR with arms that could be used to control the YAR northern tribes, or pointed North. As Robert Burrowes, an American specialist on the YAR, concluded, the Saudis 'have sometimes acted in each of the Yemens through the other Yemen'.[229]

All these Saudi manoeuvres, talks, hopes and promises resulted in few military or economic fields of cooperation between the YAR and the US in the period 1972–76. During the years following the resumption of diplomatic relations Washington provided Sana'a with only $16.8 million in economic aid and $200,000 in military aid, while Riyadh provided the YAR with more than $400 million as development assistance.[230] According to American military scholar Major John B. Lynch, Washington gave Sana'a only a limited amount of aid because it wanted 'to keep taut the string of relationship with Saudi Arabia'.[231] In March 1975, the USAID office was upgraded to full mission status and located in Sana'a. It continued a modest aid programme throughout the rest of the 1970s. The level of aid to Yemen was constantly debated in Washington with several factors in mind, but the foremost was always: what is the national interest of the US?[232] Despite all the rational analyses, the fact is that it was the oil boom of 1973[233] which gave Saudi Arabia the upper hand in the Yemeni arena and this was reflected in the YAR–US relationship of that period. It should be noted that US aid worldwide was affected by an economic recession. This, and the continued US lack of economic interest in Sana'a, meant that the US Department of State was content to leave the YAR to the Saudi programme. No big development project was undertaken by the US government in the 1970s and 1980s because such projects were no longer US policy.[234]

Bloody events in the Yemen and US concern

In 1977, in reaction to Saudi policies and in order to put some pressure on the US, President al-Hamdi visited Europe and sought French arms in 'an attempt to break out of the diplomatic pattern largely dominated by Saudi Arabia and the United States'.[235] When he returned home he contacted the US ambassador to Sana'a, Thomas Scotts, to complain that Saudi Arabia was delaying the delivery of arms under the agreement. The US then urged the Saudis to deliver some arms to Sana'a.[236] Ambassador Scotts seemed concerned about the US stance in Yemen.[237] Scotts argued for US mediation between Saudi Arabia and Yemen to protect al-Hamdi from the Saudis. This caused tension between the Department of State and the ambassador. Scotts opposed the arms delay, wanting a prompt delivery to protect al-Hamdi from the sceptical US policy. But he was told, 'We won't upset relations with Riyadh for a small country like Yemen.' In his belief, the US 'wanted to have the Yemen on the cheap and wanted the Saudis to pay for its friendship even when American interests were threatened by Aden'.[238] President al-Hamdi, who saw the Saudi pronouncements as a waste of time, became convinced he could not rely on Riyadh to reorganize and equip his army in order to establish central government control over the northern tribes who were more loyal to the Saudi money or to help him uproot the Saudi political influence in his country. He decided to break the Saudi stronghold in the YAR by forming closer relations with the PDRY.

At the height of al-Hamdi's efforts to break through this 'pattern largely dominated by Saudi Arabia and the US',[239] al-Hamdi and his brother 'Abd Allah were assassinated during the night of 12 October 1977, a few hours before his first scheduled visit to Aden to proclaim, with his southern counterpart, a new step towards Yemen unification. It was not in the interest of the KSA that Yemen unify. This incident put an end to the YAR's efforts to be independent of the KSA for about two years. Burrowes later wrote:

> Despite this event which brought Col. Ahmad al-Ghashmi, more responsive to Saudi Arabia, to power, Saudi policy toward the reorganization of the Yemeni army did not apparently change. One year later, it was observed that the YAR army was much weaker than it was in 1974. The Saudis had played political football with the program and used it ... to manipulate Yemen's politics and its leaders to their ends.[240]

On 24 June 1978 President Ahmad al-Ghashmi also met the same fate as his predecessor. According to Sana'a sources, Salem Rubiyya' 'Ali, the chairman of the Presidential Council of the PDRY, had telephoned al-Ghashmi on 23 June to inform him that he was sending a special envoy to Sana'a. When the envoy arrived in Sana'a airport the next morning, he was directed to President Ghashmi's office, where he opened an explosive-filled briefcase, killing both men.[241]

On 26 June a military struggle broke out between political factions in South Yemen, during which the 43–year-old President Salem Rubiyya' 'Ali lost his life. According to the official announcement on Aden Radio, the Central Committee of the ruling Unified Political Organization of the National Front (UPONF) had held an emergency meeting on the evening of 25 June to discuss developments in the North but Rubiyya' refused to attend and instead sent his resignation. When the meeting reconvened the next morning to discuss his resignation, Rubiyya' ordered forces loyal to him to bomb the Committee headquarters in an attempted coup; the Central Committee retaliated by ordering a military attack on Rubiyya'. Within a few hours the Committee ordered the execution of Rubiyya' and two of his close associates.[242]

In Sana'a the leading officers and political elites chose 'Abdul-Karim al-'Arashi, speaker of the assembly, as acting president for a two-month period until presidential elections could take place. On 17 July the People's Constituent Assembly elected Lieutenant-Colonel 'Ali 'Abd Allah Saleh president and commander-in-chief of the armed forces, upgrading him to the rank of colonel. The fifth president of the YAR immediately began to reorganize the divided, ill-equipped, army and to contact the sheikhs and persuade them, the political elite, to work towards permanent stability. Saleh survived an attempted assassination a few days after his election.[243] Three months later, on 15 October 1978, Saleh survived another attempt on his life by a Libyan-backed Nasserist faction headed by Colonel Mudjahid al-Kuhali. The minister of social affairs, 'Abdul-Salam Mukbil, and other senior army officers were subsequently sentenced to death; others fled the country. In Aden the execution of President Rubiyya' in June was followed by the creation of the Yemeni Socialist Party (YSP) in October as successor to the Unified Political Organization of National Front (UPONF). Elections to the Supreme People's Assembly were held in December. 'Abdul-Fattah Isma'il, a hard-line Marxist, became chairman of the Presidential Council and the secretary-general of the YSP.

Following the success of the hard-liners in the south, the NDF commenced its armed attacks inside the YAR and was calling for the overthrow of the 'reactionary' regime in Sana'a. These guerrilla operations were supported by Isma'il, who presided over the party congress of October 1978, which was attended by the NDF secretary-general, who publicly declared support for the NDF. These Yemeni developments, which made the situation critical in southern Arabia, caused much concern in Riyadh, ever fearful as it was of communist expansion in the region.

The US also became concerned, especially since three years of Saudi–US efforts to moderate the PDRY had clearly failed. The US moderating attempts began in 1974 when Republican Congressman Paul Findlay had been invited to Aden to discuss the release of an American teacher, Ed Franklin; the latter had been imprisoned for taking photographs of Aden harbour without permission during a transit tour stop of his ship. Findlay handed the PDRY foreign minister, Muhammad Saleh Muti', and President Rubiyya' a letter from US Secretary of State Henry Kissinger, which presented Washington's desire to achieve 'a just and durable peace in the Middle East'. An alleged case of espionage that same year, resulting in the imprisonment of several Americans working in South Yemen and President Ford's decision in 1975 to supply the YAR with modern US arms, brought all indirect US–PDRY communication to a halt. The establishment of relations between Aden and Riyadh in March 1976 was followed by a Saudi attempt to promote talks between Washington and Aden, but the US replacement of the British in the Masyarah air-base in neighbouring Oman and the outbreak of the Somali–Ethiopian war in the Horn of Africa,[244] which created diverse South Yemeni, Saudi and US responses, prevented any immediate dialogue. Congressman Findlay met President Rubiyya' again at the United Nations Assembly in September 1977 when the latter addressed that year's general session. According to Findlay, Rubiyya' 'restated his desire for renewed relations with the United States and suggested that I report our discussion to Secretary of State Cyrus Vance'.[245] Encouraged by Saudi Arabia, Cyrus Vance also met with the PDRY foreign minister on UN premises and it was agreed that the US would send a mission to Aden to discuss the issue of restoring relations between the two states. Between 13 and 15 January Findlay visited Aden for the second time and held talks with both Muti' and Rubiyya' on the prospects of mutual relations.[246] Findlay carried back to the Carter administration a verbal response from Rubiyya'.[247] Clearly the US was almost convinced of the feasibility of restoring relations, especially since this would offer Washington an opportunity to confront the Soviets from their only stronghold in the peninsula. In a letter dated 26 January 1978 to the US national security advisor, Zbigniew Brzezinski, Findlay wrote: 'Thanks very much for receiving Mrs Meyner, Leo Ryan and myself in regard to Palestinian and South Yemen policies. I am reassured by your statement that the Executive Branch will check further with Saudi Arabia with regard to diplomatic relations with South Yemen. This is, it seems to me, very prudent for us to have a listening post there reinforcing the one already established by the Saudis.'[248]

On 26 June 1978 a State Department official announced that the director of the Arabian peninsula desk, Joseph Twinam, 'was on his way to Aden when President Rubiyya' was deposed' and was therefore only able to visit Saudi Arabia.[249] With Rubiyya' out of the way, YSP Secretary-General 'Abul-Fattah-Isma'il consolidated his power, announcing his willingness to adopt a clear pro-Soviet line and to put PDRY resources into a confrontation with 'imperialism, reaction and conservatism in the area'.[250] Tension escalated with Oman as a result of PDRY support to a leftist revolution in Oman at a time when the NDF re-commenced its guerrilla operations in the YAR. In Aden it was announced on 5 January 1979 that the '13th June front'[251] had decided to join the NDF.[252] Moscow's position on the Horn of Africa may have been behind the Soviet willingness to enhance its presence in the PDRY. Stephen Page, a Canadian Sovietologist, saw that Moscow's loss of access to facilities in Somalia in November 1977 increased Aden's importance to Soviet strategy, leading to the creation of a more radical pro-Soviet leadership in the PDRY.[253] One month later Aden became involved in the Soviet support of Ethiopia. A small number of PDRY forces were dispatched to the battlefield near Oghadin in support of Ethiopia against the new Saudi ally, Somalia. Failure of Riyadh–Washington efforts to contain the PDRY by diplomacy resulted in the emergence of a harder US stance against the PDRY; Washington believed Moscow to be behind the crisis of June 1978 in Aden in order to block relations with the US and KSA. In this scenario, one entirely consistent with Cold War politics of the time, Moscow would have wished to preserve its foothold in the area, especially in Yemen, by any means. The US administration was therefore prepared to defend its own foothold in the YAR both militarily and politically.

The change in the government of South Yemen was viewed in Washington as a new challenge to the US strategy of reducing the Soviet role in the oil-rich area. The American Embassy in Sana'a 'viewed the political turmoil in late June 1978 from the perspective of North Yemen's vulnerability to military action from the South'.[254] The embassy strongly recommended that 'with a minimum of effort by the United States, quantities of weapons already purchased for Yemen by Saudi Arabia could be shipped by air to Yemen on an expedited basis, thus significantly improving North Yemen's defensive posture'. The US military attaché stated: 'Since Saudi Arabia was paying the bill, our only hurdle was to convince them of the feasibility of our initiative. Accordingly, a conference was arranged (with the approval of state) to be held in Riyadh in late July.'[255]

The choice of Riyadh as the venue for this conference on Yemen defence needs reflected US concern for the security of Saudi Arabia. John Ruszkiewicz, the US military attaché in Sana'a, travelled to Riyadh in late July to work out the arms deliveries with the US Military Assistance Mission in Saudi Arabia 'prior to presenting our concept to the Saudi military'. The conference, attended by representatives of a number of department agencies from Washington, discussed the US proposal to improve the YAR's defence capabilities and developed a programme for the use of the American equipment by Sana'a which meant an increase in the US presence paid for by the Saudis. This conclusion by the conference aimed at 'supplanting' the Russians completely from the YAR as well as challenging the Soviets in South Yemen.

The American media openly stated that the US was 'accelerating its military aid to North Yemen as a response to the recent tightening of Soviet influence in South Yemen' and that 'the Carter administration is also considering sending a military advisory mission to North Yemen to try to reorganize and train its army. So far, that army has not been able to make proper use of U.S. ... military equipment that Saudi Arabia is paying for.'[256] Both the US and Saudi Arabian governments expressed interest in an increase in US commitment. Instead of only supplying arms and training a few officers, the Saudis and Americans suggested that a US military advisory mission could be established in the YAR to take direct responsibility for building up the armed forces and improving the air force. With the approval of Congress, Saudi Arabia transferred from its stocks four trainer versions of the American-made F-5 fighters to the YAR. Also discussed was the possibility of 'following up the trainers with a dozen F-5 jets'.[257]

The US proposal was not welcomed in Sana'a. Both the Americans and the Saudis asked the YAR to cut its links with the USSR, but Sana'a wanted to maintain at least minimal links with Moscow. The cost was considered to be too high since the programme did not include necessary items such as aircraft, tanks, artillery and modern rockets similar to those being delivered to the PDRY by the Soviet Union. In early 1979 President Saleh told a Kuwaiti journal: 'Our current acquisition of US arms is limited and we have not received what we really need from the US.'[258] It took the Saudi government, which was not convinced of the feasibility of the new package to the YAR, three months to decide what to do. Eventually, as a result of US pressure, they submitted the letters of offer and acceptance for the new equipment in January 1979, when the situation in Iran was alarming both Washington and Riyadh more than that in Sana'a.

On 10 February 1979, US Defense Secretary Harold Brown visited

Saudi Arabia. On his arrival the Saudis suggested a larger US presence and commitment in their region – a suggestion for which Washington was not prepared. Saudi intelligence assured Brown that the Soviet threat to the kingdom was real and 'produced information that large numbers of South Yemeni tanks and artillery were moving into a remote area of North Yemen, supported by air strikes',[259] reports which the Americans were 'unable to confirm'. On 12 February Brown delivered to Saudi Crown Prince Fahd Bin 'Abdul-'Aziz a letter from President Carter to King Khaled 'suggesting periodic consultation between Washington and Riyadh on matters affecting the security of the Gulf region'.[260] Washington officials stated: 'Saudi Arabia has been urging the United States for months to take a firmer stand in the region to counterbalance Soviet influence in Afghanistan, South Yemen and Ethiopia.' In both Riyadh and Zahran, Brown held talks with his Saudi counterpart, Prince Sultan. He also made an aerial inspection of the nearby oil fields. The discussions concentrated on weapons sales for North Yemen and Sudan, which were considered 'the first tangible result of a new US pledge to consult more closely with Saudi Arabia on defence matters.' A report from Washington revealed that the United States was prepared to sell twelve F-5 fighters to Yemen and was willing to consider additional F-5s, tanks and armoured personnel carriers in a package totalling approximately $300 million, all to be financed by the Saudis. According to the same report the deal would be 'subject to Congressional approval'.[261]

Conclusion

During the period between 1972 and early 1979 the improvement in YAR–US diplomatic relations reflected an understanding between Sana'a and Washington, developed though through the KSA, the principal US ally and partner in the Arab world. Regional politics, especially the rise of the PRSY–PDRY with a red foreign policy and the departure of the British from the Gulf, increased Washington's interest in the YAR. The advent of the Johnson administration to the White House, the UAR defeat by Israel in 1967 and the subsequent change in Egypt's alliances with a drift towards the West, the implementation of the Nixon Doctrine in the Gulf and the Indian Ocean region with its two pillars the KSA and Iran, the increase of Saudi oil production to 10 million barrels per day, shifted US interest from the UAR to the KSA. US interest in the YAR, therefore, was a reflection of its interest in the KSA.

Restoration of diplomatic relations in 1972 was in the interest of both Sana'a and Washington. The YAR used these relations to reduce the pressure from both Riyadh and Aden. It also obtained technical and development assistance from the US government directly and from international donors. From its side, the US used Sana'a to break the Arab boycott against Washington, which had persisted since 1967. It also successfully used the YAR as a buffer zone between its huge oil investments in the KSA and the communist threat in the PDRY. By the beginning of 1979, it was clear that Sana'a and Washington had developed serious and sophisticated foreign policies towards each other, both having come to respect the need for a real and more direct bilateral relationship.

4

Development of a US interest in the YAR

Although the US had not heretofore had a bilateral interest in Yemen or Yemeni affairs, between 1979 and 1989 several factors persuaded Washington to adopt a Yemen policy. These were: the Cold War, which erupted into a proxy 'hot war' between the two Yemens; the role played by Saudi Arabia and its anxieties over Soviet influence in southern Yemen; US policy in the Middle East in general and its shock over the 1989 Iranian revolution; economic relationships including the aid relationship, a barometer of US interest; and, most crucially, the discovery of oil in Yemen by US firms.

The Yemeni stage of the Cold War

Tension between the YAR and the PDRY increased in January 1979, reaching a climax in February. This tension was reflected by the National Democratic Front (NDF) guerrilla attacks, military preparations in both capitals, President 'Abdul-Fattah Isma'il's tour to Syria, Kuwait, Iraq and Libya, where he secured financial support from Libya for the NDF, and several official statements from both Yemens.

The first two weeks of February witnessed frequent clashes along the YAR–PDRY borders. American sources confirmed that the Yemeni government had summoned US diplomats in Sana'a and told them that Aden, assisted by the Soviets, was attacking YAR territory. Within a few days the CIA office in Sana'a confirmed the seriousness of the situation. But the military office reported it as being exaggerated. Two weeks later US Ambassador George Lane 'decided to go along with accounts of a very serious situation and make policy recommendations to Washington accordingly'.[1] In mid-February, Washington sought informal consent from Congress to most of the items of a $390 million arms package financed by Saudi Arabia to the YAR.

During the second half of February 1979, the US government

announced 'a more active policy to shore up the security of the Arabian Peninsula in the light of events in Iran'.[2] It also expressed concern 'about the recent flare-up in fighting between North and South Yemen'. But on 27 February President Carter stressed that he did not intend to deploy US troops anywhere in the Middle East, and denied press reports that his administration had proposed setting up a military base in Saudi Arabia, making it clear that America intended to provide only encouragement to its friends in the area to defend themselves and to protect US interests against Iran and South Yemen. Yet Washington confirmed that $100 million worth of American arms to the YAR had been dispatched by air, 'mainly infantry support weapons such as anti-tank and anti-aircraft guns'.[3] On 23 February YAR and PDRY troops became engaged in open warfare. On 28 February the Department of State announced it was increasing arms supplies to the YAR for 'defensive' use against 'invading PDRY forces',[4] and notified Congress of its intention to waive the waiting period for these. The Carter administration also informed the Saudi government of its decision to deploy a squadron of F-15s and two AWACS aircraft to Saudi Arabia 'to bolster the security of Saudi airspace'. It ordered a carrier task force headed by the *Constellation* from the Seventh Fleet into the western Indian Ocean to demonstrate US concern for the security of the Arabian peninsula, and 'to deter any possible South Yemeni advance into the North, should the opportunity for this on the ground appear'.[5]

In late February and early March 1979, US military teams started to arrive in Sana'a to train the Yemeni armed forces to operate and maintain the new equipment which arrived when the war was over.[6] State Department spokesman Hodding Carter revealed that 'word has been received from diplomats in Saudi Arabia that military personnel in the desert Kingdom which borders North Yemen had been ordered to report for duty',[7] indicating that the US administration was determined to accelerate arms deliveries to North Yemen without Congressional approval 'to show United States' resolve to our Yemeni friends ... our willingness to protect vital national interests in that part of the world to our Saudi ally, and finally, to send a signal to the Soviets we were serious about meeting Soviet encroachment into the Arabian Peninsula.'[8]

On 3 March 1979, while the war was still going on, PDRY Foreign Minister Muhammad Saleh Muti' stressed that what was going on in the North was a conflict between the Yemeni people led by the NDF in the North, and the regime in Sana'a.[9] An NDF spokesperson told Aden Radio a few days later that 'the client reactionary regime in Sana'a has assembled a strong force of regular troops and mercenaries, led by a notorious warmonger [and] has attempted to recover a number of areas under the control of the revolutionary people's forces'.[10] This source expressed the will of the NDF to continue the war 'against imperialist reactionary influence and to bring about the establishment of a democratic national regime in the YAR'.

The border 'mini-war' between the two Yemeni states of 1979 in which Washington believed the North 'didn't show well'[11] unquestionably heightened the sense of insecurity in the region, alarming the US, which feared that the YAR would impose once again, as it had during the 1960s, a threat to its interests in Saudi Arabia. President Carter increased his country's involvement in South Arabian politics and offered the YAR protection and arms, which had been already 'in the pipeline',[12] against the PDRY.

David Ransom, deputy director of the Office of the Secretary of Defense at the time, confirmed that the US stance towards the YAR in 1979 was both military and political.[13] William R. Crawford, the first US ambassador to the YAR, also justified the US belief in the seriousness of the situation in early 1979. The fighting, was 'more serious than past incidents'[14] and 'clearly a carefully planned, coordinated and amply supported campaign with the apparent intention of seizing and occupying North Yemeni territory and destabilizing the North Yemen government'.

The situation in the Yemens in February and early March 1979 was viewed in the United States in terms of global Washington–Moscow relations: 'President Carter has to take a stand somewhere in the region, and he can do it cheap in Yemen because Saudi Arabia is paying all the bills'[15] Ambassador George Lane quoted Zbigniew Brzezinski as saying at that time that if the YAR–PDRY 'mini-war' had not occurred, 'the US would have wanted to invent something like it as a way of being able to demonstrate that we are serious against the Soviets who were backing their man, 'Abdul-Fattah Isma'il as pushing at the edges of a key country for us, Saudi Arabia', which was 'producing 10 million barrels of crude oil every day and hosts our military bases'.[16] Lane also indicated that the US arms package was designed to serve the security of Saudi Arabia and nothing else:

> The US was trying desperately to persuade Saudi Arabia to support the Camp David agreements [peace treaty between Egypt and Israel in 1979], and the Saudis were saying 'no'. The Saudis asked us to support 'Ali 'Abd Allah. If we didn't then the Saudis would say don't ask for our support any more, from oil to Camp David.[17]

The inter-Yemeni war of 1979 was viewed seriously in Washington because it coincided with many other events that negatively affected implementation of US foreign policy in the area. These main events

were: the Arab opposition to the Camp David agreements; warfare in
the Horn of Africa in 1977–78 as a result of the Ethiopian revolution
which announced its socialist orientation on 11 February 1977;[18] the
revolution in Iran[19] which ended the role of the Shah of Iran as a US
'policeman' in the region; the Soviet influence in Afghanistan;[20] the
growing importance of the Bab al-Mandab straits following the reopening of the Suez Canal throughout the 1973 Arab–Israeli war,
during which Sana'a declared war against Israel; the alleged transfer of
some of the Soviet Union's military capability from Somalia to the
PDRY; and the Carter administration's determination to bring about
peace between Egypt and Israel to end the Soviet influence in the
former.

Aden condemns the US naval movements

On 9 March 1979 a PDRY Foreign Ministry spokesperson confirmed
the dispatch of a US aircraft carrier to the Arabian Sea and the passage
of several US naval units through the Suez Canal to the Red Sea:

> [Aden] sees a clear indication of America's aggressive policy towards the
> peoples and countries of the Gulf and the Arabian Peninsula and the
> resolve of the imperialists to create and expand hotbeds of war and fan
> regional conflicts in an attempt to harm the national sovereignty of the
> Arab states and peoples and to push them into preoccupation with
> regional issues and conflicts.[21]

He added: 'They do it in an attempt to pave a course for Sadat to
complete the negotiations with Israel.' He viewed the US dispatch of
its warships from the Indian Ocean and the airlifted arms from the
West to Sana'a, which aimed 'to bolster up the YAR government at the
cost of the peoples revolution' as a 'flagrant interference in the internal
affairs of the northern part of the homeland' which 'exposes hostile
designs against Democratic Yemen'.[22]

Debate in the US Congress over the US arms package to the YAR

On 12 March 1979 the House of Representatives' Subcommittee on
Europe and the Middle East, chaired by Lee H. Hamilton,[23] held a
hearing on the proposed transfer of the twelve F-5E aircraft, fifty
armoured personnel carriers, sixty-four M-60 tanks and two C-130
transport aircraft to the YAR. (These transfers were considered by the
Arms Control and Disarmament Agency and other executive branch
agencies to represent a necessary and prudent response to the military

situation in Yemen.) The following witnesses were questioned during the Subcommittee session: William R. Crawford, deputy assistant secretary, Bureau of Near Eastern and South Asian Affairs of the Department of State, who had served as the first ambassador to the YAR (1972–74); David Ransom, deputy director, Office of the Deputy Assistant Secretary of Defense for Near Eastern and South Asian Affairs; James Michel, deputy legal adviser, Office of the Legal Adviser, Department of State; and Alan A. Platt, chief, Arms Transfers Division, US Arms Control and Disarmament Agency. The meeting was also attended by Joseph W. Twinam, director of the State Department Bureau of Arabian Peninsula Affairs. This meeting in itself indicated that the US was seriously concerned by events in the Yemens. The situation in the YAR was a serious threat to US interests in Saudi Arabia. The effect of the situation on US security interests was one of the major topics of the debate:

> *Mr Fountain*: I happen to agree with you, right or wrong, that the national security interests of the US are affected by what may happen there. You say Saudi Arabia's security is directly affected by the situation, and neighbouring North Yemen.
> *Mr Crawford*: Yes.
> *Mr Fountain*: How is it directly affected?
> *Mr Crawford*: Remember the million North Yemeni workers who are in every aspect of Saudi Arabia and its life. It is the strong feeling of the government of Saudi Arabia, I think shared by ours, if because of subversion – more than subversion, actual invasion – from the PDRY, North Yemen were to be destabilized to the extent that you have a hostile pro-Soviet regime in North Yemen, all of those million workers in the oil fields and every other aspect of Saudi life would be hostage to the political dictates of the government back home. In other words, they could become a very harmful force in Saudi Arabia and the Gulf. So, there lies the interest of Saudi Arabia in maintaining a government with a politically moderate orientation.[24]

Another aspect discussed was the Soviet presence in South Yemen and its influence in the area, and the failure of Washington–Aden contacts to moderate South Yemen during the lifetime of President Rubiyya'. The witnesses expressed concern about the intelligence estimates of from 800 to 1,000 Soviet advisers, about half of whom were regular military personnel, between 500 and 700 Cuban advisers, and more than one hundred East Germans, primarily concentrated on internal security intelligence.[25] They emphasized the strategic importance of South Yemen: 'You only have to look at the map to know how important the whole area is to the United States.'[26]

This fact was stressed by all the witnesses, but the complexity of the situation was clearly revealed. Like the Saudis, American officials were not sure if the arms delivered would be used to defend Saudi and US interests. Congressman Fountain stated:

I am not sure whether we are shipping to friend or foe. You have Russian advisers in North Yemen, and apparently the Saudis are concerned about the impact of the South Yemeni efforts against North Yemen. Just who will get hold of these tanks and planes, and so forth; do we know?[27]

To some Americans, the YAR was an unreliable ally because although its government was not pro-Soviet, it was not pro-Western either. This debate also indicated that the main objective of the US equipment supplied to North Yemen was political rather than military.[28] The US arms package in itself was useless, but intended simply to interrupt the YAR–Soviet military connection and to achieve a listening post in the YAR army. But following the arrival of the American military advisers, rumours spread in Sana'a that the US advisers who were training the YAR army to use the American arms were at the same time training commandos to blow up bridges in the south, and to use the Vulcan weapons against personnel and against villages. There were also rumours outside the YAR which suggested this was a part of a wider plan by the governments of the YAR, Egypt and Saudi Arabia to overthrow the PDRY government.

Political observers in Washington believed the swift American response to the situation in the YAR to be due to the seriousness of the threat to American interests in Saudi Arabia.

Southern Yemen has been raising hell throughout the region in the decade since the British left. Its radical leaders seem responsive to anyone who wants to cause the Saudis trouble. They are also well supplied with Soviet arms and have recently augmented their corps of Soviet and Cuban advisers.[29]

The eventual ceasefire mediated by the Arab League was a result of American, Soviet, Saudi, Syrian and Iraqi pressure on the PDRY. The NDF and PDRY forces returned to their bases in the South by 23 March, leaving the few border towns and villages they had occupied to YAR forces.

Yemeni talks on reunification and US response, 1979

After the ceasefire, the Arab League arranged for the two Yemeni presidents to meet in Kuwait on 11 March 1979.[30] Instead of merely discussing normalization of relations between the two states, both

Sana'a and Aden stressed that unity, 'the solution for all Yemen's tragedies',[31] was on the agenda. On 26 March PDRY President 'Abdul-Fattah Ismai'l stated that: 'the gravity of the Arab political situation arising from the signing of the treaty of surrender between the Zionist enemy and the Sadat regime will require Saudi Arabia and the Arab oil-producing countries to take practical measures to strengthen Arab solidarity. Foremost among these measures is the oil weapon as confirmation of the clear Arab stance on the Camp David agreement.' President Isma'il accused the US of creating the 1979 inter-Yemeni war 'by sending arms to the region before and after the events between the two parts of Yemen'; Washington 'did not merely aim to avert what had happened in Iran and to preserve its interests, but also to frustrate the efforts of the Arab peoples and transform the Arab–Israeli war into an inter-Arab and inter-Yemeni war, like that which happened in Lebanon.'[32]

It would seem that Ismai'l was suggesting that the US encouraged the inter-Yemeni war to threaten Saudi Arabia, to ensure it would not use the oil weapon against Washington in reaction to the Egyptian–Israeli peace treaty as it had under the leadership of King Faisal in 1973. But if this is what he thought, a pertinent question is: why was the PDRY unable to stop the NDF operations inside the YAR in order to counter the 'imperialist conspiracies' of which the PDRY cabinet spoke one day later?[33]

Instead, the YAR and the PDRY tried to counter these 'conspiracies' in their own way. Between 28 and 30 March President Saleh and his southern counterpart met in Kuwait and decided to begin a new phase in inter-Yemeni relations. On 29 March President Isma'il revealed that the PDRY had proposed a unity plan at the very beginning of the summit.[34] On 30 March President Saleh and President Isma'il announced a new unity accord. Their joint statement asserted a determination 'to consolidate the just pan-Arab struggle against the common enemy represented by the imperialist–Zionist–US alliance and treason'.[35] In the wake of the summit, as a gesture of goodwill, President Saleh dismissed his foreign minister, 'Abd Allah al-Asnadj, and his minister of culture and information, Muhammad Salem Basindwah, who were among the leaders of FLOSY. Rumours in Sana'a said that al-Asnadj opposed President Saleh's attempts to normalize relations with the south and had started cooperating directly with Saudi Arabia in order to influence President Saleh. Alarmed by this development and by the movements towards unity, Saudi Arabia promptly stopped the flow of US arms to Sana'a. The US did not welcome the unity plans because of its strong connections with Saudi Arabia and because they contradicted Washington's own plans to counter Soviet influence in the PDRY.

Minimal YAR–US relations

When the war ended in March 1979, YAR–US relations were interrupted: American interests in Saudi Arabia were no longer under
threat, and the Saudis, who had better connections with Washington
and who had financed the US arms package to Sana'a, saw that continued cooperation between Sana'a and Washington would not protect
KSA interests. This fact and the YAR–PDRY leaders' discussion of
unity, however, forced American policy to change. Political sources in
Washington revealed that:

> US intelligence organisations have concluded that the North Yemeni
> government of President 'Ali 'Abd Allah Saleh, which is receiving emer-
> gency shipments from a US arms package worth $500 millions, is likely
> to collapse within the next six months ... that US analysts are uncertain
> who will succeed the erratic and unpopular President Saleh and take
> control of the F-5e jet fighters, M-60 tanks and other weapons now
> being supplied to the North Yemeni army ... [36]

The change in US policy created misunderstanding between Sana'a
and Washington. In March 1979 rumours circulated in Sana'a said
that, with the exception of two air force personnel, all American
military advisers had left the country, and that their departure was
connected with Sana'a's efforts to obtain arms from the Soviet Union.
Consequently, during the same month, Saudi Arabia agreed to
resume the supply of American arms, thereby demonstrating that the
KSA did not dictate US policy where the strategic interests of Washington were concerned. This was subsequently confirmed by Major
Ruszkiewicz, the US military attaché in Sana'a, in his personal account
of the events in this period.[37] Despite opposition from Riyadh, the US
administration removed some constraints on the provision of military
aid to Sana'a in order to restrict military relations between Sana'a and
Moscow. This, however, was not enough to satisfy the needs of the
YAR.[38] On 12 April the *Washington Post* reported that a squadron of 12
F-5Es had been delivered to Saudi Arabia for reassembly and shipment
to North Yemen.[39] It was then said that the last items of the $390
million arms package, hurriedly authorized by President Carter when
war broke out in February, had been delivered by the US Navy and
that 'the US mobile teams in North Yemen numbering 21 men, will
continue to instruct North Yemenis in the use and care of US arms'.[40]
But part of the US arms package was delayed in Saudi Arabia.
Riyadh, fearing the influence of Sana'a on its Yemeni client tribes in
the north, which were its lever in YAR affairs, decided to constrain
the power of President Saleh and his government by restricting the

supply of American arms. The Saudis justified their position by raising the issue of the YAR–KSA border dispute and the presence of Soviet military advisers in Sana'a. This 'Saudi unwillingness to transfer the weapons either quickly or fully indicated the continuation of certain basic differences between Riyadh and Sana'a on security matters'.[41] According to Ambassador Lane:

> after the war there was a major problem between the United States and the Yemen because the Saudis were no longer interested in sending the weapons to the Yemen, because the danger from South Yemen ceased. President Saleh was terribly interested in building up his military forces so as to make sure that what happened in February 1979 could not happen again.[42]

Originally, the US and the KSA saw that it was in their interest to provide Sana'a with only a limited amount of defensive weapons to provide military protection in the event of pro-Soviet invasion. A Department of State memorandum[43] issued in August 1978, which referred to the 6 August meeting of Ambassador West with Prince Sultan, the Saudi defence minister, and Prince Sa'ud al-Faisal, stated that the scope of the military program to the YAR, 'which essentially involves accelerated and more effective introduction of already approved and funded equipment, will fall short of meeting Yemeni expectations'.[44]

The North Yemeni government continued its efforts to establish direct dealings with Washington. In mid-June 1979, President Saleh, in a letter that his top political adviser, 'Abd Allah al-Asnadj, personally handed to Secretary of State Cyrus Vance in Washington, asked for the dispatch of senior US military advisers to help train his armed forces in the use of the American equipment. He also appealed for 'a more direct US military role in the Arabian Peninsula and Gulf region'. In an interview in Washington, al-Asnadj called on Americans to 'liberate themselves from the Vietnam complex' by actively defending 'certain political values' in the peninsula. Al-Asnadj also said that 'the 30,000-man Yemeni army, which largely has been trained and equipped by the Soviet Union over the past decade, was having trouble converting to US material and methods and would benefit from a reorganization program that would be directed by US officers stationed in Yemen'. Mentioning that between thirty and fifty military instructors had been roistered on short-term postings, and that members of a military planning and command-structure team headed by Major-General Richard Lawrence stationed temporarily in Saudi Arabia had also visited Sana'a to survey defence needs, al-Asnadj said that 'Yemen would welcome a similar planning mission and predicted that permanently stationing senior U.S. officers in the area would not draw criticism from other Arab countries'.[45] According to political analysts in Washington, al-Asnadj's statements 'indicated irritation with slow deliveries of the US arms through Saudi Arabia'.[46] He emphasized that 'any increased U.S. presence in Yemen should be made in the context of the trilateral military arrangement'.[47] A few days later the *Christian Science Monitor* quoted the Yemeni envoy as saying: 'North Yemen would do nothing to undermine US peace efforts in the current Egyptian–Israeli talks to implement the Camp David agreements.'[48] By making such a statement, al-Asnadj was trying to convince the American administration of his government's commitment to the West. But his argument was not as strong as that posed by US business interests in the KSA.

Although the YAR slowed down unity talks as a result of Saudi pressure al-Asnadj's mission was not successful,[49] nor did he succeed in representing the Yemeni point of view concerning direct YAR–US contacts and he was forced to talk constantly about trilateral relations.[50] The following month YAR Prime Minister 'Abdul-'Aziz 'Abdul-Ghani travelled to the US where he met the US adviser to the president for national security affairs, Zbigniew Brzezinski, on 28 August to discuss 'the arms package, the bilateral relationship and relations as a whole',[51] according to Ambassador George Lane, who was also present. Due to the stronger Washington–Riyadh relationship, demonstrated by Saudi Arabia's helpful oil policy at a time when Washington was trying to persuade Riyadh to accept the Egyptian–Israeli Camp David agreements, US policy did not alter. Ambassador Lane stressed that during this period Saudi daily oil production reached nearly 10 million barrels at $32 per barrel, $4 less than the OPEC price.[52] No real understanding between Sana'a and Washington developed because the two countries did not share the same strategic outlook regarding threats to security. As was the case with many countries in the area, Sana'a believed the main threat to its security came from Saudi Arabia, a radical South Yemen and Israel, whereas the US believed the chief security threat to its interests in Saudi Arabia and Israel came from the Soviet Union and the radical Arabs.

US military and political arrangements successfully contained the PDRY and Soviet threats to its interests in Saudi Arabia throughout the inter-Yemeni war period of 1979. This was achieved in part through alternative strategic assets and its bases in Diego Garcia in the Indian Ocean and Masirah in the Sultanate of 'Oman, making the need to arm the YAR redundant. While opposed to the latter policy the KSA had no objections to the former. This provides one possible explanation for Washington's negative response to the YAR's demands. The events of 1978, 1979 (and later of 1986) in the two Yemens also weakened the hard-liners in the PDRY and the country as a whole, indicating that US bases around the PDRY were sufficient to protect US interests. The outcome was that the YAR felt forced to respond positively to Soviet initiatives during and after the second inter-Yemeni war of 1979.

Sana'a seeks Soviet arms and causes US concern

On 5 October 1979, YAR Foreign Minister Dr Hassan Makki confirmed that Sana'a had invited US military advisers to join Soviet experts in training his country's army. He added that negotiations were in process for a new agreement to supply the North Yemeni army with US weapons. At the same time Makki confirmed that the USSR was still supplying arms and military advisers, concluding: 'We cannot forget the role played by the Soviet Union in helping us and providing us with weapons when the revolution was under attack. We are proud of our friendship with the Soviet Union, which is based on mutual respect and the preservation of the interests of the two people.'[53] This can be interpreted as indirect criticism of the US. In Sana'a, proposals to obtain more Soviet arms were justified because the US refused to supply equipment directly; Washington only approved an annual aid budget to be spent on training YAR personnel in American military academies and on the maintenance of the US military equipment previously sold to the YAR. Yemen apparently accepted this kind of aid in order to avoid American conditions. Washington may have favoured a presence in the YAR on an equal footing to Moscow, but Makki's statement indicates that Washington had become less interested in arming and reorganizing the Yemeni army.

Two months later the US press made it clear that Sana'a had moved towards Moscow in return for more arms and military advice. The *Washington Post* commented:

> Yemen's President, having pocketed the [nearly half a billion $worth] US arms, is now taking even larger doses of Soviet arms, and advisers ... This development is no small embarrassment for Washington. The administration perhaps thought it was buying a Yemen. It turns out it may have been only renting a Yemen, for uncertain time.[54]

It seemed strange to many Western observers that what they considered to be their Yemeni ally should seek arms from their enemy. Yemeni needs were never discussed.

Despite this, the YAR continued to be of significance to the US because of its position on the Red Sea and its location between the rich oil resources of the KSA and the radical PDRY. This is why, according to Ambassador Lane, Sana'a was 'the only country in the world where in the morning the United States had a training program for Yemen pilots on the F5 planes at Sana'a airport, and in the afternoon the Soviets had a training program for Yemeni pilots on the Sukhoi 22'.[55]

Correspondence between the White House and Congress shows that YAR–US military cooperation could not be developed simply because it did not serve US national security purposes.[56]

The shift towards the USSR indicates that the YAR government believed that it was in their interests to maintain good relations with Moscow because the US was not willing to organize and equip the YAR's army without the approval of Riyadh, which footed the bill. US objectives were seen to be merely to 'minimize any further threat against Saudi Arabia, reduce Soviet influence, and counteract the PDRY's radical government'.[57] It was clearly only Washington's concern for Saudi repercussions which made it decide not to send more arms to the YAR. Al-Asnadj's and 'Abdul-Ghani's subsequent visit to Washington show that Sana'a tried to deal directly with Washington during June 1979, but when this failed the Yemeni government turned the very next month to Moscow, where a major arms agreement was signed. Between 26 and 28 October 1979, President Saleh visited Moscow personally to seek more arms. The Soviets agreed to provide the YAR with many of its military needs in order in support of their policy that aimed at 'neutralization of the ... Gulf, Red Sea and Indian ocean area'.[58]

On this subject, Robert Stookey has stressed that 'the special relationship between the United States and Saudi Arabia formed after the 1973 Arab–Israeli conflict had repercussions on Yemen–American relations'. It therefore 'became customary for the United States to take significant action toward Yemen only after close consultation with the Saudis'.[59]

David Ransom thought the Soviets were afraid of loosing their position in the North, 'so they offered a very big arms package to Yemen'.[60] When asked if he thought this was a result of the negative US attitude towards the YAR, Ransom replied:

Yes. And the Yemenis accepted [the Soviet offer], but the Soviets gave more aid and more weapons to the South than to the North and provided more advisors until 1986. In 1986, 1987 and 1988 the curves cross. Now the Soviets provide more to the North than to the South, because the South is a failure.[61]

Even though the YAR had received strong US military support, its leaders might have felt they had no choice but to remain on good terms with the USSR. If they had been expelled from the YAR, the Soviets would no longer have had any incentive to restrain Aden's military ambitions against Sana'a. Events in the Horn of Africa set a precedent: when the USSR attempted to mediate between Ethiopia and Somalia – both allied to the Soviet Union but opposed to each other – the Soviets had been expelled from Somalia in 1977. Moscow then gave all its support to Ethiopia leaving Somalia unable to receive comparable support from Washington. Somalia had been trying to seize territory from Ethiopia; the YAR, however, merely wished to protect territory it already had. The YAR leadership therefore felt it was essential to their country's security to maintain good relations with the Soviet Union.[62]

The YAR–USSR arms deal to break Saudi interference in the Yemeni affairs was the direct result of the Saudis' insensitive handling of the transfer of US arms, the diplomatic situation after the border fight and the unity agreement with South Yemen.[63] On the subject of a campaign within the US to keep the YAR pro-Western, former US Secretary of Defense Arthur Schlesinger, then Albert Schweitzer Professor of the Humanities at City University New York, wrote:

> Colonel Ali 'Abd Alla Saleh, the President of 'our' Yemen, has signed an arms agreement with Moscow. Soviet tanks, planes and rocket launchers have arrived in North Yemen. Saudi Arabia, disturbed by the turn of events, has cut back its financial aid to North Yemen. The American F-5E aircraft, M-60 tanks, Vulcan air defence systems, so imprudently rushed to North Yemen, may well, at the next spin of the dial, end up pointed at the Saudis, if not at us.[64]

President Saleh, in an interview with the Kuwaiti *al-Siyassah*, dismissed these allegations against the YAR, which never mentioned the fact that Saudi Arabia was playing with the YAR for its own objectives; the Saudis succeeded in disturbing military relations between Sana'a and Moscow and then slowed down the delivery of the US arms package in order to promote further instability in the YAR.[65]

Soviet 'strategic advance', 1984, constrains YAR–US connection

The observations of a specialist on Yemen during his visit to Sana'a in April 1984 about a Soviet preparation for what he believed to be 'another strategic advance' in the area are applicable to the situation a few years earlier:

> The Soviet Union has intervened to help the conservative government

of North Yemen crush a left wing guerrilla movement in a move largely unnoticed by the rest of the world and played down here.[66] The aid in the form of an estimated $600 million worth of arms delivered from 1979 onwards and hundred of military advisors, has enabled the Sana'a authorities to build an effective central army for the first time in the country's history and inflict defeat on the forces of the National Democratic Front which had been active throughout much of the southern part of this country for some years ... The Russians did not want to lose their foothold in North Yemen to the West without a fight.[67]

This was an accurate observation. The Soviets abandoned the NDF and even their greatest ally, 'Abdul-Fattah Ismai'l,[68] for their wider concerns in the area; in addition to preserving its interests in the YAR, Moscow sought to 'reassure the Gulf Arabs of its non-hostile intentions in the wake of the Afghanistan invasion'.[69] On the other hand, in late 1979, after direct USSR involvement in both the PDRY and the YAR, Moscow did not support President Ismai'l's policies in South Yemen[70]: instead the YAR realized the necessity of maintaining communication with the Soviet Union and accepting a Soviet presence. It was reported that Secretary-General Leonid Brezhnev was opposed to the policies of South Yemen during that period, a matter which contributed to the ousting of Isma'il in 1980. The leadership in Moscow was convinced that 'revolution was unlikely in the oil rich states of the Arabian Peninsula'.[71] Moscow sought to befriend these conservative governments and supported the fourth PDRY president, Ali Nasser Muhammad, who paved the way for the Soviet Union to establish relations for the first time ever with most of these rich states.

According to Stookey:

the Soviets have come to the conclusion, on the basis of their historical experience in various apparently radical countries, that no Arab country, including the PDRY, is a realistic candidate for membership in their community of socialist nations, given the persistent strength of Islamic and Arab Nationalist traditions. They, therefore, now seek to continue mutually beneficial relations with Arab countries regardless of their political complexion.[72]

In addition to what can be considered a shift in the Soviet position vis-à-vis the US in the Arabian peninsula, it is also possible to discern the invalidity of the old Soviet strategy of opposition to US influence in the region. Moscow was forced to adopt new policies towards the YAR to prevent the loss of a foothold in the most populated country of the area.

As a consequence of the Soviet initiative, relations between the US and the YAR soured in mid-1979 and thereafter were at best only minimal. Throughout the early 1980s the US was criticized in the YAR for its subordination of Yemeni interests to those of the Saudis, its strong support of Israel, and for the poor quality as well as the small quantity of its military and economic aid programmes. These criticisms were not as strong as they might have been because Yemenis' expectations of the US were gradually lowered.[73]

Oil

Oil prospects and the consequent US oil companies' interest in Yemen offered the US administration an opportunity to counter the growing Soviet presence.[74] Washington therefore decided to use its unrivalled economic power to implement its foreign policy in the YAR. This interpretation is supported by the facts of the long-standing rivalry between Washington and Moscow in south-west Arabia, and because Hunt Consolidated Inc. perhaps did more for US prestige and influence in the country than the Soviet arms supply did for that of the Soviet Union. In this context, one should also take into consideration the political changes in the area, especially the developments in the Horn of Africa, Afghanistan, the overthrow of the local US 'policeman', the Shah of Iran, and the announcements of the leader of the Islamic revolution in Iran, Ayatollah al-Khomeini, in early February 1979, of his intention to sever all oil dealings with the US. The outbreak of the Iran–Iraq war in September 1980 also pushed the US to encourage oil exploration in the YAR in case the war should lead to the loss of the oil from Iran and other countries of the Arabian peninsula.

Nineteen-eighty witnessed the emergence of a new era in Yemeni history when an aeromagnetic survey of the whole country by the YAR government showed sedimentary basins in areas north of Marib and in other parts of the YAR.[75] According to the published official documentation, in the same year an independent oil exploration consultant, Moujib al-Malazi, who 'happened to be in contact with the London Hunt office',[76] arrived in Sana'a to enquire about oil prospects in the country and was welcomed to compare 'geological information with the new aero-magnetic data'.[77]

Following several meetings with Yemeni officials, al-Malazi shared his findings with Dr Ian Maycock, manager of the Hunt London office, who became intrigued by the possibilities of oil in Yemen. Towards the end of the year, he briefed the company's head office in Dallas, Texas, on his findings and recommendations.[78] In January 1981, Hunt Consolidated Inc. dispatched a high-level team to Sana'a. The team consisted of Hunt senior vice-president Tom Meurer, Maycock and al-Malazi. Their trip ended badly:

After three days of waiting for official permission to visit Marib al-Djawf, Mr Maycock, the London director of our office, al-Malazi and I decided to visit the Marib-al-Djawf area to see what kind of rocks were available there. To see what the age of the rocks looked like. In the area we were caught by the army and were sent to jail in Sana'a, because we were not carrying our passports. We spent most of the day under arrest.[79]

YOMINCO intervened to release the prisoners and facilitated a tour to the western area: 'we were able to check the age of the rocks, and so we got an idea what the area looked like'.[80] The team's subsequent report was positive, and the company recognized it was involved in an area of great potential, which was 'strategically secure, economically sound and politically reliable'.[81]

Before an agreement was officially signed, a newly founded Yemen Hunt Oil Company (YHOC) conducted initial geological sampling and mapping.[82] Discussions between YOMINCO and Hunt Consolidated Inc. resulted in a draft work programme. Between 22 July and 28 July the two parties successfully negotiated a Production Sharing Agreement signed by the minister of state and chairman of YOMINCO, 'Ali 'Abdul-Rahman al-Bahr, and Raymond E. Fairchild, Hunt Consolidated's vice-president of international exploration. It covered '3.1 million acres stretching as long as from Dallas to Longvie'.[83] The concession became effective on 16 January 1982, ratified by Republican Law No. 4, 1982.[84]

This agreement specified that the Hunt Oil Company's wholly owned subsidiary, YHOC, should commence geological and geophysical work in an area approximately 200 km (124 miles) north-east of Sana'a at an elevation of about 3,000 feet. The agreement provided a six-year exploration period during which at least four wells should be drilled. Initially about half the oil revenue was to go to the Yemeni government, with its share rising as production increased.[85] Based on a projection that the discovery of commercial viability would lead to a twenty-year development period, the terms of the agreement stressed that the agreement was to be dissolved if no exploration well had been established by the end of the sixth year.[86] It was stipulated that further details about the contents of this agreement and other agreements relating to oil were not to be released.[87]

Following the ratification of the sharing agreement a seismic survey covering 1,845 km (1,146 miles) was finished by early December 1982. Additional survey later covered more than 12,000 km (7,457 miles). Maycock revealed that the computer processing of the data which continued in 1983 indicated at least 18,000 feet of sediment, and that further mapping and evaluation suggested that petroleum and reservoir rocks might be present.[88] When drillable structures were located in

April 1983, YHOC decided to drill a 'wildcat' to obtain more precise information.

The first three drills were named Alef, Lam and Meem,[89] and drilling in Alef began on 31 January 1984. During the drilling a South Korean consortium (Yukong Limited, Samwhan, Hyundai and Korean Petroleum Development corporations), obtained a 24.5 per cent interest in YHOC's concession on 29 February. Before reaching half its planned depth, Alef showed hydrocarbon. In March, drilling progressed through shale, limestone and several large beds overlying oil- and gas-bearing sandstone, and at about 13,700 ft, granite basement rock was reached.[90] Well-testing at the time showed that the first well was 'where it should be'.[91] When the initial drill stem test in the Alef field was done on 4 July[92] 1984, the YAR's oil flowed for the first time at a combined rate of over 7,800 bpd from two separate zones; several other perforations yielded natural gas at a combined rate of 55 MMcfd.[93] A nine-well Alef field programme was completed in 1985. The Alef reservoir was assessed to be approximately 300 million barrels. A feasibility study for a refinery, an export pipeline and other associated projects began.[94] On 25 September 1985 Prime Minister 'Abdul-'Aziz 'Abdul-Ghani laid the foundation stone in Marib for the first Yemeni refinery. At the ceremony Ray L. Hunt stated: 'I am confident that this will be just the first of many similar ceremonies which will take place in the years to come as Yemen assumes its rightful place as an important supplier of crude to the world markets.'[95] When the Alef field capacity reached a level in excess of 100,000 bpd, the YAR government created the Supreme Council for Oil and Mineral Resources, to be chaired by Foreign Minister Dr 'Abdul-Karim al-Iryani. In September 1985 YOMINCO was transformed into the YAR Ministry of Oil.

In late 1985, the Yemeni government approved an agreement between YHOC and a subsidiary of Exxon Corporation, Exxon Yemen Inc. Exxon was given a 49 per cent interest in YHOC's 75.5 per cent share of the concession, but YHOC remained the main operator in the Marib-al-Djawf area. The joint venture was named Yemen Exploration and Production Company (YEPCO).[96] The YAR government built a 38-mile paved road from Marib to the refinery. On 12 April 1986, the YAR celebration of the inauguration of its first refinery was attended by President Saleh, US Vice-President George Bush and the president of Hunt Consolidated, Ray Hunt.[97] Oil production started at the 10,000 bpd level required for refinery operation. As Bush confirmed, the promise of large quantities of oil in the YAR, meant greater US eagerness to 'be in partnership with the Yemeni people'.[98] In September 1986 work was begun on the YAR's first oil pipeline to the Red Sea.

YEPCO also bought a tanker, *Esso Japan*, renamed *Safer*, which was converted for floating storage.[99]

President Saleh opened the tap of Yemeni oil to the world in November 1987. Export flow started at 100,000 bpd, rising to 125,000 in January 1988, and to 175,000 by the end of the year.[100] According to some observers, the volume of the Yemeni oil find would not be big enough to affect global oil prices or the strength of OPEC, but they would be important for the economy of Yemen.[101]

By January 1990 six commercially viable fields were operating: Alef, Azal, Saif bin dhi Yazan, Asad al-Kamel, Djabal Nukum and al-Shura.[102] Meurer concluded that the Yemen 'has a lot of gas' and 'there are some ways which we can make gasoline out of it'. As for the oil prospects, he said:

> As the prices go higher we can produce more oil from the existing fields. Because we produce now around 35 percent of the oil underground. The new technology will help us to do that. Also many parts of Yemen have not been explored yet, especially the area between Shabwah and Marib.[103]

To sum up the effect of oil on the YAR–US relationship in the 1980s: oil exploration and discovery helped the US to preserve its presence and influence in the YAR and this enabled it to counter Soviet influence, as well as helping to secure a new oil source should the supplies from the Gulf and the Arabian peninsula be interrupted for political reasons; US interest in the Yemeni arena developed through the special relations that developed between US oil companies and the YAR government; and oil revenues helped the YAR to compensate part of the decline in its workers' remittances and the reduction in Saudi aid, which was affected by the Saudi objection to oil exploration in the YAR and the Iraq–Iran war. In addition to the economic benefits, the oil discovery in an area stretching southwards to the PDRY brought the question of Yemen unity to a serious turning point for the first time in modern history.

Yemeni oil increased official US contacts because, as Cultural Attaché Marjorie Ransom confirmed, 'when our private relationship expands that also affects the formal one'.[104] Washington doubled its aid to the YAR in 1984 once it became clear that there was oil, in order to exert more influence and to promote trade between the two nations. According to Mrs Ransom, aid programmes promoted more knowledge about the country and companies that sold food assistance programmes might also become interested in selling products through regular channels.[105] According to John Kelly, the US assistant secretary of state for Near Eastern and South Asian Affairs in 1990, US aid to the

YAR was generally considered to be 'in the geopolitical interest of the US' which gave 'good access for American oil companies and firms which have an interest there' and 'has tended to dilute the Soviet influence'.[106] The transcript of the press conference given by Kelly in 1990 also reveals political reasons behind the decision to double the amount of aid to the YAR since 1984:

Q. What about development assistance?
A. We provide assistance to North Yemen. The last fiscal year was about $20 million.
Q. How much [do] we get back from the $20 million every year? What gain?
A. Oh yes. Well I think over the years, the US, there has tended to dilute the Soviet influence.
Q. $20 million every year for how many years?
A. This has been up and down. That was the most recent year's figure.
Q. We don't get anything back!
A. I think we are. I think we are getting access among other things, good access for American oil companies and firms which have an interest there.
Q. Oil companies should pay then. Should they?
A. Well … We're helping a country that needs some help and development. It is in the geopolitical interest of the US.

The American use of the oil card to make closer contacts with the YAR was interrupted by the Saudi government, which claimed that the Marib oil was within its own borders and a part of its existing fields.[107] The Saudi objections apparently went unheard in Washington, for the US companies continued to explore vigorously for more YAR oil. The USA had clearly decided not to leave the YAR to the Soviets, who could not compete in developing the economy of the country. Yemeni and American officials confirmed that Saudi Arabia, which used not to have southern borders on its official maps, had laid claim to territory near Marib. A number of border clashes occurred as a result of Saudi support of some northern Yemeni tribes resisting the authority of the central government in Sana'a. Riyadh resurrected old border claims spanning the new oil fields, and a map was published which put most of the area being explored by the Yemen Hunt Oil Company area inside Saudi borders. It was later revealed that in late 1984 Prince Saud al-Faisal, the Saudi foreign minister, wrote to the YAR deputy prime minister and foreign minister of the YAR, Dr 'Abdul-Karim al-Iryani, reiterating these claims.[108] Yemeni sources commented that the Saudi attitude toward North Yemen was 'triggered by Riyadh's fear that this poor but populous country could pose a security threat if it finds itself awash with oil', explaining why it had 'revived claims to Yemeni territory where the oil was discovered'.[109] A Fellow at the US Institute of Peace warned his government that:

if American diplomacy is unsuccessful in moderating Saudi policy toward its neighbours however, then, Washington should consider publicly expressing concern about Saudi actions and providing increased security assistance to Oman and North Yemen. Washington should not remain idle when Saudi policies hurt our, as well as their own, interests.[110]

Washington, it can be concluded, did not approve of the Saudi reaction because the oil partnership created the first economic incentive for the US private sector to invest in the YAR. The growing US dependency on Middle Eastern oil meant that the YAR had a more significant position in US foreign policy by the beginning of 1984 than ever before. Yemeni oil revenues encouraged trade between the two states. On 18 December 1985, it was revealed in Sydney that the US had sold to the YAR 50,000 tonnes of American wheat 'subsidised by about $20 per tonne under the Export Enhancement Programme'.[111] The Australian Wheat Board reacted angrily to the sale claiming that 'the subsidy was specifically targeted to cut the Australian price by a couple of dollars' and that 'the US ... have paid the international Louis Grain Trading Company [an American company] a subsidy of more than $20 per tonne to beat the Australian bid'. Another sale of the same quantity took place in May 1986 and the Australian Wheat Board claimed that Washington's wheat export subsidy policies had cost Sydney $1.32 million.[112] These cut-price wheat sales to the YAR indicate that the US decided to use an economic instrument to achieve more influence in Sana'a. The importance of US subsidised wheat sales to Sana'a in the 1980s to Washington's foreign policy towards the YAR can be better understood in the light of similar sales to Egypt in the 1950s and early 1960s and the subsequent withholding of wheat shipments by the Johnson administration.

YAR–USA relations became more stable as the YAR became an object of interest to many of the major American and multi-national companies involved in petroleum exploration and production.[113]

George Bush in Sana'a

On 10 April 1986 US Vice-President George Bush arrived in Sana'a.[114] The following factors were highly relevant to his visit:

1. The Hunt Oil Company, which had its headquarters in Bush's home town in Texas, had stimulated US interest in the country. Two

years before Bush's visit, Hunt had found exportable quantities of oil for the first time in Yemen. This discovery raised Yemen's hopes of a partnership with the US. At the same time, the US government hoped that this turning point would help Yemen develop a more independent and friendly foreign policy that would take into consideration Western interests in the region.

2. The defeat of the NDF had led to a greater political stability after 1982. The way in which the YAR leadership had managed to deal with its internal political problems impressed the White House, and thus it was in the interest of the US government to show its support for President Saleh's policies.

3. The inter-PDRY conflict of three months earlier had weakened the radical government in Aden and hence Washington's hopes for a less radical government in South Yemen were renewed. Rumours in Sana'a at the time of the visit stated that Vice-President Bush tried to convince the YAR leadership and the southern ousted president, Ali Nasser Muhammad, to annex the southern territory by use of force. The visit was also a message to the radical governments of the region that friends of the US harvest stability and wealth, while those who are pro-Soviet reap death and backwardness, as his statements have illustrated.

4. The Iraq–Iran war had since September 1980 created instability in the region. Bush's visit to the YAR was another way of expressing US support for its friends and allies, and to send a message to both the PDRY and the USSR that 'we are here and we are prepared to protect our interests'.

On his arrival at Sana'a airport Bush stated:

> this is a critical year in world events, especially here in the Arabian Peninsula, where a brutal war has been waged in the Gulf area for five years, and a smaller ... but also brutal ... one was fought south of here only a few weeks ago. Yet throughout these troubled times the Yemen Arab Republic has vigorously safeguarded it stability and sovereignty.

He added that the Americans had recently 'found oil in the Yemen Arab Republic', and that 'we look forward to a close and enduring relationship' with Sana'a.[115] At a dinner hosted by the YAR vice-president and speaker of the People's Constituent Assembly, Kadi 'Abdul-Karim 'Abd Allah al-'Arashi, Bush emphasized the same points.[116] In his reply, Kadi al-'Arashi stressed that the YAR January dispute was considered by the YAR government to be an internal matter of the PDRY and pleaded the Palestinian cause.[117]

The next day, at a press conference that followed his meeting with the YAR president and other Yemeni officials, Bush said that he had discussed 'the stability of this region', and 'the same broad range issues that have concerned me throughout this trip'. He emphasized that 'this visit is an important milestone in relations between the United States and the Yemen Arab Republic' and that his country was 'committed to assisting the Yemeni people as they work to build a peaceful and prosperous Republic'.[118] The topic raised at this press conference which most interested the Yemeni people was the American definition of 'terrorism'.[119] At another event, the US vice-president called the YAR to work with the US and the sheikhdoms of the Arabian peninsula to eliminate the 'scourge' of 'terrorism'.[120] During his talks with the US vice-president the Yemeni president expressed his hope for better bilateral relations and permanent peace in the area, and argued that the US, as a superpower, should play an effective role in bringing the disputes in the area to a happy end. These points were also stressed by the YAR vice-president at a banquet in honour of George Bush.[121]

The YAR media, especially al-Thawrah, the main YAR government daily newspaper, hailed the Bush visit as the 'fruit of the YAR's constant and principled foreign policy', which was based on a 'sincere and practical commitment to positive neutrality, non-alignment, and openness to cooperative relations with the countries of the world and peaceful co-existence with their people, as well as friendly relations based on mutual respect and non-intervention in the internal affairs of others and the development of mutual interests'. It stressed that: 'Our country will remain, in its policy positions and dealings on all Arab, Islamic and international levels, a distinctive country in its sincere and practical implementation of the principle of positive neutrality and non-alignment without relinquishing independence.' Al-Thawrah went on to say that the YAR's positive neutrality was embodied in the YAR's policies on international issues and events and its dealings with other countries, and concluded 'our country has not fallen under the influence of guardianship, subservience or external control ... Our young and developing country, the homeland of the September Revolution, has not fallen into the orbit of any external power, is not hostage to anyone, nor does it have external loyalties as some others do.'[122] It was later reported that at a meeting with South Yemeni opposition leaders in Sana'a on 11 April, Bush had promised to provide them with military aid and other assistance to help them seize power.[123] Some observers believed that Bush tried to persuade the YAR leadership to allow the opposition to launch a hit and run war against the South, but that the proposal had been rejected completely.[124]

Only three countries in the area criticized Bush's visit. South Yemeni criticism of Bush's visit started a few days before his arrival in Sana'a. It was claimed in Aden that Bush's tour of the region 'carried poisonous dishes of sedition and separation'. The PDRY's main daily newspaper, *14 October*, called upon the YAR leadership to deny 'the US Administration the chance to achieve its hostile goals and to uncover Bush's intentions, which are aimed at jeopardising the ambition of our Yemen people to restore their unity through peaceful and democratic means'.[125] On the last day of Bush's visit to Sana'a *al-Thawri*, the mouthpiece of the YSP, stressed that the US vice-president had arrived in the Arabian peninsula 'after the largest US aircraft carriers roamed the seas and oceans and stayed in the Mediterranean amid an atmosphere of tension that prevails in the region following the recent increase in US provocations against the Libyan Djamahiriyah (Republic) and the launching of a flagrant and direct aggression against Libyan territory by US aircraft'. The YSP newspaper saw the Bush visit as an indication of 'the recent change of attitude of the US government towards the Iran–Iraq war'.[126]

The PDRY condemned Bush's visit to the region but avoided mentioning that he was actually in Sana'a because it was so close to home. In Tripoli, however, the visit was openly criticized because of what JANA, the official Libyan news agency, saw as an attack against al-Djamahiriah 'from the territory of the YAR'. JANA stated that, at his press conference in Sana'a, Bush 'disclosed aggressive United States intentions against the Djamahiriyah', and revealed that 'there has been a plan drawn up since the beginning of what he called the Libyan terrorism, aimed at destroying the anti-aircraft missile batteries situated on the Libyan coasts'. JANA claimed that the US vice-president had declared war against Libya 'from an Arab country which is supposed to prevent him even setting foot on its territory – let alone make his statement from it.' The Arab affairs editor of JANA considered that, by allowing Bush's statements against Tripoli, the YAR 'thus insulted itself' and suggested 'perhaps President 'Ali 'Abd Allah Saleh has not yet seen the statements which depict Sana'a as an American colony'. The Libyan agency ended its editorial criticism by saying:

> the masses of the Arab nation now demand vengeance for the insult to their dignity and their honour that has been stained by the U.S. imperialists, Zionists, and Atlantists [i.e. NATO members] on the basis that the Arab homeland as a whole is a target for the tenth crusade led by the child-killer Reagan and his Western allies. In their hateful crusade they make no distinction between one Arab country and another.[127]

In Teheran it was concluded that Bush came to the area to discuss the outcome of the 'imposed war on Iran', the deterioration of oil prices and to assure the Arab gulf states that the US would protect their security.[128]

Bush's visit to the YAR was followed by an increased American presence in the country. An American Embassy attaché estimated that the number of US citizens living in the YAR in that year rose to nearly 2,000, but 'every week or two you hear about American scholars, American journalists or American officials arriving in Sana'a'.[129] On 9 September 1986, Sana'a witnessed an exchange of notes of agreement concerning the provision of training related to defence articles under the US International Military Education (IMET) programme. This agreement (which remains classified), entered into force on 19 May 1987. As far as US participation in YAR development plans was concerned, nothing of huge importance was achieved. The US government remained unconvinced of the need to assist Sana'a with any large development project; according to YAR Foreign Minister Dr 'Abdul-Karim al-Iryani, it was ready to provide only small-scale 'technical assistance'.[130] David Ransom stated:

> The Yemeni government has always wanted us to do another road project like the Mocha–Sana'a road, a big expensive capital project. And we didn't think that was as important as the other things we do. We focused on training and technical assistance; water projects, agricultural projects, public administration projects and projects like that, but every year it was about $20 million. It's not bad.[131]

The aid relationship

Development assistance is a major form of transaction between great and small states. US assistance to the YAR between 1963 and 1967 in the form of the Ta'iz Water Project and the Mocha–Sana'a road had made a great impression on the Yemeni people because it was of a developmental nature, despite the fact that the West Germans had improved the road before: 'travellers became covered with dust and the road was never fully appreciated'.[132] The money spent on assistance to the YAR between 1973 and 1990 made much less of an impact because it concentrated on training Yemeni personnel in the US and was of a technical nature, reflecting the new US assistance policy in the YAR.[133] The YAR foreign minister commented on this in 1988:

> We can consider the US assistance in the context of technical assistance until now. It is not development assistance in the sense that it is not structural or industrial. The USAID agencies see that Yemen only needs technical assistance and not development assistance. That doesn't mean in any way that the US assistance is not of value to us, but the Yemeni people see the material value of the West German and the Netherlands assistance more than they see that of the US, because the Dutch and the German assistance includes development as well as technical assistance

... We called their (the Americans) attention many times to the fact that 'we considered the training assistance and training very important, but you must keep in mind ... that the Yemeni public will never appreciate this kind of help unless you connect it to some development assistance' ... We told them to choose two or three projects. I told them personally: 'You are in a very disadvantageous situation coming with technical assistance alone.'[134]

The 1973–90 period was characterized by an expansion of technical assistance in order, according to the USAID reports, to strengthen the capacity of key government institutions to plan, manage and provide needed services in areas such as agriculture, education and training, health and water supply. Marjorie Ransom, US cultural attaché in Sana'a 1975–78, said:

We worked with a number of different Yemeni institutions, especially to try to be responsive to Sana'a plans for university expansion, especially for higher education and training of future Yemeni faculty. We also worked in conjunction with our AID program. They had a large training program in Yemen where they sent people from all government ministries.[135]

Projects during this period included water supply projects for Ta'iz, Sana'a and several rural areas, and supporting water resources surveys and management plans; the American–Yemeni Language Institute agricultural projects in sorghum and millet, poultry and tropical and subtropical fruits; support for the Secondary Agricultural Institute in Ibb, co-financed by the World Bank; soil and mineral surveys; government personnel training; hospital training and applied health and training; rural development programmes; and earthquake disaster relief.[136]

In both 1983 and 1984 the USAID budget in Yemen reached $28 million, of which half was allocated to agriculture. The gradual increase of US assistance after 1982 was also aimed at promoting bilateral trade 'because those companies that sell food assistance programs to Yemen might also become interested in selling products through regular channels'.[137] The food programmes included 'activities such as funding technical advisors to the Ministry of Agriculture and Fisheries, training Yemenis in the United States and other countries from the secondary level to Ph.D., and implementing poultry and horticulture demonstration projects, among others.'[138]

When Vice-President George Bush visited the YAR in April 1986 he stressed that the main objective of US assistance was to develop the agriculture sector and water projects as well as to assist planning urban growth and to improve Yemeni education on all levels.[139] The YAR ambassador to the US, Muhsin al-'Aini, even tried to persuade Bush that Washington should assist with a big development project. Al-'Aini told me that when he returned to the YAR Embassy in Washington following the Bush visit, he repeated the suggestion but was again ignored.[140]

Overall, from 1973 to the end of 1989 about $392 million was provided through US grants, loans and food assistance programmes. Table 4.1 shows US economic assistance between 1959 and 1986.

Table 4.1 USAID annual economic assistance to the YAR ($000)

Year	Grant	Loan	Funds	PL 480	Total
1959–62	32,200	–	–	10,500	42,700
1973	1,708	–	–	–	1,708
1974	2,157	–	–	–	2,157
1975	2,449	1,350	–	–	3,799
1976	5,991	–	400	2,600	8,991
1977	15,319	–	500	1,000	16,919
1978	6,245	–	700	200	7,145
1979	16,553	–	1,100	300	17,953
1980	11,568	–	1,000	700	13,268
1981	14,200	5,000	–	300	19,500
1982	23,216	–	–	1,200	24,416
1983	26,755	–	–	–	26,755
1984	27,324	–	125	3,000	30,499
1985	27,448	–	200	12,000	39,648
1986	23,549	–	737	10,000	36,286
1987	22,000	–	305	15,000	37,305
1988	22,095	–	–	10,000	32,095
1989	23,300	–	–	10,000	15,300
1990	21,972	–	–	–	20,000

Source: USAID Congressional Presentations 1957–1990, USAID office Sana'a, and writer's research.

The table shows the doubling of USAID grants to the YAR after 1982. This shift reflects US economic interests from that date as a result of the positive oil indications found in the YAR. In 1985 the US government argued with Congress that the need to pay more attention to the YAR was due to the following factors:

1. Oil-surplus countries of the Gulf that had provided assistance to Yemen and employed its labour were in an economic recession and Yemeni workers' remittances had dropped from $1.5 billion in 1979 to an estimated $1.1 billion in 1984.

2. Official Arab and international aid had declined from an estimated $472 million in 1980 to less than $300 million in 1984.[141] Arab Gulf States aid to the YAR had been reduced because of a drop in oil revenue and the diversion of funds to Lebanon and the Iraq–Iran war. As a result YAR foreign exchange reserves, equivalent to twenty months of imports in 1975, fell to seven months in 1981, and by late 1983 represented only about 2.5 months' imports.

3. A $705 million YAR government deficit in 1983 had led to a reduced level of development expenditures. The YAR's Second Five-Year Plan, which began in 1983, projected that 46 per cent of a $6 billion investment budget would be provided from foreign grants and loans, and it had become likely that the plan would have to be scaled back significantly.

4. The December 1982 earthquake added a new dimension to YAR's troubled economic situation; the disaster had caused an estimated $2 billion worth of damages, and a World Bank report estimated that $620 million in public expenditure would be required in a four-year reconstruction programme for houses, roads, schools, water systems and other infrastructure.

5. The strategic location of the YAR, its porous border with Saudi Arabia and the large numbers of Yemenis working in the oil states of the Gulf underscored the importance of the YAR in terms of regional stability and its importance to US economic interests.

6. US objectives were intended to help develop, through economic and other assistance, a strong government in the YAR, friendly to its neighbours, which would enhance US interests in regional stability and security.

7. The YAR had a strong, free-enterprise tradition which was a countervailing model to the state-controlled economy of the PDRY.

8. Tangible US participation in the economic development of the YAR advanced American economic interests and objectives in the region as a whole.

9. The long-term US programme of human resources and institutional development laid a foundation for sustained national development and a stronger friendship between Yemen and the United States.[142] In addition to the listed reasons two others can be seen in the oil find in the YAR by US companies and the prospects of trade between the two states.

Despite the doubling of US assistance to the YAR in 1982 and its continuous improvement afterwards, Arab and other international donors were still more effective in development of the YAR.

Table 4.2 shows that aid flowing from Western Europe, the Soviet

Table 4.2 Arab and international aid to the YAR 1962–1980, by main supplier

Country or organization	Amount in YR
Kuwait	1,672,115,001
KSA	284,451,523
UN	244,480,000
Netherlands	196,023,595
West Germany	90,540,164
USA	68,062,243 (since 1959)
UK	38,204,790
USSR	32,931,619

Source: 'Abd Allah Barakat, *Masadir Tamwil al-Tanmiyya al-Iktisadiyya wa al-Idjtima'iyy fi al-Djumhouriyya al-'Arabiyya al-Yamaniyya*, Damascus, 1985, pp. 798–9; *YARCPO Annual Reports, Yemen Central Bank Annual Reports 1973–1990*.

bloc, China, Arab countries and the multilateral banks was greater than that of the US. Barakat, a Yemeni economist, observed that all Arab and international continuous aid has always been of a developmental and technical nature.[143] West Germany and the Netherlands, for example, both provided about as much development aid to the YAR as the US. But, unlike the Americans, the Dutch and the West Germans directed their assistance to some development projects required by the YAR government.[144] Japanese assistance to the YAR was limited because its products were present everywhere in Yemen through ordinary trade. The Japanese government, therefore, had no interest in providing the country with aid and provided only commercial credits.

According to Barakat, Arab and international loans to finance the various YAR social and economic development projects were much greater than those provided by the US.

According to USAID Congressional documents even the US training programme for the YAR in the 1980s was 'overshadowed by those of the Eastern bloc and other Arab states' because, for instance, the Soviet Union and Saudi Arabia each offered 'more than 200 undergraduate scholarships to Yemeni students every year, while US funded scholarships, both graduate and undergraduate, were between 60 and 80 every year'.[145]

On the occasion of his visit to Sana'a in 1986 Vice-President George Bush announced that the US government would increase its Food for Peace commitment to Sana'a, and said 'our total assistance to Yemen under this program will be $10 million for 1986' in order to encourage

Table 4.3 Loans to the YAR 1962–83, by main supplier

Source	Amount in million YR
Arab countries	2,867.9
UN	1,162.9
Regional funds	715.4
Soviet bloc countries	656.5
West Germany	374.2
Japan	217.0
Netherlands	94.8
France	59.3
UK	29.7
US	28.6

Source: CPO Annual Reports and Barakat, ibid, pp. 681–774.

'the use of local proceeds for lending to stimulate private enterprise'. Bush stressed his country believed 'strongly in private enterprise because that's what built' the US, and expressed his hope 'that as Yemen trusts the enormous energy of its people, and as it continues to encourage the private initiative of its people ... Yemen will have prosperity in the years to come'.[146] He did not announce any commitment to undertake a big development project, as some Yemeni officials had hoped, but merely expressed willingness to promote trade with the YAR through facilitation. The US Commercial Office in Sana'a also revealed that Washington had prepared various programmes to facilitate trade with Sana'a.[147]

President Saleh arrives in the district
of Columbia

In late January 1990 President 'Ali 'Abd Allah Saleh visited Washington where he held talks with President George Bush and other American officials. During this visit Mark L. Edelman, acting administrator of USAID, and Dr Muhammad Sa'id al-'Attar, the YAR deputy prime minister and minister of development, signed a bilateral grant agreement for $21 million. Philip Christianson, USAID assistant administrator for food for peace and voluntary assistance, signed food aid agreements for $20 million. Edelman stated that, under the Food for Peace programme the YAR would purchase from the US at a concessional price, $10 million in rice and $10 million in feed grains for poultry; local currency generated from the sale would finance infrastructure projects, build and equip an eye hospital (in cooperation with an American foundation), restore historical sites and construct a vocational school for girls. He also stated that the bilateral grant assistance of $21 million would fund ongoing USAID projects aimed at developing the YAR's agriculture and educational systems as well as a new project that would support private sector initiatives and promote trade and investment.[148] Despite the expectations of many of the US officials concerned with Yemen that the US would not increase its assistance to the YAR, and indeed that it might cut it, the YAR received an increase of nearly $10 million over the previous year. This brought US assistance for the fiscal year of 1990 to $47.5 million – the highest since the restoration of diplomatic relations, showing increased US interest in Yemen during the first seven months of 1990.[149]

The limited impact of US assistance

Since US assistance to the YAR during 1962–90 was often subordinated to Washington's global political and economic concerns and interests in the Middle Eastern area as a whole in which Yemen occupied a minor position. Thus US aid remained at a limited level and had a relatively small impact on the YAR's economic and social development during this period. The first phase of the USAID programme in the YAR reflected greater US political concern than was displayed in the 1970s and 1980s when the YAR became a friend of the US.

The trade indicators (see Table 4.4) all suggest that because US aid to the YAR was implemented within the context of the Cold War and American objectives in the Arabian peninsula, it was used to improve the US political presence in the YAR by increasing Sana'a's dependence on Washington.

Trade

YAR–US trade (including arms transfers), which began in 1972, was as shown in Table 4.4.

US exports to the YAR increased in the 1980s as a result of the increasing revenues from its workforce abroad. The large trade deficit was due in part to the KSA oil boom which attracted many Yemeni farmers to work there and to neglect their own farms. Consequently, the Yemeni government was obliged to import wheat and agricultural products from abroad. The American commercial credits encouraged Yemen to import these products from the US, and the YAR workers' remittances repaid these credits in hard currency. A report prepared by the US Embassy in 1979 stated that Sana'a was an excellent market for American products and investment due to the 'continued but

Table 4.4 YAR trade with the US 1972–86 ($million)

Year	Imports	Exports
1972	2.2	0.2
1973	9.6	–
1974	10.5	0.6
1975	8.3	0.2
1976	25.4	0.3
1977	46.4	0.6
1978	30.6	0.4
1979	214.1	1.5
1980	77.4	0.8
1981	43.9	0.4
1982	38.2	0.5
1983	107.5	0.4
1984	68.8	8.5
1985	42.2	1.4
1986	83.8	1.5
Total	808.9	17.5

Source: US Department of Commerce Highlights of Exports and Imports 1973–1986 and author's research.

uneven expansion [which] marked the economy of the YAR in 1977–78'.[150] International statistics show that the US was the fourth largest supplier of YAR imports.

Following the announcement of the oil discovery in 1984 the US facilitated trade with the YAR by opening credits in US banks for

Table 4.5: YAR imports 1983–86, by main supplier (%)

Country	1983	1984	1985	1986
Saudi Arabia	10.9	16.2	14.2	12.9
Netherlands	5.1	5.0	5.6	6.1
West Germany	4.6	4.9	5.4	5.0
US	4.2	4.3	2.7	5.9
UK	7.5	4.8	7.6	6.3
Japan	18.5	11.0	8.0	9.2
Italy	4.4	8.9	5.4	5.6
India	2.4	2.6	2.5	3.2
France	4.9	6.9	4.8	4.7
South Korea	2.5	3.6	2.9	3.5

Source: IMF, Direction of Trade Statistics Yearbook 1987.

Yemeni businessmen – to attract Yemeni oil revenues. As a result of a US trade promotion several agricultural commodities agreements and amendments were signed in Sana'a between 19 June 1984 and 26 July 1986. YARCPO documents showed that from 1984 to 1986 the US provided the YAR government with commodity loans worth nearly $40 million.[151] In 1985 and 1986 the Australians protested that the US was undercutting them by $2 per tonne of wheat, but the US was undeterred, making clear its intention of using this economic weapon to exert influence on Sana'a at a time when YAR oil production had started.[152] US-subsidised wheat sales in the 1980s were closely connected to Washington's foreign policy towards the YAR.

The chairman of YARCPO, Dr Muhammad al-'Attar, told me in 1988 of his hopes that trade between Sana'a and Washington would improve in the coming years. He said that since Washington imported 70 per cent of its textiles from Singapore, Hong Kong, South Korea or from Morocco and Lebanon, as well as much of its needed transformer industries goods from abroad, the YAR would have the capability to start investments in this field in the very near future.

A summary of the trade relationship between Sana'a and Washington is as follows. Remittances from Yemenis working abroad began to have a positive impact on YAR–US trade in the early 1980s. Until 1986 trade between Sana'a and Washington showed a balance in favour of the latter, demonstrating that the YAR needed the US more than the US needed the YAR. Al-'Attar confirmed that 'trade between the YAR and the USA had started to improve after the oil find in the country by American companies'. He added that his country 'used to get $5 million under the Food for Peace loans, but in 1988 this reached $20 million. In addition, the US banks offer more facilities for trade with the YAR through setting up credits'.[153]

Evolution of relations, 1986–90

Four main developments between 10 April 1990 and 22 May 1990 affected YAR–US relations: first, more oil was discovered and more American companies became involved in the country; the oil found at the border with the PDRY brought about US interest in South Yemen; second, the YAR's connection with Iraq within the frame of the Arab Cooperative Council (ACC), a new form of Arab nationalism project; third, the YAR president's first state visit to the US in early 1990, which was supposed to be an opportunity for both presidents to develop mutual understanding and attitudes towards several issues, principally the YAR's proposed unity with the PDRY and Sana'a's role in maintaining stability in the region; fourth, Yemen unity itself, which marked the dissolve of both the YAR and the PDRY to form the new ROY, which declared its adoption of YAR's foreign policy including its role in the ACC.

In the last week of January 1990 the first ever visit by a YAR president to the USA took place. President George Bush received President 'Ali 'Abd Allah Saleh in the White House, where the discussions covered a wide range of bilateral, regional and international topics. Bush expressed satisfaction that the US had been able to help the YAR realize some of its economic and development goals and noted that the US had increased the Food for Peace programme with Yemen in 1990. In response to the YAR president's plea for a just settlement to the Palestinian cause, Bush reaffirmed Washington's desire for peace and stability in the Middle East and outlined continuing efforts to find a solution to the Arab–Israeli conflict. The American president stressed his administration's belief that US diplomatic pressure on Egypt and Israel to develop a dialogue between the Israelis and the Palestinians offered the best hope for moving the peace process forward towards direct negotiations between the parties. The two presidents discussed the PDRY's and the YAR's then ongoing efforts to unite the Yemen. They also reviewed the current situation in Afghanistan and their shared support for self-determination for the Afghan people. They agreed to work together in the continued search for peace throughout the Middle East region.[154]

It was announced in Washington that the YAR would get $47.5 million in US aid in 1990.[155] This represented an increase of nearly $10 million than the previous year, despite the expectations of US officials that Washington would maintain the same level of assistance, if not actually decrease it.[156]

The third event of significance to Yemeni–US relations was YAR's decision to join the ACC. By joining this council, which was founded by Iraq, the YAR, consciously or unconsciously, was trapped by Baghdad to be involved in the latters miscalculated regional policies. News of the YAR's alliance with Iraq was received with caution in Washington. Contrary to Riyadh, Baghdad showed support for the YAR's efforts to achieve Yemen unity. This Iraqi stance successfully widened the gab and differences between Riyadh and Sana'a.

A further development relevant to the bilateral relationship was Yemen unification, which took place on 22 May 1990. In Washington this was seen as a victory for both the US and for the politically moderate YAR, which had a larger population as well as larger oil revenues than the pro-Soviet PDRY. Despite these expectations, which were coloured by Cold War attitudes, Yemen unity ultimately had an indirect negative effect on Yemen–US relations. This was due to Saudi objections to the emergence of a republican, highly populated, multi-party Republic of Yemen (ROY), which had claims on the ROY–KSA border 'Asir regions. According to Yemeni allegations, the Saudis tried to promote instability in the Yemen by donating large amounts of money to their client northern tribesmen and to some religious groups which saw unity as an anti-Islamic development and by delaying deliveries of aid to Sana'a. Iraq reacted by providing the ROY with material and political support. This stirred the old enmity between the two neighbouring peninsula states and opened the door for a closer relationship between the ROY and Iraq within the context of the newly formed ACC. When Yemeni unity was announced in Aden on 22 May 1990, it was not welcomed in Riyadh. This created a problem for Washington, which was forced to find a way of reconciling its policy towards the ROY with that of its more established and stronger relationship with the KSA in which it had greater interests.

These developments contained positive as well as negative elements that had the potential to promote bilateral YAR–US cooperation or constrain it. The products of these developments, it appears, depended on regional politics and fundamentally on the ROY's foreign policy.

Conclusion

The last phase of YAR–US relations between 1979 and 1990 created a solid base for a direct bilateral relationship between Sana'a and Washington despite the fact that the KSA continued to be the principal US ally and partner in the Arab world. This phase witnessed US protection of the YAR, when the PDRY, in late 1979, intended to destroy the YAR army and its government. It was also a period of oil discovery in commercial quantities by American companies in the YAR, an event that created a US economic interest in the country, as demonstated by the increased levels of US assistance. The US oil companies' exploration on the YAR–PDRY border, which indicated the presence of oil in the latter country, also brought about US interest in the PDRY, and thus led to the restoration of diplomatic relations between Washington and Aden a few days before the declaration of Yemen unity.

Vice-President Bush's visit to Sana'a in April 1986 and that of President Saleh to Washington in January 1990 marked a real growth in the relationship between the two governments and the two nations. Yet, regional political developments, such as the YAR's alliance with Iraq within the context of the newly born ACC, appeared to be a counter-alliance against the KSA and the GCC states; the two Yemens agreeing to form the ROY with special support from Iraq and with the ex-YAR's foreign policy, were observed with caution in Washington, forcing the State Department to find a way to reconcile its interests in both the YAR and the KSA.

This phase of YAR–US relations also witnessed increased sophistication of the YAR, USSR and US foreign policies. When Sana'a was not able to obtain all its arms requirements from the US due to Saudi obstruction, it decided to play Moscow against Washington to obtain its military needs from the former, and at the same time it promoted economic cooperation with the latter and other interested nations. Washington, realizing that Moscow was promoting its relationship with Sana'a through the late 1970s $600 million arms package to the YAR and the former's neutral stance during the second inter-Yemeni war, decided to promote its relationship with Sana'a through its companies' oil exploration in the YAR, and it successfully maintained its presence in the country through oil partnership and increased technical assistance. Moscow, calculating that it was not in its interest to encourage the PDRY's invasion of the YAR in 1979, and unable to confront the US militarily, not only opposed south Yemen's war against the YAR but also provided Sana'a with arms and military advisers needed to re-equip and organize the YAR's army. This Soviet policy towards the YAR was aimed at preventing Sana'a from falling completely under KSA and US domination.

In general, the period between 1979 and 1990 witnessed the development of US interest in the YAR and the PDRY.

5

The US and unified Yemen

This chapter covers the relationship between the Republic of Yemen (ROY) and the USA during the period that followed Yemeni unification on 22 May 1990 – when, after years of negotiations, the YAR merged with the socialist-ruled People's Democratic Republic of Yemen (PDRY) to form the ROY.[1] In many respects, relations between unified Yemen and the United States were simply a continuation of the pattern of Yemeni–US relations described in the preceding chapters, for the merger of the YAR with the PDRY, formerly on the State Department's list of notorious 'terrorist states', was viewed positively in Washington as another dimension of its victory in the Cold War. On the other hand, one major event, the Gulf War, broke with the pattern of nearly thirty years of small state–superpower interaction. For in the Gulf crisis and the US-led war against Iraq, Sana'a stood not only against Washington but against Riyadh, Kuwait and other major global and regional powers. This extraordinary policy, announced officially as 'neutrality' and a preference for an 'Arab solution' to the Iraqi invasion of Kuwait but regarded in the West and the Gulf as a pro-Saddam stance, marked the first time that Sana'a had ever been involved in international affairs beyond its borders, much less taken a position that was perceived in the district of Columbia as a threat to the interests of the United States. This risky entrance into autonomous foreign policy-making by a small, peripheral state, made highly visible by Yemen's rotation onto the 'Arab seat' in the UN Security Council, proved to be very expensive.

At the time of the Yemeni merger, Sana'a's relations with the US were apparently stable and understanding between the two states was good. Washington was providing the country with $47.5 million of development and technical assistance, which included military training and a few US F-5 fighters, which were part of a nearly $360 million arms package to the ex-YAR in 1979, delivered with US spare parts and maintenance. The Yemeni government and US oil companies were partners in oil production. US economic interest in the ROY, which started in 1984 with the Hunt oil find in north-west YAR and continued as additional US companies explored for oil in the country, was an indication that bilateral relations between the two states would witness further improvement and cooperation. The introduction of political liberties and multiparty parliamentary elections further raised Sana'a's expectations for improved relations with America. Yet regional and international politics shook these expectations.

Dominant themes

Five dominant themes determined the course of ROY–US relations from 22 May 1990 to 1993. The first was the opposing positions assumed by the US and Yemen regarding the Kuwaiti crisis. Second, there was the grave deterioration of Yemen–Saudi relations, which bottomed out with the latter's claims to ROY territories where American and European companies were drilling to produce oil and gas. Third, the end of the Cold War and the collapse of the Soviet bloc resulted in a reduction in Moscow's influence in the Middle East. A fourth, economic, theme was the discovery of more oil reserves, albeit modest, in the ROY, including the southern governorates of Shabwa and Hadramawt, and the rising involvement of additional US and Western oil companies, oil-related services and non-oil companies in the republic. Finally, instability, new economic burdens and armed actions in the new republic were followed in April 1993 by an historic experiment in multi-party elections, the first in the Arabian peninsula, and in May 1994 by an inter-Yemeni war that destroyed the military machine of the former socialists, who revolted against the ballot box, lost the battle in open warfare and were driven into opposition.

Yemeni and US positions towards the settlement of the Kuwaiti crisis

On 2 August 1990 Iraq invaded Kuwait. The UN Security Council met a few hours after the event, condemning the invasion and calling upon Baghdad to withdraw its forces from the Sheikhdom. Yemen, the Security Council's only Arab member, abstained from the vote. In the Arab foreign ministers' meeting in Cairo during the first week of August 1990, the ROY allied itself with Sudan, Tunisia, the PLO and Jordan, in a collective attempt to find an inter-Arab solution to the crisis. But this solution was dismissed by the US, on the grounds that Iraq's military superiority constituted a threat to the states of the region.[2] In subsequent Security Council meetings Yemen expressed its opposition to the invasion and the annexation of Kuwait, but it opposed the use of 'all necessary means' to free Kuwait. In one case, Sana'a voted for the air embargo against Iraq, but this was only agreed to after the US pledged to prevent a KSA decision to expel nearly a million Yemeni workers. In spite of the pledge, however, Washington was able to delay the Saudi decision for only a month.[3]

The invasion of Kuwait put Sana'a, which was allied with Iraq within the Arab Cooperation Council (ACC), in a difficult position: Yemen appeared to share with Baghdad the frustration regarding US policies towards the PLO and the Palestinians, as well as a nationalistic vision of the future of the Arab world and Arab wealth. Sana'a appeared to believe that the use of force against Baghdad would be discriminatory, would strengthen Israel's and the KSA's domination of the Arabian peninsula, and would heighten the KSA's interference in Yemeni affairs. Yemeni decision-makers thought that other issues, such as the illegal occupation of Palestine and the 1934 Saudi seizure of the Yemeni region of 'Asir, should be given the same consideration as that of Kuwait. They argued that the US and the UN did not deal with other occupying powers in the same way. The Yemenis were also convinced by President Saddam Hussein's argument that the Kuwaitis and the Americans had been plotting against his government since 1989 because Washington wanted to prevent Iraq from becoming a significant military threat to Israel and other US allies in the region, while Kuwait sought to end the border dispute with a weaker Baghdad.[4] The ROY supported an inter-Arab solution that opposed Saddam's occupation of Kuwait, because it had faith that Arab mediation could persuade President Saddam to withdraw from Kuwait. The US, however, did not believe that such an effort would free Kuwait and protect Western interests in the area. This resulted in the ROY and the US taking opposing sides regarding the settlement of the Kuwaiti question.

The ROY position towards settling the Kuwaiti crisis appeared to have seriously 'damaged'[5] the US–ROY relationship. One reason was that Yemen did not support the resolution that recommended the use of 'all means necessary' to free Kuwait. David Mack, the US assistant secretary of state, stated in a 10 November 1993 Worldnet interview:

> The United States believes that there is a contradiction that Yemen, which is a country that has taken place and courageously has witnessed democratic developments, that they are continuing to support one of the worst dictatorships in the whole world and which has repeatedly shown non-respect of international law and basic human rights.[6]

Grave deterioration of Yemeni–Saudi
relations

The period between August 1990 and late 1993 witnessed a major deterioration in ROY–KSA relations, to a point almost as low as that in the 1962–70 Yemen civil war. The lowest point of this deterioration was reached in April 1992, when the KSA warned non-American oil companies operating in the bordering desert and waters of the ROY that they were drilling in a disputed area, and that Riyadh maintained 'the right to take the appropriate action to preserve its territorial rights'.[7] Ostensibly, the ROY–KSA crisis was a result of the ROY's stance towards the Iraqi invasion of Kuwait on 2 August 1990: but while this was a major factor, Sana'a–Riyadh relations had been suffering setbacks since late 1979 when President Saleh first attempted to crack the KSA influence in his country. It was exacerbated by the president's serious efforts to bring about Yemen unity in the 1980s and the united Yemen's attempts to bring about democratic developments in the 1990s.

This new deterioration in ROY–KSA relations, it seemed, raised French and US concerns. In May 1992 Washington issued a statement that called the two neighbouring peninsular states to settle their differences through negotiations and peaceful means.

The US government's position, which was followed by a message from President Bush to President Saleh with a similar content, seemed to have put strong pressure on the ROY to negotiate the 'undefined borders'. On 16 July 1992 the ROY Presidential Council discussed the arrangements for the preliminary meeting with the Saudis, which was due to take place in Geneva on the 20th of the month.[8] 'The meeting was a success, and we agreed to prepare for the first round of negotiations,' Minister al-Dali confirmed.[9] Other rounds of negotiations were held in Sana'a and Riyadh in 1992 and 1993.

That the ROY successfully addressed the border dispute with the KSA was an indication that Sana'a was developing a new policy towards the US. Although it is expected that Sana'a and Riyadh could reach a similar agreement over time, a final demarcation of borders, even if it were to come, would be unlikely to naturalize their relations.[10] Several factors will continue to constrain trust and cooperation between the two governments: the different political systems and their dissimilar roles in regional politics; the long-standing border dispute and history of Saudi intervention in Yemen's internal affairs; the expulsion of nearly a million Yemen workers from the KSA; and more importantly, Yemen's adoption of political pluralism, democracy and a free press after its unification day on 22 May 1990.

Further oil discoveries and the role of US companies

Despite its contrary position on the 'correct' policy for dislodging Iraq from Kuwait, the new Yemeni government of 22 May 1990, with its combined leadership, sought more cooperation with the US, especially in the oil sector.[11] Thus, prior to the Gulf crisis, US oil companies became extensively involved in oil operations throughout the ROY. Although the Gulf Crisis dried up US and GCC aid to Yemen, Sana'a's diplomatic difficulties with Washington did not affect the activities of US oil companies in Yemen. Contrary to what was expected by some observers, more US companies entered the country even though production was not increasing significantly. Table 5.1 lists oil concessions and operators.

Table 5.1 Oil concessions and operators, 31 December 1993 (US companies underlined)

Block/place	Operator/notes	Area (km²)
1 Amakeen	Exxon + Sun Oil (There were 'oil shows' when, in December 1992, Sun Oil drilled its second well. The company signed an initial sharing agreement with US Exxon. According to the agreement, Exxon's share is 85 per cent of the concession.)	2.182
2 Al Mabar	UAE's Crescent + British Clyde + Indonesia Petroleum. (Drilling started in early October 1992.)	4.019
3 Jardan	Chevron + Italian AGIB (Drilling started in early October 1992.)	2.953
4 Iyad	Nimir (The concession was awarded to Nimir in September 1991. Initial estimates of reservoirs were around 300 million barrels. Production had re-started in September 1992 with 12–15,000 bpd being produced. In November 1993 the production was 6,000 bpd. According to oil experts production should start with 100,000 bpd, which should be 50 per cent of the reservoir within five years. But the Saudis were keeping production low in the country for political reasons. The field was built by a Soviet pipeline to Rodhoum on the Gulf of Aden. Nimir Petroleum is a company registered in the Cayman Islands. The Saudi family were the principal share holders in Nimir. Between $500 and 750 million was paid for the signature bonus of the concession. US Arco operates the area.)	1.951
5 Jannah	Total + Hunt + Exxon + Russian + Kufpec	

Table 5.1 continued

Block/place	Operator/notes	Area (km²)
	(Before November 1993 three oil fields were discovered; progress of drilling might lead to KSA claims.)	2.180
6 Iryan	The Indonesian Kodel + Golden Spike (In late 1993 They signed a PSA with the Ministry of Oil. Geological work has started. The area was re-claimed on 1 March 1992 from the US Strake Trading, Norway's Blysted, and KSA's Jamjoom. Licence was terminated after the group had failed to fulfil obligations. KSA was able to influence operations there because of its company's presence.)	3.224
7 Barqa	BP and Furnet. Two wells were drilled. (Furnet has a 12.5 per cent stake in both the seventh and the eighth blocks. It is a Gibraltar-registered offshoot of 'Umar Kassim al-'Esayi Trading Group, a Saudi company stationed in the KSA. KSA was able to influence behaviour there, because of the presence of its company. Operations were subject to its approval.)	4.942
8 Asakir	BP and Furnet about to start seismic works. (KSA was able to influence behaviour there. Operations were subject to KSA approval.)	4.735
9 Malik	Crescent + Japans C.Itoh + British Gas. About to drill. (Operations subject to KSA approval.)	4.728
10 E/Shabwah	Total found three oil fields (Secessation was possible due to Yemeni instability and KSA's efforts.)	11.864
10-B —	Pecten + Clyde + Ansan Skiffs + OMV found several oil fields. (Under possible secession.)	
S-1 Damis	Netherland's Shell + Japan's Sodec (Shell drilled its first well in Jan 1993. Block S1 and S2 were situated between blocks 4 & 5 claimed by the KSA.)	4.484
S-2 Uqlah	A. Occidental + Consolidated Contractors International CCC (Found oil shows after drilling four wells.)	02.808
11 Sirr Hazarelf	ELF found small quantities. (Work was delayed in mid-1989 and ceased in April 1992. The company asked the Yemeni government for guarantees because of existence of the mines in the western area of the block as well as by KSA threats.)	47.217

Table 5.1 continued

Block/place	Operator/notes	Area (km²)
12 N/Sanau	Binham + Arco + Tullow + Coplex (Coplex is a Yemen subsidary of Binham. Undertaking seismic works and about to start drilling (KSA claimed the area).	15.940
13 Al Armah	Open (Red Eagle left after it failed to pay signature bonus.)	7.417
14 S/Masiela	Canadian Oxy +CCC + Pecton (Under threat of possible secession. Production was expected to start with 120,000bpd in September 1993, but actual production in November did not exceed 54,000 bpd.)	35.548
15 Mukkalla	Oman's Alsa'id Alqawi (Signed a production sharing agreement in early 1993. Area under threat of possible secession.)	6.954
16 Qamar	Nimir with Arco the operator, undertaking seismic works and about to drill the first well. (Under attempts and threat of possible secession.)	10.404
17 Aden/Abyan	Open	19.375
18 Marib/Al Jawf	Yemen Hunt + Exxon + Yoking (The main concession operated by the two companies. Production from November 1989 ranged between 155–230,000 bpd. In late December 1992 and in November 1993 production was around 180,000 bpd. Gas reserves were estimated at 20 trillion cubic feet in late 1992. KSA claims were 30 miles north of the concession.)	8.445
19 Jawf	Open	4.223
20 Upper Jawf	Philips + Uaeipc (Both left after concluding the seismic work, which showed the existence of gas.)	4.222
21 Central Highl.	Open (Under KSA threat.)	22.660
22 Al Zaydiah	Mayfair (Undertaking seismic work.)	9.015
23 Antufash	Open (BP+Amoco operations were halted by KSA threat in April and August 1992. The companies left after drilling one well which showed modest quantity of oil.)	13.040
24 Al Kathib	Adair signed PSA.	9.972
25 Hudaydah	Open	6.015
26 Moccha	Open	4.020
27 Al Jambiya	Open	5.250

Table 5.1 continued

Block/place	Operator/notes	Area (km²)
28 North Belhaf	Jalik + Adair (Signed PSA, but failed to pay signature bonus.)	3.771
29 South Sanau	Nimir (Under KSA claim.)	11.055
30 Habroot	Petrocanada + UK Lasmo + Total + Amoco (Under possible KSA threat.)	12.083
31 Rama	Open	13.014
32 Howarime	UK Clyde + The Norwegian Norsk Hydro + The Netherlands Oranja-Nassan Yemen and local Hadramout Ansan Skiffs. (They drilled an exploratory well.)	6.924
33 Al Furt	Nimir with Arco the operator. (Seismic work completed and drilling is about to start. Under possible KSA threat.)	6.017
34 Jeza	Open (Under possible KSA threat.)	7.943
35 Hood	UK Lasmo + British Gas+ Japan's Idemitsu Kosan + Coplex + the local Hood Oil (Under possible KSA threat.)	7.395
36 Thamud	Open (Under possible KSA threat.)	10.660
37 Marait	Open (Under possible KSA threat.)	6.966
38 Damqavet	Open	
39 Socotra	British Gas undertaking seismic survey.	
40 —	Open, originally a relinquished area of Canadian Oxy.	

Sources: Yemen Oil Exploration Board reports; Muhammad ba-Matraf, Director of explorations at the board; Dr 'Abd al-Sattar Nani, Director of Research; author's research; *Economist*, 11 and 25 July 1992; Petro Finance Market Intelligence Service, *Yemen: Border Disputes and Relations with Saudi Arabia*, Washington, DC, May 1992.

The table shows that in late 1993 American oil companies were seriously involved in most of the ongoing oil explorations in the ROY.

Marib oil reserves exceeded 1.2 bb. The total gas reserve in Marib was estimated around 20 bcf.[12] In November 1993, the US ENRON signed a letter of intent with the Yemeni Oil Exploration Authority to develop the gas avialable in the Marib–al-Djawf basin.[13]

The next production area is at south Masila (block 14) where Canadian Oxy is operating. (American Occidental owns 30 per cent of that Canadian oil company.) Reserves in the discovered fields were estimated in December 1992 at 1.2 billion barrels. Exports began in September 1993. A third production area was Aydah at block 4, where the American Arco was operating for the Saudi Nimir company. Serious production started in September 1992 at a rate of 12–15,000 bpd.

Total oil production in Yemen from blocks 4, 8 and 18 amounted to 232,000 bpd. This figure, multiplied by Yemen's share (62 per cent), makes a total of 144,000 bpd. Yemen's daily local consumption of 65,000 bpd, subtracted from its daily exports of 144,000 bpd, yields a daily income of $1.3 million, based on an average price of $16[14] per barrel. Therefore, its 1993 income from oil was $475 million.[15]

Other US companies, such as Sun Oil, Hunt-Exxon (operating in conjuction with French Total), Arco, Phillips, and American Occidental found oil and gas in blocks 1, 5, 16, S2 and 20; reserves were under calculation. Work in Chevron's wildcat at block 3 began in October 1992. In other blocks the US companies Arco, Toto, Adair, Mayfair, Beltin, Amoco, and Canadian Oxy[16] were all involved in different stages of the oil and gas exploration and production process. The following US oil-service companies were operating in the ROY in July 1992: Caltex, Yemen Crest, Haliburton-Oilfield Services, Haliburton-Geophysical Services, Western Geophysical, Nabors, and M.I. Drilling Fluids Company (a division of Dresser–Haliburton).[17] In the minerals field, the United States Geological Survey (USGS) contracted with the Yemen Mineral Exploration Board in early 1992 to prepare maps that would show the volcanic areas where gold could possibly be found.[18] Gold had previously been found in Hadramawt.

The only successful non-American oil company was the French Total, which found oil and gas in block 5 (with Hunt and Exxon) and in block 10 (with Amoco), where four wells have shown positive results. These wells were not yet on production in late November 1993.

It was evident that more US oil and oil-services companies had become involved in the ROY after 1990, and that more oil had been found in the country. This might have implied that the US interest in Yemen would increase, thus leading to an improvement of bilateral relations. A side-effect of this development was the increased dependence of the ROY on US companies. Yemen was likely to be tied to the US more tightly than at any time previously.

When, in the early 1980s, American Hunt, Exxon and other Korean partners seriously explored for, and then discovered, oil in the ex-YAR, their operations were significant to the West from both an economic and political standpoint. A number of factors contributed to this: there were fears of the spread of the Iraq–Iran war to the GCC states and of possible threats to the flow of Gulf oil; exports of Iranian

Table 5.2 Mineral concessions through 5 December 1993

Block	Company/notes	Mineral expected
Sa'dah	Now open. UK Cluff have just relinquished the area	Gold
Tabak at Shabwah	UK Cluff. Reconnaissance completed, exploration about to start	Poly-metals; lead, silver and zinc
Al-Djabali	Netherlands Billiton was negotiating the concession in light of the feasibility study which was finalized in December	Lead, silver and zinc
Al-Baidah	German–French MetalEurope obtained the concession	Gold
Shiharah	MetalEurope obtained concession	Gold
Wadi Medden	Irish Meridian International initiated, on 16 October 1993, its exploitation of 6 km and its exploration of another 300 km of the concession	Gold
North Ma'bar	South African, Anglo-American was in contact with Yemeni authorities over the concession	Gold
East Dhamar	South African, Anglo-American was in contact with Yemeni authorities over the concession	Gold
Al-Hamoura	Now open. Reconnaissance was completed by Romanian companies	Zinc
Wadi Falhan at al-Djawf	UK Ansan Wikkfs has obtained concession and was undertaking reconnaissance	Gold
Wadi Ribat at Al-Buka'	UK Ansan Wikkfs has obtained concession and was undertaking reconnaissance	Gold
Bahrah at Djahm	UK Ansan Wikkfs has obtained concession and was undertaking reconnaissance	Gold

Source: 'Uthman Nu'man, vice-chairman of Yemen Mineral Board, 16 December 1993 and author's research.

oil had decreased as a result of its anti-Western policies; Soviet arms were flowing into the YAR at the expense of Washington's influence; in the southern borders of the YAR there was a pro-Soviet Yemen which was considered to be a communist base in the Middle East; above all, former-North Yemen, which was a buffer zone between the PDRY and US interests in the KSA, went on to develop a special relationship with the US and KSA. However, by 1993, these US and Western concerns and interests had ceased to be valid; Yemen's income from the oil sector was uncertain and US oil companies' operations became less important to the US and the West.

Sana'a's efforts to find more oil[19] as a resource to develop its economy had clearly made Yemen dependent on US oil companies[20] and US intentions. This meant that the ROY was gradually losing its limited freedom of mobility when dealing with the only superpower left in the world.

End of the Cold War

Yemen entered a new phase with the formation of the Republic of Yemen on 22 May 1990. Important factors that facilitated unity at the time were the collapse of the USSR after a nearly half a century of tension with the US, and, as a consequence, the containment of Moscow's influence in the world, especially in the Arabian peninsula and the Horn of Africa. But a side-effect of the collapse of the communist bloc for Yemen was that Russia and China became more interested in the KSA at a time when Sana'a–Riyadh relations were severely deteriorating. After unification, it appeared that the ROY was unable to develop cooperation and understanding with the Saudi Kingdom, and Yemen's opposition to US and the KSA's policies towards Iraq during the Iraqi invasion of Kuwait created sharp political differences between Sana'a and Washington. These ROY–US differences were expensive for Yemen: Washington's interest in the country was modest, the oil flow to the West was no longer seriously threatened, and the Soviet bloc was no longer a rival of the US in the Middle East.

In late 1993, US policy on Yemen was a minor component of its overall Middle Eastern policy. The US maintained a strong relationship with the KSA and the other oil-rich sheikhdoms of the Gulf, and was concerned to contain 'Islamist radicalism' and anti-Israel and anti-Western policies and sentiments. At this time, it appeared that Yemen was economically weaker than ever before due to the loss of Arab and American aid and the lack of economic and military significance. Sana'a was becoming less important politically to Washington and it had never been that important

Instability and war against democracy in ROY

The issue of stability and the development of democracy in the ROY played a role in determining relations with the US. The deterioration of relations between Yemen and Saudi Arabia, the inter-Yemen differences created by Iraq's invasion of Kuwait and the Yemen leadership's sympathy with President Saddam Hussein, together with Yemen's weak economy had certainly created problems for the new Yemen. These problems, coupled with the KSA's influence over the northern tribes and traditional and militant totalitarian forces interested in a bloody war against democracy, created instability in the ROY. The eruption of the fear of the unknown in Yemen was intensified when the fever of political violence and instability started escalating to alarming levels in 1992. Armed attacks against senior officials became common, and yet Yemen's security system was unable to combat the saboteurs or bring the culprits to justice.

In early November 1992, the ROY vice-president and leader of the Yemeni Socialist Party (YSP), 'Ali Salem al-Bidh, who had departed for the Southern governorates in late July, returned to Sana'a from Aden. It was clear that differences between the YSP and the president were still very great. In mid-October the YSP Political Bureau held its first meeting in Aden since unification. This was a show of support to the YSP secretary-general, as well as an indication that the YSP leadership was united.

On the other hand, the Yemeni press reported in late October and early November 1992 that parliamentary elections would not take place before the end of the supposed transitional period (22 May 1990 to 21 November 1992). The Supreme Elections Committee (SEC) indicated on 19 October that it was still facing difficulties, and that preparations for elections needed several months to be concluded. A few days later the leaders of the ROY agreed to extend the transitional period, and pledged to prepare for elections on 27 April 1993.

The postponement of parliamentary elections for 184 days, the continuously rising inflation and the related decline of the Yemeni currency's value against the US dollar, the outbreak and suppression of demonstrations in the major cities of the ROY in late 1992 and the mounting rivalry between the two ruling parties all combined to push the country to the edge of possible disintegration.

Elections and their aftermath

The US was, however, supportive, at least in its rhetoric, of the democratization process. The US ambassador clearly stated from the beginning of his mission in the ROY that the US was interested in the newly united Yemen's efforts to achieve internal unity, democracy and economic and political freedom.[21] Yemen has been the only state in the Arabian peninsula to embark upon the road of democracy, a journey that involved the maintenance of a free press, operating a multi-party system and accepting visits from human rights observation missions; but democracy could not develop easily in a contained environment, or flourish in the absence of law and order. A contradiction existed between working for a successful democracy within Yemen and its attempts to settle differences with Saudi Arabia. There was a contradiction too between US support for Yemen's democracy and Washington's alliance with the KSA against any threat whatsoever. Without the Clinton administration's promotion of democratization in the GCC states, democracy in Yemen would continue to displease the KSA and thus would have a negative effect on the development of ROY–US relationship.[22]

The Yemeni national elections of 27 April 1993, involving over two million voters and 3,700 candidates for 301 constituency-based seats in the Chamber of Deputies, were regarded as 'free and fair' by international, including American, observers. After intense campaigning by President 'Ali 'Abd Allah Saleh's General People's Congress (GPC), the co-ruling Yemeni Socialist Party, the Islamist-tribal coalition known as the Islah ('Reform') Party led by Shaikh 'Abd Allah Bin Hussayn al-Ahmar, several pan-Arab and numerous local parties, and independent candidates over the shape of the new ruling coalition, the results showed that the GBC won 122 seats, Islah 62 seats, the YSP 57, independents 46 and the Ba'th 7. Three Nasiri parties each gained 1 seat, the religious-aristocratic al-Huq party had 2, and 2 remained to be decided. The elections thus indicated a genuine contest and mandated a coalition government in which the YSP's al-'Attas remained prime minister and al-Ahmar became speaker of parliament.

Once it was clear the elections were going forward, the US offered some official support, and the Western media in general responded favourably.[23] An embassy memorandum in April 1993 stated that:

> Since Yemeni leaders decided to try democracy as the best way to sort out the division of power following the unification of North and South in 1990, the Post has made democratization its number one mission. We have shaped nearly every program to strengthen Yemen's emerging democratic institutions and to underline U.S. support for this development ... Whatever foreign policy differences may exist between Yemen and the U.S., we have encountered almost unlimited demand among Yemenis for American support in building democratic institutions. Their receptiveness and enthusiasm belies the idea that the Arab world is somehow culturally unsuited for democracy.[24]

Among the US official visitors during the campaign and election season were James Zogby of the Arab–American Institute, who reminded Yemeni audiences of the long road to universal suffrage and free elections in the US,[25] and Deputy Assistant Secretary of State David Mack, who said cautiously that he was 'instructed to congratulate [the] Yemeni people and government' and to express US encouragement and support for the process.[26]

To demonstrate its support for the electoral process, USAID committed nearly $500,000 (mostly for American staff and their travel expenses) to the Washington-based British–American International Foundation for Electoral Systems (IFES), and two affiliates of the National Endowment for Democracy, the National Democratic Institute for International Affairs (NDI), and the International Republican Institute (IRI) to assist election officials and observers. However, none of these projects contributed demonstrably to the electoral process. IFES technical advice to the Supreme Elections Committee – co-financed by the European Community, the UK and the Netherlands – procured 5 million ballots and ink, 6,000 ballot boxes and seals, voting screens and 230 voting booths,[27] and held training sessions for pollworker trainers. But booths and other equipment arrived after voting day, and the design and execution of training sessions were also way beyond schedule. The IRI conducted some studies of the Yemeni parties' media and campaign activities and helped recruit sixteen American, Dutch, German, Bahraini and United Arab Emirates observers, all funded by their respective governments. The team of observers included fewer Arabic speakers than expected because of neighbouring states' reluctance to have their citizens observe the process. The NDI also collected information, then offered to help a hastily organized Yemeni nongovernmental organization, the National Committee for Free Elections (NCFE) to train local volunteers as independent election monitors. Its plans to organize volunteer monitors for each of 7,000 polling stations were stymied by partisan squabbles within the NCFE, retraction of SEC approval for its activities, and NDI's own late start and lack of familiarity with the Yemeni environment.[28]

Ever mindful of Saudi and Kuwaiti concerns, the US was cautious in its endorsement of the Yemeni elections. Ambassador Mack stressed that 'one election does not make a democracy', and that US support was more likely to consist of corporate investments than government aid. Yemen must take further steps towards democracy before satisfying US standards, and in any case should not consider their experience a 'blueprint' for neighbouring countries,[29] who have the right to choose the style of 'democracy' that best suits their internal environments. In fact, he suggested that Kuwait's limited-franchise balloting (excluding women and others) in August 1992 should, perhaps, have been a model for Yemen.[30] Announcing a token $1.7 million increase in US assistance, Ambassador Hughes later made it clear that progress towards normalization of ties with Washington depended on improvement in Yemen's relations with its Gulf neighbours.[31]

Six months after the elections, however, the two former ruling parties failed to agree on the division of government posts between themselves and the Islah, never mind coming to an agreement on development strategy. As the riyal continued to plummet against the dollar, Yemen's leadership seemed no closer to directing its attention to the deepening economic crisis and the pending World Bank Structural Adjustment Programme. US interest was indicated by USAID's installation of electronic voting equipment in parliament (which, unfortunately, was abandoned after one or two experiments, in favour of old-fashioned paper ballots and show-of-hands); a conference on Yemen by Chemonics, Inc., the USAID contractor for the 'Democratic Initiatives' in the Middle East programme, in mid-September; and by Al Gore's informal meeting with al-Bidh in Washington in August.[32] When former US President Jimmy Carter made a private visit to Sana'a in September 1993, he told an appreciative Yemeni audience that it was time to 'put the Gulf Crisis behind us' and 'cement relations with those who took an opposing view'.[33] Still, economic relief from the US or its Gulf allies remained but wishful thinking on the part of the Yemenis.

A desire for improved relations with the US and the Gulf did help to produce the only discernible policy change in the post-election period, symbolized by the replacement of Foreign Minister 'Abd al-Karim al-Iryani by Mohammad Salim Basindwa. The new foreign minister disavowed Yemen's Gulf War stance, and devoted his attention to achieving a rapprochement with the Gulf monarchies. His limited successes – indicated by the painfully slow progress in Yemeni–Saudi border negotiations, another round of Saudi letters to Hunt, Elf Acquitaine and other international oil companies warning them against operations in Yemen[34] – showed that the restoration of friendly ties with the Gulf, a condition imposed by the US for improved US–Yemeni relations, would be measured in years rather than weeks or months.

Although reconciliation took place between the YSP and the GPC as the country was preparing for its first parliamentary elections, this reconciliation and the stability resulting from it did not last long. In August 1993, the vice-president returned from the US and settled in Aden. When he was subsequently re-elected vice-president by the new parliament, however, he forwarded a number of conditions to be fulfilled before he would take his oath. The YSP sent these 'eighteen points' to the president of Yemen. By November 1993, these conditions had still not been fulfilled, al-Bidh remained in Aden, and YSP sources reported several assassination attempts against the vice-president and three of his sons. The al-Bidh family survived these attempts, but in October a nephew of the vice president, Kamal al-Hamid, was assassinated. In November 1993, a southern colonel named al-'Absi was murdered on the road between Ta'iz and Hudeida. Instability and insecurity also assisted gunmen in stealing and attempting to steal several vehicles owned by foreigners, including automobiles owned by a US diplomat, a German researcher and a German expatriate involved in developmental aid. Carjackings occurred even in the heart of the Old City of Sana'a. The hijacking record for the period 1 January 1993 until 31 October 1993 was as shown in Table 5.3.

Table 5.3 Hijacking record for the period 1 January 1993 to 31 October 1993

Event	Foreign victims	Local victims
Hijacked vehicles	136	310
Attempts at hijacking	44	170
Persons kidnapped	8	63
Car thefts	31	102
Killed during hijacking	–	6

Source: Ministry of Interior, Sana'a; Yemen Times, 28 November 1993, p. 16.

The interior minister, Yahya al-Mutawakil, though highly qualified and much admired, appeared unable to continue his earlier efforts to maintain security and put an end to such acts. The reason for this was clearly the fact that many of those terrorists and sabotagers were protected by influential sheikhs, officials and army officers, as was pointed out by the minister himself earlier in the year. In conclusion, the security situation of November and December 1993 was similar to that in October 1992. A few days after the beating of his deputy, Philips, and the hijacking of his vehicle near Dhamar, Hayes R. Mahoney, the US cultural attaché and director of the USIS office in Sana'a, was kidnapped on Thursday 25 November 1993 as he was getting into his car after a British Airways party at a city centre hotel. A week later, Mahoney was freed in the Jahm area of Marib province east of Sana'a. It was said that the five kidnappers were acting on orders from 'one of the tribal chiefs of the area who justified his act on the grounds that he had demands to make to the government'. Mahoney was the first US diplomat to have been kidnapped in Yemen in recent years, but tribesmen pursuing local quarrels with oil companies and the government have carried out a string of abductions of foreigners. Two American Hunt Oil employees were held for four days in May when twenty-five men from the Hashid tribe ambushed their car east of Sana'a. They were seeking the release of a clansman who had killed a police officer. Six men, employees of French Total, were held for two days in April. A Japanese dam expert was abducted in February and a Canadian oil employee in January. In early December a German engineer was kidnapped for a short while near the province of Dhamar. Twenty-three European tourists were briefly held hostage east of Sana'a in October by a tribal leader seeking concessions from the government.

The government warned in February that it could not guarantee the safety of foreigners, and in September it announced plans to set up a special force to protect the employees of foreign oil companies. Oil companies have hired extra guards and often use helicopters to avoid driving through lawless areas. Even Hunt, in the latter half of 1993, were threatened by acts such as the firing of several rocket-propelled grenades (RPGs) at pumping stations near Razeh by the kidnapper of Mahony. The company was also prevented from drilling in the 'Thu Reidan' field. In sum, the growing tension between the two principal armed players on the political stage put the country once again on the edge of political upheaval. Salim Saleh Muhammad, a member of Yemen's five-man Presidential Council, was the first senior Yemeni official to acknowledge publicly that the union that had been declared in May 1990 was not working; he suggested federation as an alternative. He said on 25 November that divided Yemen into a federation of self-ruled regions could settle the country's political turmoil. He expressed the belief that the three-year-old merger of the north and the south would not survive, and said that a split was certain if Sana'a did not accept Aden's proposals for political, economic and social reforms. 'If our 18-point proposal is not implemented, there will be a separation: they will rule Sana'a and we will rule Aden,' Mr Muhammad said. But he ruled out the possibility of civil war.

In November 1993 the growing internal crisis attracted the attention of the United States. The office of US spokesman, Michael MacMurray, released the following statement on 10 November:

> The United States Government has followed closely recent unsettled political events in Yemen, a nation which took an important step toward democracy with its successful parliamentary election in April 1993. The Yemeni elections – the first multi-party elections in the Arabian Penisula – marked an important development in the history of the region, consistent with United States support for democratization.
> The United States Government supports strongly the unity of Yemen

as being in the best interests of the Yemeni people, and the people of the region as a whole. The United States also supports progress toward greater popular participation in government, democratization, and economic reform leading to a free market system in Yemen.

At the time of unification in 1990 the Yemenis themselves made their wish to build a new nation, with new and better institutions. The United States welcomed this effort. In light of recent events, in which this new chapter in the development of Yemen has been strained in internal disagreements, the United States wishes to make clear its [wish] that there must be a peaceful resolution of all political issues through dialogue among all interested parties. This will allow the process of further democratization and institution building to continue.

On 19 November 1993, US Ambassador Arthur Hughes delivered a letter to the Yemeni President from the US administration and showed him satellite photographs of northern and southern troop movements. The letter expressed deep US concern over the continuation of the political crisis and its effects upon stability in Yemen. The letter also renewed US support for unity, democracy, and economic reform in the country. A further expression of US concern came when the American ambassador delivered another letter to Vice-President al-Bidh in Aden in which he once again expressed his concern over the current political situation and showed photographs of troop movements.[35] It appeared that the US ambassador's mediation efforts in both Sana'a and Aden in late November 1993 were fruitful and well timed. The US succeeded in calming down the tension that existed in 1993. US efforts in 1993 clearly played an important role in preventing a military confrontation between the armies of what had previously been two Yemens in 1993.

'Unity enhancement war' and the US position

The 1994 inter-Yemeni fighting ended officially on 7 July 1994. The beginnings of the war can be traced back to 21 February of the same year, when the YSP leadership attempted but failed to destroy the Al-'Amaliqah forces stationed in Abyan. The result of that attempt was a clear indication that the YSP could never win in a military encounter. The recent inter-Yemeni fighting, however, led to the crushing of the military machine of the first and last ruling Socialist party in the Arab world. By merging with the former YAR, the ex-PDRY leaders thought in 1989 that they could 'stoop to conquer', sidestepping the effects of the third tidal wave of democracy that destroyed their major ally, the USSR. The ostensible results of the war were: the continuation of Yemen unity, the formation of a united military and security establishment and a united Yemeni decision-making front. The entry of the government forces into Mukalla and the strategic parts of Aden took place on 4 July, US Independence Day, a powerful symbol in the history of Sana'a–Washington relations. Despite the hasty interpretations expressed in the statements of some US officials (such as that of Ambassador Robert Pelletreau, the US assistant secretary of state, who told journalists in both Oman and the UAE in response to questions that Aden was still very far from being reached by the northern forces and that the southern forces were highly trained), the US position was supportive of Yemen unity, its democratic initiatives and the internal Yemeni dialogue:

> We have felt from the beginning that unity was a concept that was in the interest of the people of Yemen. And we believe that unity should be rebuilt beginning with an end to the fighting and a restoration of political dialogue.[36]

On 6 June 1994, at the concluding session of the GCC meeting, which took place near the Yemeni borders, Christine Shelly, the US Department of State assistant spokesperson, emphasized that the GCC role should be a positive one and that Yemen's problems could not be solved through military means. This statement can be taken as a message to certain members of the GCC. The timing of the statement can also be seen as means of assuring the parties in the Arabian peninsula that the US was following the situation and that it would do its best to talk to the disputing parties so that the war did not affect neighbouring states. A statement by the Department of State spokesman, Michael MacMurray, which was issued before Aden's surrender to the government forces, stressed the importance of ending any sort of heavy bombardment of Aden and urged both parties to continue dialogue. The statement's warning that further military operations would lead to urgent action by the Security Council was a warning to both sides that further fighting would only lead to more civilian injuries, especially given that all the defences of the secessionists had already fell apart. Some YSP leaders, who then contacted the US Embassy in the UAE, assured me that the US played an important role in ending the war at this stage, thereby saving the city and the country further unnecessary human and material losses as well as helping the secessionists to leave the city peacefully.

In interviews published in Sana'a on 6 July 1994, several Yemeni politicians and university professors agreed that Yemen unity was one component of US policy towards Yemen. The principal leader of the secession attempt, and a founder of the League of the Children of Yemen and vice-president of the secessionist southerners, 'Abdul-

Rahman 'Ali Al-Djifri, admitted in an interview published in London later in September that secession did not gain any US support:

> Before the eruption of fighting, I was not aware of the US position. It broke out just a few hours before my scheduled arrival in Sana'a to hold talks with the US Assistant Secretary of State at the US Embassy. The US declared stance during the war was correct, but, it seemed, there was another undeclared position, which doesn't agree with the facts of the situation. If wrong information reached the Americans, we hope this information can be corrected. Unfortunately, this stance represents a rare case of a clearly self-contradictory US stand.[37]

Further to the fact that Sana'a and Washington had a long history of bilateral relations and understanding, and the fact that Washington showed its resolve to its allies and friends, a US Peace Institute official assured a seminar at London University's School of Oriental and African Studies (SOAS) on 23 September 1994 that 'Washington has long campaigned for President Saleh due to the interests of the US Hunt and Exxon and the successful democratic initiatives which led to the 1993 elections'.

Also, following the recent internal strife, Washington showed its support and enthusiasm for democratization, reconciliation and the new ROY approach as represented by seven Presidential Council points, which were issued by the Council in July 1994. On 7 July 1994, the Presidential Council pledged to implement republican decree No. 1/94 regarding the general amnesty. Its seven points were: willingness to compensate those who had lost their properties as a result of the 'rebellion'; according to Cabinet regulations continued commitment to democratization and pluralism; guarantee of the freedom of the press; respect for human rights; commitment to a market economy and resort to dialogue within the context of respect for 'constitutional legitimacy' in order to solve any political differences as well as avoidance of any kind of violent acts in political relations; restoration of normal public life in those areas that had suffered as a result of rebellious and destructive acts; workers in the civil service sector were to return to their posts and start work again on a normal basis as quickly as possible; and eagerness to broaden popular participation in government and to introduce a system of local government that would guarantee extensive powers for administrative units.

The statement issued by the Yemeni Presidential Council confirmed that 'the unity of Yemen can only mean security and peace' for the Arabian peninsula and Gulf regions. It pledged, moreover, to work with 'all friendly Muslim and non-Muslim states' for the good of their peoples, their security, and their development. The US administration lent its encouragement and support to the Presidential Council's statement and the seven points it included, as well as to the ROY's participation in strengthening the foundations of security, stability and cooperation in the peninsula and Gulf regions. According to Yemeni media coverage, US Ambassador Arthur Hughes indicated in a meeting with President Saleh following the end of the war – the first indication since the 1990 Gulf crisis – that Washington was seeking to resume its aid to the ROY.

In contrast to the US stance, the KSA seemed to provoke – and even to support financially – the attempt to split Yemen apart again. In our opinion, the USA's supportive attitude to Yemeni unity appears, in the light of the end of the operation known as the 'unity enhancement war', to have foiled the attempt made by the sole power in the southern governorates (since 1986) to drag Yemen and Saudi Arabia into conflict during the internal Yemeni war of May–July 1994. A study of the outcome of the Yemeni crisis and of the rebellion against the two constants of democracy and unity also leads to the conclusion that Saudi Arabia played a major role in these events. The events centre on a rebellion led by influential figures in the YSP against the results of the 27 April 1993 general election. It was a rebellion, therefore, against the will of the Yemeni people as symbolized by the House of Representatives, the 1991 Constitution and thus the democratization process as a whole. This rebellion was a refusal to accept 'pluralist democracy', an attempt to impose a democracy in which 'geographical area' and 'resources' should be given representation. The rebels asserted, as was maintained by the former vice-president, that an agreement made in private between himself and the president while their motorcade was passing 'through the tunnel' in Aden in 1989 had been betrayed; additional 'excuses' for the rebellion were that 'the armies should not be merged until everything has been agreed on' and that the idea of a 'division between three' (parties) was unacceptable 'because we have been a state'. It became clear that Riyadh and other states of the GCC had interfered in Yemen's affairs, and that the involvement of Riyadh, in particular, in Yemen's internal crisis had hastened the destruction of the YSP's military arm and curtailed the potential of Yemen's regular forces. In addition, a close examination of the Saudi role, both before and during the conflict, leads to the conclusion that the part played by the KSA in the annihilation of the YSP military capability and in that party's resorting to a disgraceful rebellion against democracy, unity, legitimacy and Yemen's highest principles, perhaps aimed at achieving a goal – namely, that of replacing the YSP by its own supporters in a position of authority over the southern region or a part of it.

Following the end of the war, Sana'a began to make efforts to 'turn over a new leaf' in the history of Yemen's bipartite relations and in its relations with the Gulf States. A letter from the Yemeni president to the Saudi king, immediately after the latest war in Yemen, confirmed Sana'a's desire to iron out differences and problems relating to the border question by means of dialogue and talks.

In the sphere of oil production and the role of US oil companies, Hunt resumed the pumping of around 185,000 barrels per day from its Safir Field in the Marib–al-Jawf Basin in July 1994, while production by the Canadian–US company in the al-Masilah Basin reached 150,000 barrels per day on the day when military operations ceased. Production in the Shabwah region remained at a low level. Meanwhile, reports spoke of commercial discoveries in the Jinnah Field, where two of the companies holding concessions, Hunt and Exxon, are American. Discoveries were also reported in the concession areas of the UK company, Clyde, and the French firm Total. The role of US oil companies in Yemen both before and after the war confirms the continuing growth of US economic interests in the ROY.

As for Yemen's internal political situation, the conclusion of the war in favour of 'unity and constitutional legitimacy' in July 1994 represented the end of the second crisis caused by the former vice-president's going into retreat in Aden. It also eased efforts aimed at putting an end to Yemen's internal political crises and enabled Yemenis to resume the tasks of economic, social and political development. This was to be achieved by a practical application of the principles of experience and equal citizenship, using the capabilities and qualifications of all Yemenis. The conclusion of the war also meant the end of an important stage in the history of Yemen–US relations, and the beginning of another stage that relies on repairing all aspects of the Yemeni edifice, and on the cooperation of all Yemenis, of whatever persuasion, in achieving this goal. This means putting into practice the contents of the statement made by the president of the Republic of Yemen, Lieutenant-General 'Ali 'Abd Allah Saleh, following his unanimous re-election to office at the beginning of October 1994 in accordance with the constitutional amendments passed by 252 out of 259 deputies. This statement pledged to continue reform and democratization, and to secure the freedom of the press and respect for human rights. It also pledged to build the economy and the state's civil institutions, to uproot corruption and those responsible for it, and to continue concerted efforts to normalize relations with neighbouring states, in particular Saudi Arabia. The president appointed the well-known Yemeni economist and administrator, 'Abdul-'Aziz 'Abdul-Ghani, who had successfully directed the three-year programme and several five-year plans in the former YAR, to form a coalition government. In this government, Islah's share was eight ministries out of a total of twenty-three, the most important of which is the Ministry of Education. For its part, Washington appointed Mr David Newton as its new ambassador to Sana'a. In a hearing before the US Congress Foreign Relations Committee on 29 September 1994, Newton affirmed that his 'principal task would be to encourage the Yemeni Government to heal the wounds caused by the recent internal conflict, by promoting the national reconciliation as President Saleh himself has pledged'. The second US ambassador to the Republic of Yemen also indicated his willingness to encourage good relations between the ROY (which is undertaking democratization) and its neighbours. Yet how can Yemeni–Saudi relations improve if not at the cost of democratization in the Yemeni arena?

At the end of a farewell meeting between Saleh and the first US ambassador to the Republic of Yemen, Arthur Hughes, the president awarded Hughes the Unity Medal. This event both symbolizes Yemen's grateful appreciation of the role of the USA in safeguarding its unity and anticipates the continued strengthening of Yemeni–US relations.

Conclusion

The contradictory ROY–US positions regarding the settlement of the Kuwaiti question and towards Iraq in 1990 demonstrated that Yemen's pro-Iraq orientation, which placed Washington and Sana'a at cross-purposes for over three years, had come to an end. Yemen's differences with the GCC states and the US would continue to be costly, isolating and harmful for Sana'a. ROY–KSA negotiations on the border dispute, although they might end with a final demarcation agreement, were unlikely to improve Sana'a–Riyadh relations as long as their different political systems persist, and as long as the regional and international balance of power continued to be the same. Hence, Sana'a–Riyadh political differences would continue to constrain the Sana'a–Washington relationship.

However, there were counterbalancing factors. One implication of Washington's support for Yemen's political pluralism and its pressure on both the ROY and the KSA to negotiate their border disputes was that the US had no interest in destabilizing Yemen, but the KSA appeared to have just such an interest. This indicated a significant divergence of US–KSA interests in the ROY. Moreover, the increasing involvement of US companies in the Yemeni economic sector at a time when the country was suffering from aid cuts and scarce resources made Sana'a more dependent on US oil companies. Thus, Yemen was unlikely to recover without their support. Meanwhile, the corresponding collapse of the USSR and the deterioration of both ROY–KSA relations and ROY–US relations left Yemen with no other allies to depend on. This strengthens the belief that Saudi economic assistance to Yemen will inevitably restrict democratization in the ROY, which is the only chance for internal Yemeni stability and progress.

In the period 1990–94 the ROY continued to be of marginal importance to Washington – to influence regional and US contingency planning rather than policy towards the region and Yemen itself. This was compounded by the ROY's short-lived Arab nationalist foreign policy, itself exacerbated by Yemeni popular support for Iraq during the Gulf crisis and the US response to it. Having declined in importance to Washington, Sana'a became incapable of using its relationship with the US for its own interests. Also, the collapse of the communist bloc and the disappearance of the USSR from the Middle East eliminated Yemen's long-standing ability to exploit the superpowers' rivalry for its own benefit. Sana'a therefore lost a considerable portion of its limited freedom of mobility when dealing with the United States.

Saving Yemen from disaster, poverty and instability needed reasonable policies and urgent remedies for the country's accumulating political, social and economic problems; maintaining a unified Yemen required serious efforts towards democratization, a factor which widens the gap with neighbouring Saudi Arabia. One of the options available to Yemen was to try to repair its relations with its neighbours. It is ironic that, had it been able to repair its relations with the KSA and GCC states, Yemen would not need the US as it does today.

Conclusion

Global, regional, and internal factors all affected the relationship between Yemen and the United States. Yemeni foreign policy, and especially its relationship with the US, have thus been conducted in the context of the bipolar US–Soviet balance of power for most of the twentieth century, but were deeply affected by the demise of the USSR in the late 1980s. Global strategic rivalries affected Yemen, which tried, in varying ways and at different times, to gain benefit from these rivalries. Moreover, US–Soviet rivalries were played out by proxy between North and South Yemen. The end of the Cold War and the disappearance of the USSR's influence in the area removed one great power's resistance to Yemeni unity but also denied the united Yemen part of its limited freedom of manoeuvre when dealing with the only remaining superpower. At the regional level, itself profoundly affected by developments in the global arena, Yemen's location at the south-western tip of the Arabian peninsula situates it in a political and strategic position that cannot be separated from other dramas in the Middle Eastern theatre: anti-colonial struggles, US rivalry with other powers for influence in the region, the Arab–Israeli conflict, the Iranian revolution, and Desert Storm. The single most significant regional influence on Yemeni–US relations has been its northern neighbour, Saudi Arabia, whose vast oil wealth the US has sought to protect and which has exercised a hegemonic policy towards Yemen. The Yemeni–Saudi–US 'triangle' was bent out of shape by Yemen's self-declared neutrality in the 1991 Gulf war; the economic and political repercussions of this stance are still being felt. Finally, circumstances within Yemen, from its republican revolution through the development of the oil industry, unification with the PDRY, parliamentary elections and 1994 internal Yemeni military encounters have themselves been influenced by, and in turn fed back into, the regional and international arenas, shaping Yemeni foreign policy in general and its relations with the US in particular.

In conclusion, this chapter reviews the constants and themes in Yemeni–US relations: the Cold War, the triangular relationship with Saudi Arabia, broader US policy in the Middle East and US oil interests. It looks for continuities in the role of Yemen in US foreign policy and in Yemeni policy towards the US, because it is such continuities that make this study a case in point of superpower–small state relations. But it also takes into account Yemen's audacious, and ultimately very costly, failure to adopt the US–Saudi position in the conflict between Iraq and Kuwait. The consequences of Yemen's effort at autonomous foreign policy in the regional and global arena underscore the limited freedom of small states to exercise discretion in foreign affairs.

The Cold War

The revolution in North Yemen, which resulted in the declaration of the YAR, developed into a regional crisis of serious dimensions which the limited presence of both the US and the USSR was unable to prevent. The subsequent civil war in the Yemeni arena allegedly threatened the stability of the conservative pro-Western countries in the Arabian peninsula as well as the flow of cheap oil to the Western world. The impact of this revolution, therefore, was not confined to Yemen but implicated Saudi Arabia, the Hashemite Kingdom of Jordan (HKJ), Egypt and Britain. The existence of the YAR offered the UAR the opportunity to promote revolution in the region under the flag of Arab nationalism and provided the USSR with the chance to challenge both US and UK influence there. Thus the Yemeni civil war in the 1960s led to an internationalized crisis, and the involvement of the superpowers themselves.

When the KSA decided to supervise and support a counter-revolution in a YAR that depended on UAR support and protection, the YAR sought USSR backing as well as US recognition to prevent the KSA and the UK from restoring the deposed ruling family. Moscow recognized the republic and offered it political support, thereby antagonizing Washington. The US government also feared that Sana'a would join the Arab nationalist movement, which was allied to the Soviet bloc, in its drive to counter Western dominance. When the civil war in the YAR began, as a consequence of the revolution and the counter-revolution backed by Saudi Arabia, US policy was greatly influenced by the Soviet, Egyptian, British and Saudi policies. Since the Kennedy administration saw the Yemeni revolution as a communist threat in the peninsula, it made friendly gestures towards the YAR and recognized it. Meanwhile the Kennedy administration cooperated with Egypt in the search for a peaceful solution that would avoid any sort of confrontation between the parties involved; and which would remove the Soviets from peninsula affairs. Yet the change in the American administration brought about a different US policy towards the UAR and the YAR. The Johnson administration indirectly encouraged the counter-revolutionary forces and the conservative element in the Yemen; it bolstered the defences of the KSA and provided protection to this rich ally. Furthermore, the Johnson administration intervened to reduce UAR influence in the peninsula by curtailing Nasser's policy of nationalist expansion, preventing the USSR from having any real influence, and containing the Yemeni revolution so that it would not affect US allies in Saudi Arabia and Jordan.

When Israel defeated the UAR in the 1967 Arab–Israeli war, Egypt was forced to withdraw its troops from the Yemeni arena and reconcile itself with the KSA. Consequently, the US alliance with the KSA and its indirect support for the Northern Yemen royalists led in mid-1967 to the weakening of the pan-Arab and the pro-Soviet elements in the YAR. This brought Sana'a under KSA and US influence. As a result the YAR lost the ability to play Moscow off against Washington for several years. During the late 1960s, despite Sana'a's eagerness to restore relations with Washington, the US saw no need to do so. In 1971 the British completed their withdrawal from the Persian Gulf thereby creating a serious security issue for the US because of the increasing importance of oil to the world economy. This coincided with the emergence of the pro-Soviet PDRY which pledged its support for what it termed the 'people's revolution' in the Gulf.

When relations between Sana'a and Washington were eventually restored in 1972, it was largely because of these factors. Because of deteriorating relations between Sana'a and Moscow, which resulted from internal social struggles, strong Saudi influence and Moscow's alliance with Aden, the YAR tried to play off the US against the USSR in an attempt to get military and development aid from the US and reduce the role of the PDRY and the KSA in its internal affairs. Washington grasped the opportunity to confront directly Soviet penetration in the Yemeni arena, aiming to turn the YAR into a buffer zone between the Marxist South Yemen and Saudi Arabia. Because the US had no direct economic or military interests in the YAR itself, it left Sana'a's security needs for the KSA to deal with. However, as Sana'a, under KSA influence, was unable to improve relations with Moscow between 1972 and 1978, relations with Washington were minimal; the US was not concerned about events within the YAR as long as its interests in the KSA were not threatened.

The tension between the Yemens, which increased greatly from 1978–79, once more encouraged Sana'a to attempt to use the threat of Aden to exploit Cold War rivalry; this time it succeeded. The YAR obtained $US360 million package of American arms, financed by Saudi

Arabia, as well as US protection, which helped Sana'a to defeat the leftist element in the Yemeni arena. Moreover, the US position and the YAR's military and political alliance with the US in this period resulted in the USSR reevaluating its policies towards the two Yemeni states. Direct US arms deliveries to Sana'a ceased following the termination of the 1979 war between the Yemenis, and the KSA withheld important spare parts. This led to Sana'a contacting Moscow to obtain the military equipment it needed. The Soviets took the opportunity to restore their position in the country: they did not want the YAR to be completely dependent on the US.

While YAR relations with Moscow improved dut to the supply of Soviet arms demanded by Yemeni military officers, Sana'a–Washington relations improved through increased US economic assistance between 1979 and 1984. Contacts were confined to USAID technical projects, largely because there was no longer any imminent threat of attack from the PDRY. One of the factors that eased US concern was that the Soviet Union did not encourage any further tension between the Yemeni states that would comprise any threat to the KSA; although the period was characterized by economic cooperation alone, from 1979 to 1990 the YAR–USSR military relationship persuaded the US to deal directly with Sana'a, rather than through the KSA, as it had from 1972 to 1979.

Throughout its lifetime the YAR was obliged to exploit the superpowers in order to survive. In this it achieved a fair degree of success, managing to survive and develop, although it was often used by these powers for their own objectives.

The role of the Kingdom of Saudi Arabia

North Yemen–KSA relations up to 26 September 1962 were characterized by barely veiled mutual suspicion and distrust, the product of the long-standing rivalry between the two monarchical families and of territorial disputes. The YAR revolution was achieved with the assistance of revolutionary Egypt. The UAR, with its Soviet backing, was seen as the enemy of the conservative governments in the Arab world, especially of the Saudi royal family, and was perceived to be a serious threat to the security of the ruling kings and sheikhs in the area. Realizing that it could not survive without forming alliances with all the foes of the UAR, of the Arab nationalist movement, and of communism, the KSA reacted promptly to the 1962 YAR revolution: it organized and supervised a counter-revolution and pledged to restore the deposed Yemeni monarchy. The KSA sought British and Jordanian advice and assistance as well as US advice and protection. Riyadh also

prepared itself for a long encounter with the Nasserite and revolutionary elements in the YAR. This situation inevitably involved the
US, which had economic and political interests in both the KSA and
the UAR.

To safeguard the republican regime against any British or Saudi–
Jordanian aggression, the UAR supported Sana'a's request for US
recognition. Washington insisted upon a declaration that the republic
would honour existing international obligations. It also demanded that
Cairo publicly declare its support for the full content of the communiqué released by the YAR government in December 1962. Three months
later the US formally recognized the new republic and proposed a
disengagement plan to end the civil war. The Kennedy administration
had calculated that the civil war in the Yemen would stir a wider
military conflict between the UAR and the KSA – a confrontation that
would involve the US not least because of US interests in Saudi oil; it
therefore decided to recognize the revolutionary regime in the hope of
stabilizing the situation in Yemen. US recognition thus aimed at keeping the US as part of both the solution and the problem, and at trying
to solve the growing problem through diplomatic channels. It also
aimed to persuade the UAR to withdraw from the YAR.

Because US mediating efforts failed to persuade either the UAR or
the KSA to leave the Yemeni arena to the Yemenis, the Yemeni civil
war expanded and the US gave indirect support to royalists by bolstering the Saudi regime and by supporting Israel. After its defeat by
Israel in 1967, Egypt was no longer able to provide military and
economic support to Sana'a. As a result the YAR became virtually
defenceless, unable to resist the strong pressures and influence exerted
by the KSA. During the period 1967–72, when relations between
Sana'a and Washington were broken off completely, the US was content
to accept the KSA's policy towards the YAR and ignore Sana'a's
initiatives to restore relations. By 1972, however, mostly due to US
needs to contain any influence from the pro-Soviet PDRY, Washington
decided to restore relations with Sana'a.

Although Riyadh eventually announced its support for restoration
of Sana'a–Washington relations, Saudi Arabia's oil wealth and its special
relations with the US prevented the development in YAR–US relations
to the extent that was demanded by the YAR, out of fear that a stable
and strong YAR would constitute a threat to Saudi hegemony. This
led to very limited US–YAR dealings in the form of US economic
assistance. Sana'a wanted direct dealings with Washington and suggested bilateral development projects in the hope that a closer YAR–
US relationship would lessen Riyadh's heavy hand in internal YAR
affairs. This KSA policy towards the YAR meant that any significant

YAR–US military cooperation was blocked until 1979. In that year the pro-Western YAR government faced a military and political threat from the Marxist South. The KSA reacted by financing the promised US arms package. Both the US and the KSA provided military protection to the government in Sana'a; PDRY attempts to unite Yemen by force had failed before the end of the year.

With the removal of the PDRY threat to the YAR the USSR took a neutral stand between the two Yemeni states and it became clear to the Saudis that they no longer needed to deliver the rest of the arms package. They believed that organizing and arming the YAR would result in a threat to themselves. The US adopted KSA policy, and YAR approaches to Washington for further military equipment failed.

The improvement in YAR–US relations in the mid-1980s created difficulties for the KSA. American oil companies found oil in 1984, attracting for the first time US economic interest in the YAR amidst reports that there was a large oil reserve in the YAR and that Sana'a was moving towards unification with the South to form a moderate state. President Saleh visited Washington in January 1990. It was subsequently reported in Sana'a that the KSA objected to Yemeni unity and to oil exploration in the country on the grounds that oil wealth and unity would constitute a threat to Saudi hegemony in the peninsula.

At the time of unification in 1990 among clear indications of much more oil, the relationship between the two neighbouring Arab states had deteriorated to an all-time low. Yet again this adversely affected the Sana'a–Washington relationship. As has consistently happened since 1960, the ability of Sana'a to achieve freedom of manoeuvre was constrained to a certain extent by the historically stronger Riyadh–Washington relationship.

US Middle Eastern policy

US interest in the YAR was always a reflection of its greater interests elsewhere in the Middle East. By recognizing the republic and maintaining a presence in both the YAR and the UAR the US hoped to preserve its interests in the area – mainly in the KSA and the UAR. The need for cheap oil, concerns for Israeli security and a commitment to containing Soviet influence were the dominant factors underlying US policy towards all states in the Arabian peninsula in the period of this study. When the Arab nationalist movement faced a setback as a result of the 1967 Israeli victory in the Six Day War, the YAR was gradually forced to endure increasing KSA influence; yet the US showed no interest in the YAR, because it did not constitute any threat to existing US interests in the region. When, in 1972, Washington eventually restored relations with the YAR, it did so in an attempt to weaken Arab hostility to both itself and Israel. US policy towards the YAR at this time received only limited KSA support; but this was thought necessary in Washington because of the vacuum left by the British withdrawal from the Gulf and because of the emergence of the pro-Soviet PDRY as well as anti-imperialist popular fronts in other Arab Gulf states.

A sense of US concern in the area can also be observed during the 1979 inter-Yemeni war, partly because Saudi Arabia felt directly threatened. But a greater cause of US anxiety was the fact that this war came in the wake of the April 1978 revolution in Afghanistan, the signing of an Ethiopian–Soviet treaty in November of that year, the assassination of US Ambassador Adolph Dubs in Kabul in February 1979 and the fall of the Shah. These events had created the impression in the area that the US had lost all capacity to control regional events and that the oil states would have to seek accommodation with the Soviet Union in order to protect themselves.

In a prompt response to a YAR appeal, Washington provided Sana'a with Saudi-financed arms, as well as moral and political support. It also moved a naval force close to Aden and made a show of airpower over and around it, to demonstrate its determination to protect Sana'a from a PDRY invasion. This provided the US with an opportunity to reassure Saudi Arabia and other US friends in the region of its resolve. Throughout the 1970s YAR–US relations served the interests of both the US and the KSA by helping prevent the fall of the YAR government to the leftists supported by the PDRY.

Nineteen-eighty witnessed a novel form of cooperation between the superpowers. Moscow restored its position in the YAR by providing Sana'a with arms. At the same time it tried to normalize relations between the two Yemeni states. In 1984 US companies discovered oil in the YAR, and in 1986 an internal power struggle in the PDRY took place that destroyed the PDRY's ability to threaten its neighbours. These events convinced Washington that the security of its Gulf allies and its own interests were no longer under threat. The discovery of oil indicated that US interest in the Yemen might become tangible and may even lead to a direct bilateral relationship.

In general, US concern in the YAR between 1962 and 1990 was based not on specific YAR considerations, but rather on its Middle Eastern objectives in the context of the general state of Washington–Moscow relations. As the US continued to have huge strategic and economic interests in Saudi Arabia, it could only 'view the YAR from the Saudi corner'[1] because 'every country when it decides its policy with a foreign country puts into consideration its relations with other partners'.[2]

'Tangible US participation'

YAR–US relations in the 1980s were characterized by some modest USAID projects in the country, reflecting continued US interest in the country. As regards the total value of American arms received in Sana'a in 1980, it was US $316.4 million;[3] by 1990 it reached $360 million.[4] The American F-5s were present at the military show in Sana'a on the 17th anniversary of the revolution, on 26 September 1979. Nine of the twelve planes in the show were flown by pilots of four different nationalities without a common language: 'There were three Saudis, two Yemenis, two Americans and two Nationalist Chinese (Taiwanese). The Yemenis and the Saudis spoke in Arabic which the Saudis translated into English to the Americans and the Taiwanese.'[5]

US governmental and Congressional documents of the first five years of the 1980s reveal that US political interest in the strategically located Yemen increased during these years as the political stability in the Middle East became increasingly fragile and as Western dependence on Middle Eastern oil continued. The Reagan Administration stressed that in demographic and supply terms the YAR played an important role in the Arabian peninsula. The YAR's political importance was assured by its geographic position in relation to the troubled Horn of Africa and Marxist South Yemeni state. A pact signed between Aden, Tripoli and Addis Ababa in mid-1981 was interpreted in Washington as being explicitly directed at countering US influence; one of the main purposes of the USAID-financed development projects in the YAR was to strengthen forces resistant to a PDRY takeover in the sense that 'a strong government in the YAR, friendly to its neighbours enhances US interests in regional stability and security'.[6] The nature of US interest in the YAR changed after 1984, as demonstrated by USAID presentations to Congress in 1985 and 1986. These presentations, which referred for the first time to 'the potential oil resources in the ill-defined border [area]', also revealed that 'a long-term US program of human resources and industrial development seeks to lay a foundation for sustained national development and a stronger friendship between Yemen and the United States', and stressed the need for 'tangible US participation in the economic development'[7] of the YAR.

Under pressure from Saudi Arabia to limit its role in Yemen, Washington no longer wanted to supply the YAR with arms, and restricted the amount of official aid. But, bothered by USSR influence in the YAR, it permitted private-sector oil exploration. The US

Embassy confirmed that it informally encouraged and advised the US oil companies to pursue their explorations, 'because it's good for the United States.'[8] The 1980 reports of large oilfields provided the US with a new opportunity to compete with the USSR in the YAR. The Texas-based oil company, Hunt Consolidated Inc., was the first American company to drill for the Yemeni oil.

American oil interests

The nature of the bilateral interaction shows that US interest in Yemen during the period of study was little more than a reflection of US interest in other states in the Middle East. It was only in 1984, after the American company Hunt found oil in the west of the country, that the US government showed tangible bilateral interest in Yemen for the first time. Consequently the relationship improved a little because a 'private relationship promotes the official relationship'.[9] The oil discovery and reports that there was more oil in the country promoted the YAR into a different category in the eyes of the US Department of State and led to a new foreign policy involving the doubling of US aid. Vice-President George Bush's 1986 visit to the YAR, reinforced by President Saleh's early 1990 visit to Washington, was considered in the Yemen as marking the beginning of direct bilateral relations between Sana'a and Washington, as the old Saudi role between Yemen and the US was reduced.[10] Dr 'Abdul-Karim al-Iryani concluded that the US attitude changed after the oil find and added, 'the YAR has become more careful to preserve and sponsor these relations at present than at any time before'.[11]

The oil explorations in the YAR and the oil find on its borders with the PDRY led to the US cautiously welcoming the formation of a united Yemen in 1990. In addition to the oil find in the country, it is evident that 'the growing importance of the Red Sea as it appeared during the eight years of the Iran–Iraq war'[12] provided chances for cooperation between Washington and Sana'a. Sana'a continued to be in greater need of Washington than vice versa, but the US wanted in Yemen a pro-Western and pro-US government. Aware of Washington's objective, Sana'a benefited from the bilateral relations with the US.

Desert Storm and beyond

At just about the time of Yemeni unification, the world turned upside down. During the space of a year, there were radical changes in the global, regional and Yemeni arenas, and a major shift in US policy in the Middle East. In the context of international, regional and internal transformations, Sana'a appeared to have adopted a policy inconsistent with the position of a small state *vis-à-vis* a superpower. The costs of this independent policy – refusal to join the US–Saudi coalition against Iraq – brought home a lesson in the proper role of small states in international affairs.

The change in the global arena was the end of the bipolar balance of power. Suddenly, during 1989, the communist menace evaporated. It would be difficult to overstate the impact of the end of the Cold War on Yemen, for it helped create the circumstances for Yemeni unification and for Desert Storm – events which, for better or worse, altered the course of Yemeni history. Two decades of proxy East–West competition in the Yemen came to an end. The PDRY, already weakened by a disastrous fortnight of fratricide in January 1986, lost its principle source of financial and military support. US and even Saudi interests in keeping the Yemens occupied with 'containing' one another softened. Although unification negotiations predated the collapse of communism by several years, and internal economic, political and cultural factors cannot be ignored in an analysis of the factors leading to the merger of the YAR and the PDRY, the dismantling of the Berlin Wall was frought with symbolic and practical implications for Yemenis as well as for Europeans.

Likewise, although this is hardly the place to debate the global conditions influencing the events leading up to the US-led international bombardment of Iraq to force it to evacuate its forces from Kuwait, there is little doubt that diplomatic and military events would have played out differently in the autumn of 1990 and the spring of 1991 had Moscow continued to play its historic role in the Arab world. For the USA was now unchallenged in its claim to a sphere of influence over the Arabian peninsula. This tilt in the balance of power in the region towards the US and its clients among the Gulf oil monarchies, coupled with the fact that what had been North Yemen was no longer the buffer between Saudi Arabia and the old 'socialist outpost' in South Yemen, reduced Yemen's leverage considerably.

In August 1990, Saddam Hussein upset the regional balance of power. Scarcely more than two months after Yemeni unification, when Iraq invaded Kuwait, Yemen was in a difficult bind, made abnormally public by its coincidental rotation into the 'Arab seat' on the UN Security Council. Yemen's ally in the ACC, Iraq, had responded enthusiastically to unification, and now argued, persuasively in the eyes of most Yemenis, that the US and other Security Council members were applying a standard against Iraq not applied against Israel. Yemeni President Salih told US Secretary of State Baker[13] and others that Yemen favoured the concept of an 'Arab solution' to the Iraq–Kuwait crisis, and its UN ambassador argued for diplomacy rather than force to remove Iraq's army from Kuwait. When Riyadh invited US forces into its territory, Yemenis were appalled by what they perceived as hypocrisy from a regime that preached against the presence of non-Muslims, and frightened by the potential boost to Saudi claims to military hegemony in the entire peninsula.

Yemen grossly miscalculated its leverage in the crisis, its freedom to forge an independent foreign policy, its capacity to influence the outcome of the crisis and the costs it would pay for neglecting to side with its northern neighbour and heretofore benefactor. Perhaps the leadership was carried away with the euphoria of unity. Perhaps they failed to appreciate how the world had changed during the brief period since the USSR ceased to be a superpower. Perhaps they took President Bush's rhetorical commitment to a peaceful solution at face value. Perhaps the genuine sentiment on the streets of Sana'a, Aden and other cities against the oppulent Gulf monarchies left them no real choice. Perhaps they mistook the sentiments of most Arab people for the policies their leaders would choose. Certainly they misjudged the strength of the Iraqi army and the will of the Western alliance to restore Kuwait to the al-Sabahs. Perhaps Yemeni foreign policy-makers thought there was a strong moral principle at stake, a principle of diplomacy, neutrality or republicanism. Perhaps internal matters in a Third World state gave the decision-makers in Sana'a no choice; for certainly no rational calculation of self-interest would have led a small power to take a stand against a vastly wealthier neighbour allied with the great powers of the world.

The Saudis reacted furiously against what it regarded as an ungrateful beneficiary, revoking the work permits of most Yemenis in the kingdom, cancelling its military and economic assistance programmes, launching a vociferous anti-Yemeni media campaign and later renewing claims to territories generally recognized as Yemeni and warning international petroleum corporations against operating in Yemen. The US State Department under Secretary James Baker likewise undertook to 'punish' Yemen for its failure to back Washington's aims and methods in the Gulf crisis,[14] slashing its aid and in-country official personnel, although American oil firms continued exploration and production.

Whereas steps towards parliamentary democracy, most notably the multi-party elections of April 1993, gave the Clinton administration reason to reconsider its policy towards Yemen, these very developments only deepened Saudi antipathy. Just as the 1962 republican revolution had sent tremors of fear through the Saudi royal family and contributed to measured political reform in the kingdom, the 1993 elections were regarded as 'unIslamic' – in part because of the participation of women voters and candidates – and as setting a dangerous, potentially destabilizing precedent. These fears were such that both Yemeni President Ali Abdallah Salih and the Clinton administration hastened to assure the Saudis that they had no intention of exporting democracy to the KSA. Washington also let it be known that it would not pursue the matter of Saudi human rights abuses as long as Riyadh supported the 'peace process' in the Middle East.[15] Still, Saudi human rights and democratization activists seized on the Yemeni example. In a BBC interview the secretary-general of the Saudi Committee for the Defence of Sharia Rights, Muhammad al-Masa'ri, observed that although the educational level and standards of living were far higher in his country, Yemen had made far greater political progress.[16] It is no coincidence that once again Riyadh announced reforms, this time the creation of a Consultative Council, while at the same time dismissing the university faculty for offences that included the distribution of tapes of Yemeni election campaigns and parliamentary sessions.

Saudi–Yemeni relations thus remained tense throughout 1993, with border negotiations proceding fitfully toward no particular conclusion, and the Saudi and Kuwaiti media predicting – and, according to some sources, abetting – the break-up of the Yemeni union.[17] Neither the change of foreign minister nor the inclusion of the Saudi-backed Yemen Islah Party in the post-election coalition government seemed to make much difference to Riyadh: Riyadh and other GCC states financed a secession attempt led by the YSP secretary-general in mid-1994. An inter-Yemeni encounter did more than blostering the Yemen unity. With its commitment to the KSA, Washington seemed responsive to take former President Jimmy Carter's advice to put the differences surrounding Desert Storm behind them.

To some extent, Yemen's Gulf war policy was the exception that proves the rule in great power–small state relations. In radically altered global, regional and internal circumstances, Yemen took a gamble and lost. Subsequently, however, its relations with the US resumed their normal pattern: Yemen as a minor concern to the US. There are thus certain recurrent themes that characterize the relationship.

Recurrent themes

Yemeni influences on regional and US policies

An important theme of this study is how Yemeni policies affected the region, and how in turn regional problems and relationships in the Middle East region affected the US and its policies. In 1962 the revolution forced the YAR to depend on the UAR and the USSR.

This dependency led the YAR to adopt Egyptian foreign policy and, to an extent, the anti-US policy of the USSR. From the moment the YAR became a government committed to republican, revolutionary, anti-colonialist and anti-imperialist policies it sided with the so-called progressive Arabs against the monarchical and conservative Arabs as well as against the West. This created concern in the Arabian peninsula and in the Middle East as a whole, and opened up the area for an encounter between the so-called 'conservative' and 'progressive' fronts in the region. The revolution in North Yemen led to a subsequent change in the Saudi government and its internal policies: Crown Prince Faisal became prime minister and initiated reform in both the internal and external policies.

Reconciliation between North Yemeni republicans and royalists and the establishment of closer relations with the KSA in 1970 alarmed the PRSY, which turned to the USSR for arms and protection. Sana'a's ability to defeat the radical element in the YAR in 1968 led to the advent of a more radical government in the PRSY. Restoration of YAR–US relations in 1972 had a similar effect. The negotiations following the inter-Yemeni war in 1972 on the issue of uniting the two Yemens led to Saudi alarm which in turn led the KSA to seek US and Western military equipment and advice. The reunification discussions of late 1979 again created alarm in the KSA. Military cooperation and closer relations with the PDRY throughout the 1980s led to greater KSA dependency on US and Western protection.

The 1962 YAR revolution tempted the UAR to involve itself in Arabian peninsula politics and to challenge Western influence. This involvement drained Egyptian capabilities and adversely affected its military capacity against Israel. In this respect the YAR indirectly contributed to the defeat of the Arab nationalist and radical elements in Egypt and the Arab world.

YAR policies clearly affected the region, and, in turn, the regional problems derived from or caused by the Yemeni revolution also affected US policy towards the YAR and the region as a whole. YAR alliances with the UAR and the USSR in the 1960s, which Sana'a deemed necessary for its survival, were perceived in Washington to be aggressively anti-American. Washington therefore supported its existing allies in the region and counteracted potential YAR influence by bolstering the defences of US-friendly states. UAR success in constraining and severing YAR–US relations in 1966 and 1967 lay behind US neglect of the YAR for the five years following the UAR withdrawal from the country. The defeat of the anti-US element in the YAR in 1968 made Sana'a of less concern to Washington. Regional developments, of which the most important were the withdrawal of the British from the Gulf in 1971, the rise of a pro-Soviet South Yemen in 1969, severance of the two-year-old PRSY-US relations in 1969 and the pro-Nasser revolution in Libya on 1 September 1969, which was followed by the Libyan nationalization of US oil companies, all paved the way for US political interest in the YAR. YAR–US diplomatic relations were therefore restored on 1 July 1972 and USAID projects were resumed.

Saudi Arabian ability to influence the YAR throughout most of the 1970s made the US deal with Yemen through the KSA. There continued a trilateral relationship until 1984, when the YAR was able to reconcile with the PDRY and cooperate with the USSR, and when US oil companies discovered oil. YAR–PDRY rapprochements in the 1980s and the deterioration of YAR–KSA relations during this period persuaded the US to pay more attention to bilateral relations with the YAR. When YAR–PDRY unity took place on 22 May 1990, the US showed some caution, though it congratulated the Yemenis on their achievement. This caution was mainly due to KSA reservations because it saw Yemen unity as a threat to its own security.[18]

These reservations were underscored by Yemen's position in the Gulf war in 1990, by its elections in 1993 and by its crushing of a 1994 YSP attempt, with Saudi support, to re-proclaim a southern Yemeni state. Despite its fledgling oil industry Yemen was economically crippled by the loss of Saudi, Kuwaiti, Iraqi and American aid and by the twin problems of plummeting remittances and skyrocketing unemployment in the wake of the 'desert storm' and 'unity enhancement war'. United Yemen, a country with easily twice the population of Saudi Arabia, torn for all of its brief history between democracy and domestic chaos, and having once shown its lack of concern for its northern neighbour, was now regarded far more than ever as a threat to Saudi security.

YAR exploitation of superpower rivalry

Another dimension of this study is how global strategic rivalries and intersections affected the YAR and how it tried, in varying ways and at different times, to benefit from these rivalries. In 1962 the YAR sought both US and USSR recognition and support to bolster its position against British and Saudi opposition. Its efforts with the US failed at first because of the republic's commitment to the Arab nationalist movement, which, the US believed, opened the area to Soviet influence, and was thus a threat to US–Western interests in the region.

The Soviet Union, influenced by the Yemeni Left, hesitated in providing the YAR with arms after the coup of 5 November 1967. A

Yemeni delegation to Moscow returned empty handed, but when republican Sana'a warned Moscow that the country was due to fall under US influence if the royalist seige captured the capital, the USSR provided the YAR with arms including 24 MiG 19s and many Russian pilots and military experts who, with Syrian pilots, operated the new arms and bombers.[19] In 1968, when the YAR government launched a war against the leftist opposition and relations with the USSR deteriorated, the YAR tried to replace Moscow with Beijing: it was reported that Premier Al-'Amri cancelled a scheduled visit to China in early March 1968 after a meeting with the Russian ambassador in Cairo.

Following the defeat of this siege, which was supported by the KSA and the US, Sana'a tried to benefit from its relations with the USSR. Increasing KSA influence, however, weakened Sana'a–Moscow relations. In 1972, amidst deteriorating relations between Sana'a and Moscow and the latter's alliance with Aden, the YAR tried to exploit the Cold War superpower rivalry in order to get military and development aid from the US. It failed because Washington's response was to turn the YAR into a buffer zone between the Marxist South Yemen and pro-Western Saudi Arabia, therefore dealing with Sana'a trilaterally through Riyadh.

The tension that escalated from 1978 to 1979 between the two Yemens pushed Sana'a to play off Washington once again against Moscow and Aden. This time it succeeded, obtaining American arms (financed by Saudi Arabia) and US protection, which played a decisive role in helping Sana'a survive an attack from the Marxist and Arab nationalist opposition movement. Though US military sales to Sana'a ceased once the inter-Yemeni war was over, by the end of 1979 the YAR had persuaded the USSR to provide it with an arms package to strengthen its army and achieve security. The Soviets were responsive because they did not want the YAR to fall completely under US influence.

The YAR used its position between its southern neighbour controlled by the British before 1967 and the PDRY after 1970, and its northern oil-rich Saudi neighbour to acquire political support, military assistance and economic aid from both the USA and the USSR and successfully maintained this policy throughout the 1980s. Although efforts to play two regional powers, Iraq and Saudi Arabia, against each other in 1989/90 served Yemen unity, in 1990/91 these efforts failed because while Saudi Arabia remained a favoured client of the US, Iraq had lost its superpower patronage.

Yemen in US Middle East policy

US policy towards the YAR within overall US policy in the Middle East is an important theme running through this book. As has been seen, US concerns in the Middle East were to prevent the oil resources of the Persian Gulf falling under the domination of forces hostile to the US and the West, and thus to protect the KSA and other Arabian peninsula states as well as to counter the communist penetration in the region, and to protect Israel.

In the 1960s, US policy towards the YAR was a stepchild of its policy towards the UAR and the KSA. In the 1970s, the US restored relations with Sana'a in the light of the British withdrawal from the Gulf and the appearance of the pro-Soviet PDRY as well as the flourishing of pro-Moscow fronts which were willing to overthrow the pro-Western governments of the Arabian peninsula. In this period, Washington became interested in Sana'a in order to use it as a buffer zone between its economic interests in the KSA and the political hostility of PDRY. This became clearer in 1979, when Washington provided the YAR with arms as well as moral, political and military support to help it counteract a PDRY invasion. Apart from the oil discovery in the mid-1980s, US interest in the YAR throughout the 1980s continued to be a reflection of US interest in the KSA. From this perspective, the Yemen played only a small part in US foreign policy towards the Middle East.

After the Gulf war, strengthened US interest in the Saudi Kingdom did not reduce Yemen to something like a minor irritation to the US. Although the need to offset Soviet influence was absent, the US had political and economic reasons to improve relations with Yemen. It showed support to Yemen's unity, constitutional legitimacy and disapproval of the YSP's 1994 attempted secession. One incentive for the US to establish good relations with Sana'a in the 1990s, it appears, is its desire to see Islamists contained in the most populous part of the Arabian peninsula. In addition, Hunt and other American firms have continued to operate in the Yemen, and the embassy has continued to look out for their concerns. Although it was obvious to everybody that Yemen needed foreign companies' investment and technology badly, and that little US diplomatic effort would be needed to secure their presence in the country, this did not mean that Yemen was in no position to influence US foreign policy directly.

Another area of American policy in the Middle East in which, despite Saudi objections, Yemen appeared to have a potential role was the Democratic Initiatives project of USAID and the State Department. This multi-faceted programme had components contracted to or through the National Endowment for Democracy, to the private consulting firm Chemonics, and to the Consortium for International Development. It included projects to support parliamentary development, judicial reform and independence and to strengthen women's position and role in politics and public service. Under these initiatives, staff and consultants to the International Republican Institute and the National Democratic Institute visited Yemen during its election season to write reports and conduct election monitor training sessions, and American Congressmen, judges and others met with their Yemeni counterparts. Although it was poorly funded and staffed in comparison with Democratic Initiatives projects in Egypt, Jordan and elsewhere, a slow but steady stream of American visitors reported in the Yemeni press created the impression locally that the United States was deeply concerned with the progress of democratization in Yemen.

These initiatives may have led Sana'a to overestimate the level of world, and US, interest in its domestic politics. Yemenis imagined that the world was watching its elections in 1993. When, during yet another dispute with the president, Vice-President Ali Salim al-Bayd made a personal visit to the US and was received by Vice-President Al Gore, his fellow Socialists trumpeted American support for the YSP. Jimmy Carter's and François Mitterrand's visits in the autumn of 1993 were also treated as evidence that the eyes of America and Europe were on developments in Yemen. This had the positive effect of applying a kind of indirect pressure on the post-unification governments and others not to abandon promises to respect pluralism, press freedom and human rights. In this context, any improvement of Yemeni–Saudi relations in the near future could cost Yemen its very limited remaining opportunity for democratization.

The US in Yemeni foreign policy

A further theme is how Yemen's relations with the US fitted into its overall foreign policy, especially as regards Saudi Arabia and South Yemen, first under the British and then under the NLF and YSP. US recognition of the republic did not fulfil these Yemeni hopes of ending KSA and British support for the counter-revolution because of the YAR government's commitment to the Arab nationalist movement, which was a threat to the security of the KSA, and which was perceived as a potential threat to the British position in Aden and the protectorates.

As the American record of relations with the moderate republicans during the first phase of diplomatic relations shows, the YAR, though under Egyptian influence, attempted to use the US diplomatic presence to counter UAR domination. In 1972 the YAR sought an alliance with the US to resist the KSA and PDRY influence. This alliance proved fruitful because it prevented the defeat of the YAR by PDRY-supported leftists. In a prompt response to a YAR appeal that coincided with events in Iran and Afghanistan, Washington provided Sana'a with the military, moral and political support to protect it from a potential PDRY invasion.

The YAR–US relationship deflected PDRY pressure until 1979 and convinced the USSR in the 1980s to adopt a friendly attitude towards the YAR contrary to the wishes of its PDRY ally. While it obtained military equipment from the Soviets to strengthen its army, the YAR tried to acquire more economic aid from the US. Economic cooperation between Washington and Sana'a resulted in the 1984 discovery of oil in commercial quantities by an American company, an event which created the start of serious US economic investment in the YAR. Although at times the YAR's policy towards the US was forced upon it by both regional and international events, it did achieve a degree of freedom of manoeuvre in determining its own foreign policy towards the KSA and the PDRY. The YAR also temporarily achieved some economic benefit from its relationship with the US.

The end of the Cold War and the aftermath of the Gulf war elevated relations with the United States to something like an obsession in Yemeni political reasoning, precisely because these same developments reduced US concern for Yemen to a new low, but it also left Sana'a with few options for attracting US attention. Perhaps naïvely, many Yemenis assumed that the US would provide strong support for its democratic experiment. One area of potential concern to the US was the ongoing potential for instability in a country plagued by inflation and unemployment and lurching from one political crisis to the next. Unlike Riyadh, which seemed both willing and able to stir conflict and dissention within unified Yemen by funding and perhaps arming conflicting elements, Washington's interest was in stability in Yemen as an aspect of overall stability in the peninsula. This interest was reiterated in a statement from State Department spokesman Michael MacMurray on 10 November 1993, when the 'new chapter in the development of Yemen has been strained by internal disagreements'. He continued that the United States wished to make clear its position that 'there must be a peaceful resolution of all political issues through dialogue among all interested parties. This will allow the process of further democratization and institution-building to continue.'[20]

The Yemeni people's impact on world politics

The role played by the Yemeni people in affecting domestic, regional and international policies also merits examination. To a considerable extent the 1962 revolution was the result of the widespread deter-mination of the Yemeni people to improve their living conditions by supporting the overthrow of the socially and politically backward monarchy. Throughout the lifetime of the YAR the majority of Yemenis in the republic were influenced by pan-Arab, anti-colonialist, anti-imperialist and anti-Zionist ideas. This clearly influenced the YAR government in the early to mid-1960s, when it embraced the Arab nationalist and pro-Soviet ideology of Nasserite Egypt. In turn the UAR gave large amounts of military and economic assistance to the YAR in order to weaken the hitherto united front of conservative pro-Western monarchies and sheikhdoms in the Arabian peninsula. This drained UAR resources and, after the defeat by Israel in 1967, it lost its position as leader of the Arab nationalist movement. The UAR's defeat meant, in effect, the defeat of Arab nationalism in the Middle East; this served US interests at the expense of USSR interests. Having lost its Egyptian foothold in the region, the USSR was forced to turn to the PDRY. Strengthened by Soviet military assistance, the PDRY became the source of ten years of instability within the YAR. From 1967 the YAR began to make overtures towards the US. But it had to work hard to quell internal criticism of its pro-Western initiatives from the strong nationalist and socialist elements in the country and the government itself.

After the restoration of relations with the US in 1972, all YAR governments tried to distance themselves from a public alliance with the US because of popular support for the Palestinian and other Arab nationalist issues. The geopolitical position of the YAR between the anti-US PDRY and the anti-USSR KSA, directly influenced YAR foreign policy. In 1979 US military and political assistance helped Sana'a to deter a PDRY invasion, but this did not prevent the YAR from obtaining Soviet arms partly because of the nationalist and anti-KSA element in the country which sought to resist the Saudi influence. This continued until the very end of the republic's life. Unification in 1990, achieved despite initial opposition from the KSA and only cautious support from the USA, brought with it a possible opportunity for the Yemeni people to benefit from foreign economic aid and invest-ment and the possibility of greater freedom to determine Yemeni foreign policy. It also brought an unprecedented degree of democratic freedoms, which the Yemeni population experienced when the former

YAR and PDRY rulers were preoccupied with their own worries, rivalries and campaigns against each other throughout 1990–94.

Thus the economic and political aspirations of the Yemeni people may have played only a relatively small part in affecting the foreign policies of the various countries involved in the Yemeni arena during this period but their voice could never be completely ignored by Yemeni governments.

Religious differences and YAR–US interaction

Religious differences within the Yemeni arena and within the Arabian peninsula also merit attention. Religious sectarianism and extremism played a hidden yet important role in determining the nature of the Yemeni-US interaction. In the 1960s the Shafi'is (Sunni sect of Islam) through their contacts with the Sunni Egyptian leadership, played a major role in organizing the revolution. They had paid a high price hitherto, since they were deprived of all their rights as citizens under the pre-republic Zeidi imams and during their exile to the colony of Aden. Zeidi attempts in the mid-1960s to reconcile the YAR with the KSA and the royalist camp were undermined by the majority Shafi'is, who considered such a reconciliation as anti-Shafi'i; most of the Shafi'is joined Arab nationalist and socialist parties because they saw that allying with these forces would best serve their interests. This religious conflict put further constraints on YAR–US relations throughout the 1960s. Though the Shafi'i element was defeated in the YAR in August 1968 when the Zeidi government crushed the Nasserite and the Arab Nationalist Movement, the religious factor continued to act as a constraint on YAR–US relations. In June 1969 the Arab Nationalist Movement's radicals seized power in the PDRY. Some of the key leaders of the new government in Aden were originally Shafi'i from northern Yemen. This cannot be separated from what happened eight months earlier in Sana'a, on 23–24 August 1968. That year the Marxist Shafi'is in Aden severed relations with the US. They also supported a guerrilla warfare in the central areas of the YAR. Their influence inside the politically unstable YAR made the US cautious in its dealings with the YAR throughout the 1970s and the 1980s. In the 1970s, 1980s and early 1990s, Zeidi–Wahhabi differences between Yemen and Saudi Arabia formed a barrier to cooperation and trust. The Saudis used their stronger alliance with the US to constrain Yemeni–US inter-action. It is in this context that religious factionalism within the Yemeni arena influenced its foreign policies towards the US throughout the period of the study.

Between 1992 and 1994 the YSP, despite its political failure and bankruptcy, managed to secure short-lived popular support by playing on old Shafi'i–Zeidi differences. The ensuing instability caused by the YSP attempts to postpone parliamentary elections delayed an expected post-elections improvement of Yemen–US relations.

In 1993, following its elections, Yemen was the first Arab country to include an Islamist party, the Islah, as the third partner in an otherwise secular ruling coalition. Ironically, this took place in the context of Saudi opposition to party pluralism in Yemen and patronage of the most fundamentalist, Wahhabi-leaning faction of Islam. Yet given Western fears of the rise of Islamist radicalism in the Middle Eastern arena, Yemen would be regarded in some circles as having, possibly, set an example to other countries in the region on how to contain religious fundamentalism by giving it both voice and responsibility.

Superpower–small state relations

The main comparative dimension of this study is that of superpower–small state relations: the role small powers play in the diplomatic, economic and foreign policy of larger ones, and the degree of freedom of manoeuvre that small states have in determining their own foreign policy. By examining Yemeni foreign policy throughout the period 1962–93, it is evident that it was shaped by domestic, regional and superpower influences. The backwardness of the country, its weak economy, large population, religious differences, the political and economic aspirations of the people, and its geographic position in a highly volatile and unstable Middle East – one of the main battlegrounds of the Cold War – all influenced the foreign policy of the YAR. Policy was also shaped by the nature of the Yemeni decision-making process. But the external policies of the post-1962 republic, were, to an extent, similar to those of the pre-1962 monarchical, conservative Yemen.

In 1962, the new republic tried to develop contacts with modern industrialized Western society, especially the US. This was only partly successful. Egyptian intervention, civil war, a close military relationship with the USSR, an alliance with the Arab nationalist movement, a commitment to fighting colonialism, imperialism and Zionism, and border and ideological disputes with the KSA all affected the YAR's interaction with the US. In 1962 the YAR had no choice but to ally itself with the UAR and the USSR. Without Egyptian assistance and protection and subsequent Arab and Soviet military support it was unlikely that the republic would have survived. In the 1970s it was seriously threatened by both the monarchical pro-US KSA and the radical pro-Soviet PDRY. Though the YAR was destined to fall under Saudi influence, the pressure from the PDRY on its southern borders forced it to adopt a more consistently balanced policy towards the US and the USSR. In 1979, Sana'a was expected to fall to the invading forces of the PDRY and NDF, but this was prevented by the assistance and protection of both the KSA and the US. The new USSR policy towards the YAR from late 1979 gave the YAR a limited ability to manoeuvre and maintain relations with both the US and the USSR: it received economic cooperation with Washington and military assistance from Moscow. This enabled the YAR to achieve political stability and economic development throughout most of the 1980s.

The YAR emerged in a period of high-level international and regional instability, and during a period of Cold War when the Arabian peninsula was penetrated by the two superpowers. Internal YAR political instability was mostly the result of superpower penetration in the form of massive military aid to their client states in the area. The superpower presence and their influence on the regional powers' policies, therefore, placed constraints on the foreign policy of the YAR and other small states of the region.

The domestic environment played a major role in determining the nature of Yemeni–US relations. For example, the large Yemeni population, in comparison to other states of the Arabian peninsula, was one of the considerations in the minds of Washington's policy-makers in their dealings with Sana'a. Yemen, as the most highly populated country in the Arabian peninsula, with a republican, anti-monarchical, pan-Arab, anti-colonialist and anti-imperialist orientation, created fear in the surrounding, less populated and more conservative, Arabian peninsula states. It also prompted UK and US concern over the security of their interests in the Gulf region. These two major powers and their allies in the Arab world all collaborated to defeat the republic, whether by restoring the royalist government or, at the very least, moderating the Yemeni government in order to prevent it from supporting Egyptian (and later Iraqi) threats towards Western interests in the region. Once this objective was achieved (after the Arab military defeat by Israel in 1967) Sana'a fell under the influence of the KSA, and as the USSR developed its support to the PDRY, military cooperation with both the US and USSR became more difficult because of Saudi fears of a more populated and well-equipped Yemen.

Yemen's geographical position also affected its foreign policy. In the 1960s the YAR, which controlled the southern entrance of the Red Sea, lay between the KSA, a US ally, and the SAF, a colony of the UK. Once the YAR formed an alliance with the UAR it faced war from both northern and southern fronts. In the 1970s and 1980s, the YAR had the pro-Soviet PDRY and pro-American KSA on its borders. This placed constraints on the YAR's ability to interact freely with both the US and the USSR. US policy-makers saw the YAR in this period as merely a suitable buffer zone between the PDRY and their interests in the KSA.

Above all else, the weak Yemeni economy affected its foreign policy decision-making process. The civil war in the 1960s debilitated its agricultural economy, leaving it dependent on Egyptian aid throughout the 1960s. But UAR economic capabilities were drained by the Yemen civil war and especially by its defeat in the Six Day War. It was forced to withdraw its forces from the YAR, thus pushing the republic in the 1970s into becoming highly dependent on the KSA. This dependency inevitably put limits on YAR foreign policy. Throughout the 1970s, military and political YAR–US interaction was largely dictated by KSA–US dealings, and a trilateral relationship was forced upon the YAR. Because of its weak economy the YAR had no option but to accept a Saudi-financed US arms package during its second war with the PDRY in 1979, as this served the security purposes of the KSA. When Sana'a applied for additional US supplies to reorganize and re-equip its army this was denied, largely because both the KSA and the US used their aid to influence the foreign policy of the YAR. When the weakness of this policy became apparant in the Gulf crisis of 1990, the retaliation against Yemen was swift and severe. No longer a beneficiary of its rich northern neighbour, Yemen was plunged into economic crisis and thrown back on its own limited economic resources.[21] While a dependency theorist might argue that in the long run this situation would favour genuine development, in the short run it left Yemen in deep water without a lifejacket.

In conclusion, despite the beginnings of tangible US participation in the economy of the country after the discovery of oil, as a small state Yemen attempted to maintain independence and stability and develop its economy based upon its own resources. Yemen was forced to accept 'limits to its options from larger regional powers as well as the "great power" allies of its regional neighbours and the limitations of these great powers' interests'.[22] Dependence and reliance on the developed world for expertise, trade and capital means that the independence and freedom of manoeuvre of a small state are severely circumscribed, but not entirely absent.

Appendix 1

Main actors

Table 1.1 Primary YAR actors, 1962–1990

1962–1967	President 'Abd Allah al-Sallal
1967–1974	Chairman of Presidium Council 'Abdul Rahman bin Yahya Al-Iryani
1974–1977	President Ibrahim Muhammad Al-Hamdi
1977–1878	Ahmad Hussein Al-Ghashmi
1978–1990	'Ali 'Abd Allah Saleh

Table 1.2 South Yemen primary and secondary actors, 1967–1990

Secretary-General President of the People's Supreme Congress	Foreign Minister	Ambassador to UN
President Qahtan Al-Sha'bi (1967–69)	Seif Al-Dali'i (1967–69)	'Abd Allah Al-Ashtal
Secretary-General 'Abdul-Fattah Isma'il	Ali S. Al-Bidh (1969–71) M. S. 'Awlaki (1971–73) 'A. Al-Dali (1973–78)	'Abd Allah Al-Ashtal
President Salim Rubbiyya' (1969–78)	M. Muti'(1978–)	
Secretary-General and President 'Abdul-Fattah Isma'il (1978–79)	M. Muti'	'Abd Allah Al-Ashtal
Secretary-General and President 'Ali Nasser Muhammad (1979–86)	M. Muti Salem Saleh 'Abdul-'Aziz Al-Dali[1]	'Abd Allah Al-Ashtal
Secretary General 'Ali Salem Al-Bidh President Heidar Al-Attas (1986–1990)	'Abdul-'Aziz Al-Dali	'Abd Allah Al-Ashtal

[1] Minister of State for Foreign Affairs

Table 1.3 Secondary YAR actors, 1962–90

Prime Minister		Foreign Minister		Amb. to US		Amb. to UN	Other actors
Al-Sallal	27/9/1962	Muhsin al-'Aini	27/9/1962	Al-'Aini	Al-'Aini		M. Zubairi, Spiritual Leader
Al-Sallal	31/10/1962	'A. Al-Baidani	31/10/1962	1962–1967			Nu'man, Speaker of Al-Shoura Assembly
Dhaif Allah	25/4/1962	M. Ya'koub	25/4/1962				Al-Ahmar, Paramount Sheikh of Hashid Confederation
H. Al-'Amri	10/2/1964	H. Makki	10/2/1964				
H. Al-Djaifi	3/5/1964	'A. Al-Iryani[3]	3/5/1964				
		M. Al-Sirri	3/5/1964				
		I. al-Djurafi[4]	3/5/1964				
H. Al-'Amri	6/1/1965	'A. Hamim	6/1/1965				'Uthman, Acting President (1966)
A. Nu'man	20/4/1965	M. Al-'Aini	20/4/1965				
H. Al-'Amri	20/7/1965	M. Yakoub	20/7/1965				
M.'Uthman[1]	20/7/1965						
H. Al-'Amri	16/4/1966	H. Al-Djaifi	16/4/1966				
Al-Sallal	18/6/1966	M. 'A. Sallam	18/6/1966				
Al-Sallal	12/10/1967	Al-Sallal	12/10/1967				
M. Al-'Aini	5/11/1967	H. Makki	5/11/1967				
H. Al-'Amri	21/12/1967	H. Makki	21/12/1967				
H. Al-'Amri	14/9/1968	Y. Djaghman	14/9/1968				
H. Al-'Amri	3/4/1969	H. Hubaishi[2]	3/4/1969				
		A. Barakat	3/4/1969				
A. Al-Kurshmi	2/9/1969	Y. Djaghman[3]	2/9/1969	Gaghman			
		A. Barakat	2/9/1969				
M. Al-'Aini	5/2/1970	M. Al-'Aini	5/2/1970				
A. Nu'man	3/5/1971	A. Nu'man	3/5/1971			Al-Thawr	
H. Al-'Amri	23/8/1971	'A. Al-Asnadj	23/8/1971				

M. Al-'Aini	18/9/1971	M. Al-'Aini	18/9/1971	18/9/1971	Sheikh 'Abd Allah Al-Ahmar
A Al-Hadjri	31/12/1972	M. Nu'man	31/12/1972	31/12/1972	
H. Makki	3/3/1974	'A. Al-Asnadj	3/3/1974	3/3/1974	Sultan Ahmad 'Umar, founder of National Democratic Front (NDF)
M. Al-'Aini	21/6/1974	M. Al-'Aini	21/6/1974	21/6/1974 Al-Mutawakil	
'A. Ghani	26/1/1975	Y. Djaghman[3]	26/1/1975		Speaker al-'Arashi, Acting President
		'A. Al-Asnadj	26/1/1975		
'A. Ghani	30/5/1978	'A. Al-Asnadj	30/5/1978		
		H. Al-'Amri (Dr)	21/3/1979	Al-Iryani 1982–84	
'A. Ghani		'Ali Al-Thawr	15/10/1980		Sallam
Al-Iryani (Dr)	15/10/80	M. Al-Asbahi	11/1980		Basindwah
'A. Ghani	11/1/1983	Al-Iryani (Dr)	1984	Al-'Aini 1985–90	Sallam

[1] Deputy Prime Minister [2] Deputy Prime Minister for Foreign & Economics Affairs [3] Deputy Prime Minister for Foreign Affairs [4] Deputy Foreign Minister

Deputy Prime Minister
Deputy Foreign Minister

Table 1.4 Unified Yemen primary and secondary actors, 1990–93

President/Vice-President	Prime Minister	Foreign Minister	Rep. at US	Rep. at UN
'Ali 'Abd Allah Saleh	H. Al-Attas 5/1990	Al-Iryani 'A. Al-Dali	M. Al-'Aini	Al-Ashtal
'Ali Al-Bidh (1990–)	H. Al-Attas 5/1993	M. Basindwah	M. Al-'Aini	Al-Ashtal

Table 1.5 US actors

President	Secretary of State	US officials/diplomats involved in Yemen
John Kennedy (1961–63)	Dean Rusk (1961)	Parker T. Hart, Ambassador to KSA and Minister to Yemen, 1959–62 Robert Stookey, US Chargé d'Affaires in Ta'iz, 1960–January 1963 John Badeau, Ambassador to Cairo and the YAR, 1962–63 James N. Cortada, US Chargé d'Affaires in Ta'iz, February 1963–August 1964
Lyndon Johnson (1963–69)	Dean Rusk (1963)	Ambassador Ellsworth Bunker Philip Talbot, Secretary of State George McGee, under-Secretary of State Ambassador Talcott Seelye, Director of Arabian Peninsula Desk R. W. Komer, National Security Advisor Senator Hickenlooper Bourque Zbigniew Brzezinski, National Security Advisor Raymond Hare, Assistant Secretary of State, 1966 Harlan B. Clark, US Chargé, August 1964–August 1966 Lee F. Dinsmore, US Chargé, Sept. 1966–June 1967
Richard Nixon (1969–74)	William P. Rogers (1969) Henry A. Kissinger (1973)	Robert McLintock, Second Secretary (returns to work in the American Interests Section of the Italian Embassy in Sana'a on 20 April 1970) William R. Crawford, Jr., First US Ambassador, December 1972–July 1974
Gerald Ford (1974–77)	Henry A. Kissinger (1974)	Thomas Scotts, Second US Ambassador, January 1975–April 1978 Congressman Paul Findley Joseph Twinam, Director of the Arabian Peninsula Affairs

Jimmy Carter (1977–81)	Cyrus R. Vance (1977) Edmund S. Muskie (1980)	George M. Lane, Third US Ambassador, October 1978–July 1981 David Ransom, US Chargé 1977–8 L.Colonel John Ruszkiewicz, US Military Attaché Harold Brown, US Secretary of Defense
Ronald Reagan (1981–89)	Alexander M. Haig, Jr. (1981) George P. Shultz (1982)	David E. Zweifel, Fourth US Ambassador, October 1981–January 1984 William Rugh, Fifth US Ambassador, 1984–1986 Theodore H. Kattouf, Sixth US Ambassador, 5 July 1987–9 July 1988 Charles Dunber, Seventh US Ambassador, July 1988–June 1991
George Bush (1989–93)	James A. Baker III (1989)	John Kelly, Assistant Secretary of State David Mack, Assistant Secretary of State Arthur Hughes, Eighth US Ambassador to the ROY, September 1991–
Bill Clinton (1993–)	Warren Christopher (1993)	Ambassador Arthur Hughes

Appendix 2

Important dates in Yemen's recent history, 1962–94

1911	Yemen and Turkey sign the Da'an treaty
1918	North Yemen obtains Independence
1934	Yemen–British and Yemen–Saudi Wars
1946	US recognizes Yemen
1947	Prince 'Abd Alla, Imam Yahya's third son and ambassador to all the world, returns from the US with a supplementary agreement to the 1946 Friendship and Commerce Treaty
1948	Aborted revolution against the Hamid al-Din Rule
1955	Aborted revolution against Imam Ahmad
1959	US stations diplomatic mission in Tai'z
1962	Imam Ahmad dies and Al-Badr succeeds him
1962	Successful revolution against the imamate
1967	North Yemen severs relations with the US
1967	Corrective Movement ends al-Sallal rule
1967	Southern governorates become an independent state (PRSY)
1968	Defeat of the left in the YAR
1969	Leftists take over power in South Yemen
1969	PRSY cuts diplomatic relations with the US and West Germany
1970	PRSY becomes PDRY
1970	Royalists and republicans reach a compromise in the YAR
1970	YAR and KSA restore diplomatic ties
1972	First YAR–PDRY War
1972	YAR and US resume diplomatic relations
1974	13 June Corrective Movement ends al-Iryani rule
1976	Leftist opposition in the YAR forms the National Democratic Front (NDF)
1977	Third YAR president, Ibrahim Al-Hamdi, assassinated
1978	Fourth YAR president, Ahmad Al-Ghashmi, assassinated
1978	Second PRSY/PRDY president, Salim Rubiyya', executed
1979	Second YAR–PDRY War
1984	US Hunt discovers oil in North Yemen

1986   Internal political strife in the PDRY and third Southern Yemeni
       president, 'Ali Nasser, escapes to the YAR
1987   YAR exports oil
1990   PDRY and US establish diplomatic relations
1990   YAR and PDRY merge to form ROY
1993   First democratic parliamentary elections in United Yemen
1993   Canadian Oxy begins its oil exports from Hadramawt, a southern
       governorate
1994   Inter-Yemini war leads to defeat of YSP military machine; new
       government coalition formed by the GPC and Islamists; YSP
       forced into opposition

Notes

Introduction

1. For a recent account of PDRY–US relations see Halliday, *Revolution and Foreign Policy: The Case of South Yemen 1967–1987*, pp. 79–98.

2. Works on US foreign policy consulted include Link and Catton, *American Epoch*; McCormick, *American Foreign Policy and American Values*; Kegley and Eugner, *American Foreign Policy Pattern and Process*; Spanier, *American Foreign Policy Since World War II*; Raymond L. Garthoff, *Detente and Confrontation: American–Soviet Relations from Nixon to Reagan*; *Dead Ends: American Foreign Policy in the New Cold War*; Avon, *The Imperial Republic, the United States and the World 1945–1973*; Kolko, *The Limits of Power, the World and United States Foreign Policy 1945–1954*; Nye, *The Making of America's Soviet Policy*; George, *Managing U.S.–Soviet Rivalry: Problems of Crisis Prevention*; Ambrose, *Rise to Globalism, American Foreign Policy 1938–1980*; Hoffmann, *Primacy or World Order: American Foreign Policy Since the Cold War*; Johnson, *Superpower: Comparing American and Soviet Foreign Policy*; Gaddis, *Strategies of Containment: A Critical Appraisal of Postwar American National Security Policy*; Stookey, *America and the Arab States: An Uneasy Encounter*.

3. The doctrine aimed at providing assistance to countries which need such assistance in order to keep them neutral, if not pro-US, countries.

4. Yemen's alliance with Italy during the Second World War, the long-standing rivalry between Yemen and Saudi Arabia, and the tensions of the Cold War in the post-Second World War years all further increased American interest in the Kingdom of Yemen.

5. Kegley and Eugner, *American Foreign Policy: Pattern and Process*, p. 37.

6. Link and Catton, *American Epoch*, p. 705.

7. Ibid.

8. *US Department of State Bulletin*, 15 June 1953, p. 831.

9. Stookey, *America and the Arab States: An Uneasy Encounter*, New York, 1975, p. 180.

1. North Yemen–US contacts before 1962

1. An account of early Yemeni–American contact is presented in Eric Macro's work, *Yemen and the Western World Since 1571*, pp. 21–71.

2. Sanger, *The Arabian Peninsula*, p. 237.

3. Bidwell, *The Two Yemens*, p. 112.

4. Aden consul's despatch to the Department of State, 15 September 1920, Sinclair (ed.), *US Documents on the History of South West Arabia: Tribal Warfare*

and Foreign Policy of Yemen, Aden and Adjacent Tribal Kingdoms 1920–1927, pp. 390–3.
5. Ibid., pp. 75–105.
6. Ibid., p. 263.
7. Sanger, *The Arabian Peninsula*, p. 38.
8. Sinclair, *US Documents*, p. i.
9. Ibid., p. 234.
10. Ibid., pp. 269–83.
11. Ibid., pp. 297–314.
12. See, for example, the Aden consul's dispatch of 15 September 1920, ibid., pp. 390–3.
13. Sinclair, *US Documents*, pp. 413–16.
14. Ibid.
15. Ibid.
16. Ibid., pp. 398–402.
17. Cherruau visited Imam Yahya several times before the end of 1922, but then as representative of French interests. See his report to the American consul in Paris entitled 'Yemen', pp. 12–40.
18. Ibid.
19. Ibid., pp. 398–402.
20. Ibid.
21. Sinclair, *US Documents*, pp. 165–7.
22. Sanger, *The Arabian Peninsula*, p. 235.
23. Twitchell, *Saudi Arabia*.
24. FO 371-12999.
25. Ibid.
26. Sanger, *The Arabian Peninsula*, p. 240.
27. Author's interview with Ahmad al-Shami, a former foreign minister of the Yemeni royalists, Sana'a, 1984. It is interesting to note that some Ford trucks, dating to the 1920s (manufactured in Canada), were in fact found at the Citadel of Zabid. Pers. Comm. D. Warburton.
28. *Times*, London, 7 September 1963.
29. See FO 371-11445.
30. Salem, *Takwin al-Yaman al-Hadith*, pp. 304–9.
31. A reference to the dual principle of American foreign policy enunciated in President Monroe's message to US Congress on 2 December 1823. The doctrine stated that the American continents, especially Latin America which revolted against Spain and was recognized by the US, were not to be considered any longer as a field for colonization by European powers. President Monroe announced that Washington would not interfere in European affairs but would view with displeasure an attempt by the European powers to subject the nations of the New World to their political systems. *The Columbia Encyclopedia*, p. 1195.
32. For a more recent account about the Italian role in the Yemen 1926–43 see Al-Djurafi, *al-Muktataf min Tarikh al-Yaman*, pp. 250–2; Hollingworth, *The Arabs and the West*, p. 116.
33. Safran, *Saudi Arabia: The Ceaseless Quest for Security*, pp. 61–5.
34. 'The Operations in the Yemen,' *Journal of the Royal Central Asian Society*, Vol. 21, July 1934, p. 28.
35. Ibrahim al-Rashid, *Yemen Enters the Modern World*, pp. 19–20.

36. Salem, *Takwin*, p. 334.

37. Peterson, *Yemen, The Search for a Modern State*, p. 61.

38. Interview with Al-Shami, 1984.

39. Sanger, *The Arabian Peninsuala*, p. 249.

40. See report by Captain Djamal Djamil, an Iraqi adviser to the Yemeni government, to the minister of foreign affairs in Baghdad, 12 October 1947, FO371-68322.

41. Ibid.

42. Ibid.

43. It seemed that Great Britain, through Iraq, encouraged the Yemeni army officers to undertake the coup of 1948. The competition between Britain and the US over Yemen reached its climax at that period as Djamil had illustrated. Ibid.

44. Ibid.

45. Interview with al-Shami.

46. The most important organizations of the movement were: Hayat al-Nidal (1935–36), Fatat al-Fulayhi (c.1935), Nadi al-Islah in al-Hudjariyah (1935), al-Katiba al-Ula (1938–40), Shabab al-Amr bil Ma'ruf wal-Nahyi 'an al-Munkar (1941), Hizb al-Ahrar al-Yamaniyyin (1944–45), Djam'iyyat al-Islah (1944), al-Barid al-Adabi (1945), al-Djam'iyyah al-Yamaniyah al-Kubra (1946–48), and al-Ittihad al-Yamani (1952–62). Douglas, *The Free Yemeni Movement 1935–1962*, p. 239.

47. 'A letter from 'Abd-Alla 'Ali al-Hakimi to the Secretary General of the Arab League', 19 October 1946, in *Al-Hikmah*, vol. 17, no. 2, Aden, February 1988, pp. 83–6.

48. Dated 27 February 1946. Al-Rashid, *Yemen Enters the Modern World*, p. 22.

49. It failed on 28 March. Al-Thawr, *Thawrat al-Yaman 1948–1968*, pp. 106–16.

50. *Thawrat 26 September: Dirasat wa Shahadat lil-Tarikh*, vol. I, 1986, p. 44.

51. Al-Rashid, *Yemen Under the Rule of Imam Ahmad*, p. 15.

52. Hoogstral and Kunz, 'Yemen Opens the Door to Progress'.

53. Yemen Legation's statement, Washington Middle East Institute's Yemen Files.

54. In a letter to the British Foreign Office from R.W. Baily of the British Embassy in Washington dated 18 January 1954, Fo371-109983.

55. Safran, *Saudi Arabia*, pp. 61–5.

56. Ibid.

57. FO371-114800.

58. FO371-127056.

59. Ibid.

60. Ibid.

61. Document No. 423, *Foreign Relations of the United States, 1955–1957*, p. 750.

62. Ibid.

63. US Department of State, Central Files, 786H.56/3-2856.

64. Document no. 424 in ibid., pp. 751–2.

65. Fo371-127056.

66. Document No. 425, *United States Foreign Relations 1955–1957*, pp. 752–4.

67. Ibid., p. 754.

68. Department of State, Central Files 646C.86H/1–1157.

69. Eisenhower Library, Whitman File, NSC Records, ibid., p. 755.

70. O'Ballance, *The War in Yemen*, p. 103.

71. In this year Imam Ahmad showed willingness to be reconciled with the British over the southern areas issue. He officially announced that he wanted to share with the British the revenues of oil if found in the southern occupied areas:

'what we want from the English is not so much. It is stability that we want. To keep everything just as it is. We know why the English insist on keeping these areas ... they are hoping to find oil in some areas of the south. I believe that the English think that if the oil is found they can keep it for themselves, but this is impossible. We must get our share of it.' Cited in *al-Nasr*, no. 144, 15 February 1957, as quoted by Djuzeilan, *al-Tarikh as-Sirri li al-Thawrah al-Yamaniyah 1956–1962*, pp. 30–1.

72. Wenner, *Modern Yemen 1918–1966*, p. 187.

2. Initial YAR–US contacts

1. Badeau, *The Middle East Remembered*, Washington, DC, 1983, p. 199.

2. 'Abdul-Wahid al-Zindani, *Arab Politics in the United Nations*, p. 187.

3. The members of the first command council were Colonel Abd-Allah Al-Sallal (president), Colonel Hamud al-Djaifi, Captain 'Abdul-Latif Dei-Allah, Captain Muhammad Kaid Seif, Captain Muhammad al-Makhidhi, Lieutenant Muhammad Mufarrih, Lieutenant 'Ali 'Abdul-Mughni, Major 'Abdullah Djuzaylan (members). Sana'a Radio, 27 September 1962.

4. The YAR's *National Charter*, 1982.

5. Peterson, *Yemen: The Search for a Modern State*, p. 68.

6. The attempt took place on Sunday 26 March 1961.

7. Sana'a Radio, *Thawrat al-Yaman 1948–1968*, p. 132.

8. According to Zeidism in Islam the candidates for the imamship should fulfil 14 conditions or requirements: they are to be male, freeborn, taxpayers, vigorous in mind, sound in all senses, perfect in their limbs, just, pious, generous, endowed with administrative ability, 'Alawi, Fatimi, brave, learned. Although the best candidate for the post, 'Ali Al-Wazir, being blind in one eye, failed the Zeidi conditions. See also Muhammad An'am Ghaleb, *Nizam al-Hukm wa al-Takhalluf al-Iktisadi fi al-Yaman*.

9. *Thawrat 26 September: Dirasat wa Shihadat li al-Tarikh*, vol. 2, 1987, pp. 139–42.

10. Ibid.

11. First oral history interview with Ambassador Parker Hart by Dennis O'Brien for the John F. Kennedy Library, Arlington, Virginia, 15 April 1969, 27 May 1969 and 10 June 1970, p. 13.

12. John F. Kennedy Library, White House Central File, Box No. 6, CO 320 Yemen.

13. Ibid.

14. *House of Commons: Parliamentary Debates*, vol. 666, 31 October 1962, cols. 327–8.

15. Ingrams, *The Yemen: Imams, Rulers and Revolution*, pp. 140–5.

16. Ibid.

17. Schmidt, *Yemen: The Unknown War*, p. 189.

18. On 17 February the British legation at the city of Ta'iz was closed following a week's notice given by President al-Sallal.

19. See American Legation in Ta'iz airgram no. 66, dated 26 January 1963.

20. Al-Zindani, *Arab Politics in the United Nations*, p. 189.

21. *Al-Ahram*, Cairo, 25 April 1983.

22. Al-Baidani, *Azmat al-Ummah al-'Arabiyah wa Thawrat al-Yaman*, p. 389.

23. Ahmad, *Al-Dawr al-Misri fil Yaman*, p. 118.

24. McMullen, *Resolution of the Yemen Crisis, 1963: A Case Study in Mediation*, p. 1.

25. Halliday, *Arabia Without Sultans*, p. 119.

26. Ibid.

27. Sheikh al-Ahmar's father Hussein al-Ahmar, and his brother Sheikh Hamid al-Ahmar, who called for a republic in Yemen, were killed by the imam in the prison of Hadjah in 1959.

28. Mansfield, *The Arabs*, p. 364.

29. Ambassador Hart, oral history interview, p. 13.

30. O'Ballance, *War in Yemen*, p. 88.

31. Khadidjah al-Haysami, *al-'Alakat al-Yamaniyyah al-Sa'udiyyah*, p. 129.

32. *Al-Djumhuriyyah*, Tai'z, 15–23 October 1962.

33. Zabarah, *Yemen, Traditionalism Versus Modernity*, p. 95.

34. Ambassador Hart, oral history interview, p. 19.

35. Oral history interview with Chester L. Cooper conducted by the Kennedy Library, 6 May 1966, p. 59.

36. According to Hart (oral history interview), the total American community in Ta'iz at the time of the revolution was between 100 and 130.

37. Ibid., p. 15.

38. Ta'iz was the base of foreign diplomatic missions as well as Imam Ahmad 1948–62. This situation continued for a few years after the revolution due to civil war.

39. Author's interview with Dr Robert Stookey, Austin, 30 January 1990.

40. Cortada, *The Yemen Crisis*, p. 2.

41. Ibid., p. 16.

42. Ibid., p.1.

43. Ambassador Hart, oral history interview, p. 16.

44. Stookey, *Yemen: The Politics of the Yemen Arab Republic*, p. xv.

45. Author's interview with Dr Stookey.

46. Ibid.

47. Schmidt, *Yemen: The Unknown War*, p. 204.

48. Heikel, *Sanawat al-Ghalayan*, pp. 920–2.

49. Badeau, *The Middle East Remembered*, p. 199.

50. In the words of Stookey.

51. Stookey, *America and the Arab States: An Uneasy Encounter*, p. 183; Peterson, *Conflict in the Yemens and Superpower Involvement*, p. 4.

52. McMullen, *Resolution of the Yemeni Crisis*, p. 2.

53. Gause, *Saudi-Yemeni Relations*, p. 60.

54. See oral history interview with John Badeau, conducted as part of the Kennedy Library's Robert F. Kennedy Oral History Project, 1969, p. 27.

55. Badeau, 'A Role in Search of a Hero', pp. 132–6 in Rehmy, *The Egyptian Policy in the Arab World, Intervention in Yemen 1962–1967: A Case Study*, pp. 114–15.

56. Ibid.

57. Ibid.

58. White House Central File, Box no. 6.

59. Badeau's telegram to Washington, 1 October 1962.

60. Ibid.

61. Author's interview with Ambassador Muhsin al-'Aini, Washington, DC, 7 February 1990.

62. Ambassador Badeau's report to the department, ibid.

63. Bruce Conde (his American name) said that al-Badr was to start a counter-revolution, and told journalists in Aden airport that he was going to join al-Badr in the northern borders of the country to assist him in regaining his throne. Conde was a former American army officer who became an intelligence major in the 82nd Airborne Division in North Africa. His first contact was with the Crown Prince of Yemen Muhammad al-Badr during the early 1950s when he sent al-Badr a letter asking for some stamps. When he received a reply from al-Badr, he asked to visit Yemen. Imam Ahmad sent him an invitation to visit the country in 1953 and, after abandoning his American passport, he was given a Yemeni one by the Consulate in Cairo. After settling in Sana'a, Conde became preoccupied with the stamp business. When the 1955 attempted coup took place Conde was the first foreigner to congratulate Seif al-Islam Abd-Alla on being the new imam. In 1958 Conde converted to Islam and changed his personal name to Abdul-Rahman. During his stay in Sana'a he managed to visit Djidda and Beirut several times and maintained friendly contacts with members of the American as well as the British embassies. Imam Ahmad expelled him from the country in 1959 and there is no explanation of how he returned to Yemen before the revolution. In 1962 he joined the royalist forces and became Bourbon Conde. On 28 September 1962 Conde and British pilots who were operating the small Yemen Airline managed to escape with a plane to Aden, where he made the statement mentioned above. Among the passengers were two members of the Revolutionary Command Council, Muhammad Kaid Seif and Ali Muhammad Sa'id. Members of the ex-Free Yemeni Movement considered him to be an American spy, while others, like Ahmad al-Shami, a former royalist foreign minister, believe he was and still is a sincere friend of the Yemeni royal family. According to a British report by the Ta'iz delegation, dated 4 October 1957 (FO371-127066) Bruce Conde was a freelance writer of corny travelogue articles, reporting for *Lands East* at that period. The report added that Conde first came to Yemen in 1953 and returned to Beirut, where he wrote for the *Daily Star*, in October 1956. The report also mentioned that Conde's 'image of himself was as an American Lawrence' and complained that he 'worked as bear-leader for the Western journalists who were invited to Yemen to see the British aggression'. In 1990 Conde was living in Morocco.

64. Al-Baidani, *Azmat al-Ummah al-'Arabiah*, p. 379.

65. Ibid.

66. Author's interview with Dr Stookey.

67. Ibid.

68. Ibid.

69. Ibid.

70. Ibid.

71. Schmidt, *Yemen: The Unknown War*, p. 185.

72. Ibid., pp. 486–7.

73. Author's interview with Dr Stookey.

74. Ibid.

75. Al-Baidani, *Azmat al-Ummah al-'Arabiah*, pp. 486–7.

76. 'Abdul-Rahman al-Baidani replaced al-'Aini as foreign minister in this month.

77. Author's interview with Ambassador al-'Aini.

78. Author's interview with Ambassador Talcott Seelye, Washington, DC, 19 February 1990.

79. *New York Times*, 11 October and 5 November 1962.

80. *Times*, London, 27 November 1962.
81. Cortada, *The Yemen Crisis*, p. 8.
82. *Times*, London, 27 November 1962.
83. Badeeb, *The Saudi–Egyptian Conflict Over North Yemen 1962–1970*, pp. 61–7.
84. Heikal, *Nasser: The Cairo Documents*, p. 196.
85. White House Central File, Box no. 6.
86. 29 November 1962.
87. *US Department of State Bulletin*, vol. 63, pp. 44–5.
88. *US Congressional Record, Senate Records*, vol. 109, part 10, pp. 1366–9.
89. Ibid.
90. *Daily Telegraph*, 11 December 1962.
91. 'Yemen', *Deadline Data*, 9 December 1962.
92. *Daily Telegraph*, 15 December 1962.
93. *Al-Ahram*, 28 November 1962.
94. Heikal, *Sanawat al-Ghalayan*, pp. 923–4.
95. Ibid., pp. 925–6.
96. Dawisha, 'Intervention in the Yemen: An Analysis of Egyption Perception and Policy', p. 50.
97. Ambassador Hart, oral history interview, p. 16.
98. Ibid.
99. Al-Thawr, *Thawrat al-Yaman 1948–1968*, p. 137.
100. A translation of the Egyptian communiqué is in Schmidt, *Yemen: The Unknown War*, p. 187.
101. 'Al-Baradduni, *al-Yaman al-Djumhuri*, p. 435.
102. Oral history interview with Chester L. Cooper conducted by the Kennedy Library, 6 May 1966.
103. *Department of State Bulletin*, vol. 68, 7 January 1963, pp. 11–12.
104. Theodore Sorensen, *Kennedy*, p. 534.
105. Schmidt, *Yemen: The Unknown War*, p. 185.
106. Seale, 'The War in Yemen: Did Nasser Lure the US Out on a Limb?', p. 10.
107. *US Congressional Record, Senate Records*, vol. 109, part 10, pp. 1366–9.
108. Author's interview with Dr Stookey.
109. Ibid.
110. *Guardian*, 20 December 1962.
111. Cortada, *The Yemen Crisis*, p. 9.
112. Ibid., p. 8.
113. Ibid., p. 9.
114. Ibid., pp. 9–10.
115. Ibid., p. 10.
116. *UN General Assembly, Seventeenth Session, Official Records*, vol. 3, New York, 1962, pp. 1225–41.
117. Ibid., pp. 1230–1.
118. Ibid.
119. Ibid., pp. 1233–4.
120. Ibid.
121. Al-Baidani, *Azmat al-Ummah al-'Arabiyah*, p. 550.
122. Author's interview with Ambassador al-'Aini.
123. Schmidt, *Yemen: The Unknown War*, p. 199.

124. See *UN General Assembly, Seventeenth Session, Official Records*, vol. 3, 1962, pp. 1225–41.

3. Relations breached and restored

1. Badeau, *The American Approach Towards the Arab World*, p. 135.
2. Author's interview with David Ransom, Washington, DC, February 1990.
3. In several telegrams from US Ta'iz embassy to the US Department of State dated 14 September 1964, *National Security File*, vol. II.
4. *Yemen* (an administrative history, prepared by the US Department of State for the White House at the close of the Johnson administration).
5. Al-Baidani, *Azmat al-Ummah al-'Arabiyyah*, p. 491.
6. *Al-Djumhuriyyah*, Ta'iz, 12 January 1963.
7. Ibid., 18 January 1963.
8. Riyadh–London relations were broken off during the Suez crisis in 1956. According to Safran, in June 1963 a British military mission arrived in the KSA to help improve the training of the Saudi National Guard and later that year they provided planes, pilots, and surface to air missiles to the Saudi army. Safran, *Saudi Arabia: The Ceaseless Quest for Security*, p. 97.
9. *New Republic*, 23 January 1963, p. 10.
10. *US Department of State Bulletin*, vol. 68, no. 21, January 1963, pp. 90–91.
11. Author's interview with Ambassador al-'Aini.
12. Oral history interview with Ambassador Badeau, p. 16.
13. *US Department of State Bulletin*, 28 January 1963, p. 91.
14. *American University of Beirut Bulletin*, 19 January 1963.
15. Ibid., 28 January 1963.
16. Ibid., 2 February 1963.
17. Ibid., 7 February 1963.
18. Cortada, *The Yemen Crisis*, p. 13.
19. Ibid., p. 16.
20. Ibid., pp. 18–19.
21. Seale, 'The War in Yemen: Did Nasser Lure the US out on a Limb?', p. 10.
22. Halliday, *Arabia Without Sultans*, p. 122.
23. First oral history interview with Ambassador Hart, pp. 18 and 39.
24. Author's interview with Dr Stookey.
25. Author's interview with Ambassador al-'Aini.
26. McMullen, *Resolution of the Yemeni Crisis*, p. 11.
27. Letter from President Kennedy to Crown Prince Faisal of Saudi Arabia, *Department of State Bulletin*, vol. 68, no. 1231, 28 January 1963, pp. 144–5, Annex 9.
28. McMullen, *Resolution of the Yemeni Crisis*, p. 2.
29. Ibid.
30. Ibid.
31. US Department of State, *Yemen*.
32. Quoting an unofficial translation of the letter, released to this writer by the US Department of State.
33. Ibid. In this letter Nasser assured President Kennedy that the UAR was 'in possession of the documents proving that some American pilots participated in the

transportation of troops and equipment from Jordan to Saudi Arabia to the Yemeni borders'.

34. Cortada, *The Yemen Crisis*, p. 21.
35. Ibid., p. 21.
36. Oral history interview with George McGhee conducted by the Kennedy Library, 13 August 1964, p. 13.
37. In telegrams from US Ta'iz Embassy to the US Department of State dated 14 September 1964, *National Security File*, vol. II.
38. Ibid.
39. McMullen, *Resolution of the Yemeni Crisis*, p. 11.
40. Ibid., p. 11.
41. Gause, *Saudi–Yemeni Relations*, p. 63.
42. Press conference given by Dr Ralph Bunche, *Guardian*, London, 5 March 1963.
43. Ambassador Hart, oral history interview, p. 50.
44. Former US ambassador to Brazil and India, who was successful in helping to settle the Dutch–Indonesian conflict. Cortada, *The Yemen Crisis*, p. 21.
45. Oral history interview with Ambassador George McGhee, p. 13.
46. US Secretary Dean Rusk's News Conference, 8 March 1963, *Department of State Bulletin*, vol. 68, no. 1239, p. 437.
47. US Department of State, *Yemen*.
48. McMullen, *Resolution of the Yemeni Crisis*, p. 50.
49. Ibid.
50. *National Security File*, vol. II.
51. McMullen, *Resolution of the Yemeni Crisis*, p. 51.
52. The UN mission in the YAR was established in June and began its operation on 4 July. Ibid., p. 46.
53. *American University of Beirut Bulletin*, 2–19 January 1963.
54. Grayson, *Saudi–American Relations*, p. 95.
55. US Department of State, *Yemen*.
56. US Department of State instructions to US embassies in London, Cairo, Djiddah, Taiz and Bahrein, 23 July 1964, *National Security File*, vol. II.
57. Safran, *Saudi Arabia*, p. 119.
58. US Department of State, *Yemen*.
59. Ibid.
60. Ibid.
61. *American University of Beirut Bulletin*, 14 April 1964.
62. US Department of State, *Yemen*.
63. Ibid.
64. The US ambassador in Cairo was also the US ambassador to the Yemen after the YAR revolution. In Sana'a, James Cortada, the US chargé d'affaires, was accorded the rank of minister on 16 October 1963.
65. US Department of State, *Yemen*.
66. *National Security File*, vol. II.
67. Ibid.
68. US Department of State, *Yemen*.
69. *National Security File*, vol. II.
70. *Al-Thawrah*, Sana'a, 11 November 1963.
71. *National Security File*, vol. II.
72. Schmidt, *Yemen: The Unknown War*, p. 200.

73. Grayson, *Saudi–American Relations*, p. 97.
74. Ibid.
75. Ibid., p. 97.
76. *National Security File*, vol. II.
77. Ibid.
78. Ibid.
79. *National Security File*, vol. II.
80. Ibid.
81. Ibid.
82. *National Security File-Country File*, vol. II.
83. US Department of State, *Yemen*.
84. Ibid.
85. Ibid.
86. Bidwell, *The Two Yemens*, p. 210.
87. Al-Haysami, *Al-'Alaqat al-Yamaniyyah al-Sa'udiyyah*, p. 168.
88. Ibid.
89. *National Security File-Country File*, vol. II.
90. Ibid.
91. Ibid.
92. Ibid.
93. Interview with Al-'Aini.
94. O'Ballance, *The War in Yemen*, p. 148.
95. Gause, *Saudi–Yemeni Relations*, p. 96.
96. Ibid., p. 97.
97. Mosher, 'Nasser's Drive for South Arabia'.
98. *Department of State Bulletin*, vol. 53, no. 20, September 1965, p. 476.
99. *Reporter*, 9 February 1967, pp. 24–7.
100. US Department of State, *Yemen*.
101. Badeau, *The American Approach Towards the Arab World*, p. 146.
102. US Department of State, *Yemen*.
103. *Al-Hayat*, Beirut, 22 February 1966.
104. Ibid.
105. Safran, *Saudi Arabia*, p. 121.
106. Ahmad, *Al-Dawr al-Misri fi al-Yaman*, pp. 418–19.
107. US Department of State, *Yemen*.
108. Ibid.
109. Ambassador Hart, oral history interview, p. 35.
110. Ahmad, *Al-Dawr al-Misri fi al-Yaman*, p. 320.
111. Al-Baidani, *Azmat al-Ummah al-'Arabiah*, pp. 314–24.
112. Ibid.
113. US Department of State, *Yemen*.
114. *Weekly Compilation of Presidential Documents*, 27 June 1966, p. 820.
115. US Department of State, *Yemen*.
116. *National Security File-Country File*, vol. II.
117. Ibid.
118. Ibid.
119. The documents suggest that 'Uthman demanded $700,000 a month from Washington to help the so-called 'moderate republicans' resist UAR influence in the YAR.
120. Ibid.

121. *American University of Beirut Bulletin*, 5 August 1966.
122. Author's interview with Ambassador William Stoltzfus, London, 1 June 1990.
123. Dobert, 'Development of Aid Programs to Yemen'.
124. *USAID Annual Report*, Sana'a, 1988.
125. So called because they were the first Yemeni students the imam allowed to study abroad and most of them were destined to organize the 1962 revolution. The names the memorandum listed were: (1) Muhammad 'Abdul-'Aziz Sallam; (2) Ahmad 'Ali al-Muhanni; (3) Muhammad Khushafah; (4) Muhammad Fay'; (5) Muhammad 'Ali Zabarah; (6) Hussein Salah al-Din.
126. *US Embassy/Taiz Study* dated 17 April 1965 as paraphrased by Dr Robert Burrowes in 1978.
127. Ibid.
128. *National Security File*, vol. II.
129. Ibid.
130. In 1971, the YAR invited foreign contractors to tender for the rehabilitation and improvement of the Sana'a–Taiz road, which the Americans did not use any asphalt in as the Chinese did in other similar roads.
131. Author's interview with Dr al-Iryani, September 1988.
132. Ibid.
133. *National Security File*, vol. II.
134. *Al-Siyasah*, Kuwait, 17 September 1966.
135. US Department of State, *Yemen*.
136. *Al-Siyasah*, Kuwait, 30 October 1966.
137. US Department of State, *Yemen*.
138. Ibid.
139. Ibid.
140. Ibid.
141. 'Abd-Allah, *Memoirs*, pp. 67–8.
142. US Department of State, *Yemen*.
143. *National Security File-Country File*, vol. II.
144. Interview with David Ransom.
145. Author's interview with YAR ambassador to the UN, Muhammad 'Abdul-'Aziz Sallam, New York, 20 February 1990.
146. Ibid.
147. Ibid.
148. US Department of State, *Yemen*.
149. Ibid.
150. In a talk with Brigadier Muhammad 'Ali al-Akwa', the military leader of the 5th November 1967 coup and ex-director of the YAR Intelligence Service, Sana'a, September 1988.
151. Qasimiyyah et al., *Al-Siyasah al-Amrikiyyah wa al-'Arab*, p. 171.
152. Hamroosh, *Kissat Thalatha wa-'Ishreen Yuliu: Abdul-Nasser wa al-'Arab*, p. 2.
153. US Department of State, *Yemen*.
154. Ambassador Hart, oral history interview, pp. 61–2.
155. Badeau, *The American Approach Towards the Arab World*, p. 146.
156. Ambassador Hart, oral history interview, p. 60.
157. The KSA participated in paying Egypt $154 million annually out of a total Arab subsidy of $266 million.

158. According to US Department of State, *Yemen*.

159. *New York Times*, 13 December 1967.

160. The full text of the communiqué is cited in Al-Thawr, *Thawrat al-Yaman 1948–1968*, pp. 188–9.

161. Ambassador Hart, oral history interview, p. 15.

162. It is worth noting that the Soviet Union, influenced by the Yemeni Left, hesitated in providing the YAR with arms after the 5th of November coup of 1967. A Yemeni delegation to Moscow, it was said, returned empty handed, but when Republican Sana'a faced real danger a delegation headed by the Yemeni vice-premier, Hassan Makki, visited Moscow in early December and achieved success. The USSR provided the YAR that month with arms, including 24 MiG 19s, and many Russian pilots and military experts who, with Syrian pilots, operated the new arms and bombers. For more details see Nadji, *al-Tarikh al-'Askari li al-Yaman 1939–1967*. After the lifting of the siege, relations with the USSR deteriorated and the YAR tried to replace Moscow with Beijing, but it was reported that Premier Al-'Amri cancelled a scheduled visit to China in early March 1968 after a meeting with the Russian ambassador in Cairo.

163. US Department of State, *Yemen*.

164. Ibid.

165. The republicans insisted that the conditions for ending the civil war were to maintain the republic and to exclude the return of any member of the Hamid al-Din family.

166. Yodfat, *The Soviet Union and the Arabian Peninsula*, p. 3.

167. US Department of State, *Yemen*.

168. Author's interview with David Ransom.

169. Ibid.

170. Ibid.

171. President 'Abdul-Rahman al-Iryani, 30 July 1968, *ME/2837/A/5/*, 2 August 1968.

172. Ibid.

173. *Record of the Arab World*, Beirut, p. 190.

174. Ibid.

175. Ibid., September 1969, p. 2645.

176. Ibid.

177. Malone, 'The Yemen Arab Republic's Game of Nations', p. 545.

178. Author's interview with David Ransom.

179. To the Saudis, Yemeni unity was a serious threat to their security. They saw that a united Yemen or a strong YAR would endanger KSA security and integrity of Saudi territories. Halliday (*Arabia Without Sultans*, p. 115) observes that the external American pressure and the tribal and military forces pushed the post-1962 North Yemeni Republic 'in a direction radically different from the popular trans–formation possible at the start'. He adds that 'North Yemen became a component of the capitalist world, with a pro-imperialist foreign policy and economic relations, and capitalist relations at home'.

180. See 'Background for Vice President Bush on US–Yemeni Relations', a tele-gram from the US Embassy in Sana'a to the US Department of State; *New York Times*, 9 April 1970.

181. In 1970 this writer was employed for several months by the American Catholic Relief Service (CRS), to monitor the distribution of the American ship-

ments of flour and dried milk throughout Tihama. The Yemeni people much appreciated the American relief in that very difficult period. It is of importance to note that the famine of 1959 in the same area forced the imams to seek American aid for the first time. The American aid at that time was followed by the establishment of the first US diplomatic and aid missions in the country.

182. *Al-Thawrah*, Sana'a, 26 May 1971; *Financial Times*, London, 27 May 1971.

183. Author's interview with David Ransom.

184. Ibid.

185. Grayson, *Saudi–American Relations*, p. 103.

186. YAR Prime Minister Muhsin al-'Aini revealed in late 1974 that the country had not received any Soviet arms since 1970. *Al-Hawadeth*, Beirut, 18 January 1973; *Arab Report and Record*, London, 16–31 January 1973.

187. Author's interview with David Ransom.

188. Quoting the first president of the People's Republic of South Yemen (PRSY), Kahtan Muhammad al-Sha'bi, as reported, *ME*/3605/A/7, 9 February 1971.

189. *Al-Thawrah*, Sana'a, 18 October 1972.

190. Author's interview with Ambassador Muhsin al-'Aini.

191. Ibid.

192. Author's interview with David Ransom.

193. 'Remarks by Secretary Rogers', *Department of State Bulletin*, 7 August 1972.

194. Ibid.

195. Ibid.

196. *Al-Thawrah*, Sana'a, 2 July 1972.

197. Ibid.

198. *Al-Thawrah*, Sana'a, 18 October 1972.

199. The YAR prime minister in 1972 later revealed in an interview with this author that Sana'a was keen to resume diplomatic relations with the US because of its great need for foreign assistance, and that the Italian ambassador who looked after US affairs during the interregnum had personally told the YAR chairman of the Presidential Council, Kadi 'Abdul-Rahman al-Iryani, that Sana'a would receive a great deal of US aid if it resumed political ties.

200. Author's interview with Ambassador al-'Aini.

201. *International Herald Tribune*, Paris, 11 July 1972.

202. *Department of State Bulletin*, 7 August 1972.

203. Author's interview with Ambassador al-'Aini.

204. A letter from Robert A. Stein, US chargé d'affaires to the YAR prime minister, Sana'a, 30 September 1972; a letter from YAR Foreign Ministry to the American Embassy, Sana'a, 29 January 1973 in *US Treaties and Other International Agreements*, 1973, pp. 853–7.

205. Department of State, *US Treaties and Other International Agreements*, 1974, pp. 715–18.

206. *Al-Nahar*, Beirut, 2 December 1970.

207. As of the beginning of December 1970 South Yemen's official name became the Peoples' Democratic Republic of South Yemen (PDRY) in Socialist bloc style, as a consequence of the left's accession to power on 22 June 1969.

208. *Al-Nahar*, Beirut, 2 December 1970.

209. *14 October*, Aden, July–August 1972.

210. The YAR's northern tribes fall into two tribal confederations: Hashid and Bakil.

211. A leading tribe of the Bakil confederation.

212. Author's interview.

213. *Al-Hayat*, London, 1990.

214. Halliday, *Revolution and Foreign Policy 1967–1987*, pp. 116–17.

215. The Saudis are Wahhabis, from the Sunni sect of Islam, while the ruling governments of the YAR were Zeidis, from the Shiite sect of Islam.

216. *Financial Times Supplement*, London, 27 November 1984.

217. According to the YAR census results of 1986 the total population of the country was 9,274,173. 'Central Planning Organisation Statement', Sana'a, 1988. Until recently the KSA did not announce the size of its population.

218. Badeeb, *The Saudi–Egyptian Conflict Over North Yemen 1962–1970*, pp. 98–9.

219. *International Herald Tribune*, 29 April 1976.

220. Ibid., Paris, 3 August 1975.

221. Ibid.

222. Burrowes, *The Yemen Arab Republic: The Politics of Development 1962–1986*, pp. 80–5.

223. Ruszkiewicz, 'How the US Lost its Footing in the Shifting Sands of the Persian Gulf – a Case History in the Yemen Arab Republic', p. 64.

224. *Daily Telegraph*, London, 5 August 1975.

225. Ruszkiewicz, 'How the US Lost its Footing', p. 62.

226. Author's interview with US ambassador to the YAR 1978–81, Dr George Lane, Worcester, MA, 16 February 1990.

227. *ME/5156/A/8–9*, 11 March 1976.

228. Ibid.

229. Burrowes, 'The Other Side of the Red Sea and Little More: The Horn of Africa and the Two Yemens', unpublished essay, 1990.

230. *Middle East Yearbook*, p. 233.

231. 'The Superpowers' Tug of War Over Yemen', *Military Review*, Volume 61, no. 3, March 1981.

232. Author's interview with US ambassador to the YAR 1983–1987, Dr William Rugh, Washington, DC, 9 February 1990.

233. It was reported that the oil boom of 1973 increased Saudi revenues by 400 per cent, nearly $22.5 billion. At the end of May 1975, Riyadh's gold and foreign exchange holdings surpassed those of the US for the first time, reaching about $20.5 billion against the Washington holdings of about $16.7 billion. In 1976 Saudi oil production rose to 8.7 million bpd, and in 1980 to 10 million bpd. Grayson, *Saudi–American Relations*, p. 182.

234. David Ransom, Arabian Peninsula Desk officer in the US Department of State, confirmed in early 1990 that the Yemenis constantly asked the US to undertake a big capital project, but this was no longer US policy. Author's interview.

235. Burrowes, *The Yemen Arab Republic: The Politics of Development 1962–1986*, p. 182.

236. *Air International*, 19 January 1978.

237. According to Burrowes, who worked in Sana'a during this period. Scotts resigned in mid-1978 for personal reasons.

238. Author's telephone interview with Dr Robert Burrowes, Washington, DC– Seattle, WA, 21 February 1990.

239. Burrowes, *The Yemen Arab Republic: The Politics of Development 1962–1986*, p. 182.

240. Ibid.

241. *Al-Thawrah*, Sana'a, 30 June 1978. This author travelled to Sana'a following al-Hamdi's assassination to report for the Kuwaiti daily *Al-Siyasah* to interview President al-Ghashmi and other Yemeni officials. Rumours in Sana'a at that time claimed that President Rubiyya', who unexpectedly attended the funeral of al-Hamdi, swore that he would take revenge on the assassins. It was later rumoured that Rubiyya's' opponents in the PDRY had exchanged his envoy's briefcase with another one. An official YSP communiqué, however, blamed Rubiyya' for the assassination of al-Ghashmi.

242. Press communiqué of Central YSP Committee, *14 October*, Aden, 29 June 1978.

243. *Al-Nahar*, Beirut, 12 September 1978.

244. The eruption of the Somali–Ethiopian war in the Horn of Africa had brought misfortune to the PDRY. The restoration of relations between Aden and Riyadh was followed by a Saudi loan of $1 billion of economic assistance, including the supply of the Little Aden refinery with crude oil, but the diverse responses towards the Somali–Ethiopian war, inter-PDRY factional rivalry, and the Cold War between the superpowers caused the PDRY's reconciliation with its influential and wealthy Arab neighbour to fail.

245. Findlay, *They Dare to Speak Out*, p. 9.

246. Ibid, pp. 5–12; Halliday, *Revolution and Foreign Policy*, pp. 83–90; Peterson, *Conflict in the Yemens and Superpower Involvement*, pp. 1–2.

247. Findlay, *They Dare to Speak Out*, p. 10.

248. White House Central File, Box no. 5032.

249. *New York Times*, 27 June 1978.

250. Quoting Secretary-General 'Abdul-Fattah Isma'il's statement following the YSP Central Committee meeting, October 1978.

251. Northern army officers and politicians who fled the YAR after the failure of the Libyan-backed attempted coup against Saleh on 15 October 1978.

252. *ME/6010/A/1.*

253. Page, *The Soviet Union and the Yemen*, p. 71.

254. Ruszkiewicz, 'How the US Lost its Footing', p. 66.

255. Ibid.

256. *Washington Star*, 25 July 1978, p. 1.

257. Ibid.

258. *Al-Rai al-'Aam*, Kuwait, 25 January 1979.

259. *United States Arms Policies in the Persian Gulf and Red Sea Areas: Past, Present and Future. Report of the American Staff Survey Mission to Ethiopia, Iran and the Arabian Peninsula*, p. 77.

260. A report by Norman Kempster from Zahran, *International Herald Tribune*, 12 February 1979.

261. Ibid.

4. Development of a US interest in the YAR

1. Ruszkiewicz, 'How the US Lost its Footing', p. 72.

2. *Middle East Survey*, 28 February 1979.

3. See Ambassador Crawford's testimony, *Proposed Arms Transfers to the YAR*,

Hearing Before the Subcommittee of Europe and the Middle East of the Committee on Foreign Affairs of the House of Representatives, pp. 6–8.

4. Ibid.
5. Halliday, *Revolution and Foreign Policy*, p. 87.
6. See *Gist*, Bureau of Public Affairs, Department of State, April 1979.
7. *Daily Telegraph*, London, 1 March 1979.
8. Ruszkiewicz, 'How the US Lost its Footing', p. 72.
9. *14 October*, Aden, 4 March 1979.
10. *FBIS*, Washington, DC, 7 March 1979.
11. Author's interview with Ambassador George Lane, Worcester, MA, 16 February 1990.
12. Author's talk with president of AIYS, Dr Sheila Carapico, Richmond, VA, February 1990.
13. Author's interview with David Ransom.
14. *Proposed Arms Transfers*, pp. 6–8.
15. Ruszkiewicz, 'How the US Lost its Footing', p. 66.
16. Author's interview with Ambassador Lane.
17. Ibid.
18. On 1 September 1977 the Carter administration withdrew its offer of US arms to Somalia when the latter was at war with Ethiopia over the Ogaden issue.
19. On 1 February 1979 Ayatollah al-Khomeini returned to Iran from France. See *ME/6032/A/6*, 31 January and 2 February 1979. In a statement following his arrival he confirmed that the new government would no longer deal with the Western oil consortium. Iran Radio quoted some revolutionary sources that the Islamic government intended to increase oil prices by some 30 per cent. *Al-Siyasah*, Kuwait, 2 February 1979.
20. In April 1978 the government of Afghanistan was overthrown in a military coup and a new government was established under the leadership of the People's Democratic Party of Afghanistan.
21. *ME/6064/A/2*.
22. Ibid.
23. And attended by Benjamin S. Rosenthal, Donald J. Pease, Gerry E. Studds, Michael D. Barnes, L.H. Fountain, Paul Findlay, Millicent Fenwick and Larry Winn.
24. *Proposed Arms Transfers*, p. 35.
25. Ibid., p. 20.
26. Ibid, p. 27.
27. Ibid., p. 34.
28. *Proposed Arms Transfers*, p. 37.
29. *International Herald Tribune*, 17–18 March 1979.
30. *ME/6065/A/1*.
31. *ME/6082/A/2*.
32. *Al-Kifah al-'Arabi*, Beirut, 26 March 1979; *FBIS*, Washington, 27 March 1979.
33. Ibid.
34. *ME/6082/A/2*.
35. *ME/6082/A/3*.
36. *Guardian*, London, 12 April 1979.
37. Ruszkiewicz, 'How the US Lost its Footing', p. 72.

38. *Financial Times Supplement*, 27 November 1984.
39. *Washington Post*, 12 April 1979.
40. *MEED*, Cyprus, 9 May 1979.
41. Katz, 'North Yemen between East and West', p. 105.
42. Author's interview with Ambassador Lane.
43. *Department of State Briefing Memorandum on US–Saudi Cooperation in the YAR*, 8 July 1978.
44. Ibid.
45. *International Herald Tribune*, 14 June 1979.
46. Ibid.
47. Ibid.
48. *Christian Science Monitor*, 19 June 1979.
49. On 14 April the NDF said that the Saudis through cutting the financial aid to Sana'a and through their influence in the Islamic front had succeeded in delaying the unity talks. President Isma'il indicated on the 27th that the YSP Central Committee had fully realized that 'imperialist circles, through their agents in our homeland would not stop their conspiracies against the Yemenis and the diversification of their interference in the internal affairs of the Yemeni people, in an attempt to accomplish their goal – to destroy the gains of our Yemeni people'. *ME/6094/A/9*; *ME/6104/A/1*.
50. Al-Asnadj recently revealed the disagreement he had with the YAR president, 'Ali Saleh, for he believed that any arms dealings with the US should be through the KSA. He claimed that President Saleh was importing Soviet arms from different sources while he was dispatched to Washington to negotiate direct YAR–US military cooperation. He also claimed that the Yemeni president paid $300 million on one occasion in cash for Soviet arms, a matter of which he did not approve and which led to his expulsion from the government. See *al-Magallah*, London–Djiddah, 7–13 November 1990.
51. 'White House statement' in *Public Papers of the Presidents, Jimmy Carter*, vol. II, 1978, p. 1485; author's interview with Ambassador George Lane.
52. Ibid.
53. *Al-Rai al-'Aam*, Kuwait, 5 October 1979.
54. *International Herald Tribune*, 24 December 1979.
55. Author's interview with Ambassador Lane.
56. Letters dated 3 and 4 April and 30 May 1979, signed by the following Congressmen: Les Aspin, Michael D. Barnes, Don Bonker, Dante B. Fascell, Floyd J. Fithian, William H. Gray III, Lee H. Hamilton, Leon E. Panetta, Donald J. Pease, Joel Pritchard, Benjamin S. Rosenthal, Stephan J. Solarz, Gerry E. Studds, Jonatham Bingham and C.D. Long.
57. Ibid.
58. *Al-Thawrah*, Sana'a, 29 October 1979.
59. Stookey, *Arabian Peninsula, Zone of Ferment*, pp. 106–7.
60. Author's interview with David Ransom, January 1990.
61. Ibid.
62. Katz, 'North Yemen between East and West', p. 106.
63. Burrowes, *The Yemen Arab Republic: The Politics of Development 1962–1986*, p. 105.
64. *New York Times*, 20 April 1980.
65. *Al-Siyassah*, Kuwait, 13 February 1980.

66. Five factors led to the defeat of the National Democratic Front in 1982. They were: 1. USSR and USA military, political and economic support; 2. Soviet disapproval of the NDF war against Sana'a for fear that Sana'a might ask for direct American assistance; 3. large-scale assistance given to the YAR army by the powerful Bakil and Hashed confederations which got subsidies from Saudi Arabia; 4. the limited appeal of the NDF beyond the immediate border area; 5. the defeat of the NDF coincided with the extremely heavy flooding that occurred in the Southern Yemeni state during this year, which, it appeared, pushed the PDRY to compromise.

67. Halliday, 'Russians Help to Defeat Left-wing Guerrillas'.

68. Ismai'l was originally from North Yemen, where the Shaf'i sect to which he belonged was deprived of its political rights by the Zeidi imams. The North Yemenis in the south were treated contemptuously and as foreigners with no political rights until 1967. Anti-Northern sentiments continued in South Yemen after 1967 and the anti-left orientation in the North following the Egyptian defeat in the North may have been behind the very strong appeal of Marxism-Leninism for the YSP secretary-general, 'Abdul-Fattah Isma'il, who became the symbol of the radical leftist element in both the South and the North. President Isma'il started the year 1979 with the conclusion of a two-year cooperation agreement between the Committee for the Defence of the Revolution of Cuba and the People's Defence Committee of the PDRY; the PDRY attended the Comecon as an observer; between 16 and 17 September Isma'il received the Soviet prime minister, Aleksei Kosygin, and by the end of the year a twenty-year friendship cooperation treaty was signed between the PDRY–USSR governments, ratified by the PDRY parliament on 10 February 1980. In the last weak of September 1979, in an interview for the American TV company NBC, Ismai'l expressed his hope that the USA would 'benefit from the lesson it had learnt in Vietnam' and that it should not attempt to learn it again in any other region, particularly in the Arabian peninsula. On 29 November he invited Ethiopian President Mengistu Haile Mariam and they signed a Treaty of Friendship and Co-operation on 3 December. Despite all that, South Yemeni politics, the anti-Northern sentiments, the attitude of Arab nationalist countries like Iraq and Syria which had good relations with Moscow, and the Saudi–US stance in the YAR forced Moscow to set Ismail and his policies aside, and he was forced to resign in April 1980 and leave for Moscow on 28 June.

69. Safran, *Saudi Arabia: The Ceaseless Quest for Security*, pp. 387–8.

70. In fact Isma'il tried to communicate with Saudi Arabia, Oman and other Arab countries to break the isolation of his government, but all his efforts failed because of his reputation as an atheist in an Islamic society and Communist hardliner. Even his ally during the 1979 inter-war, Colonel Mu'ammar al-Kadhafi, left President Isma'il in his corner. In June 1979 the Libyan president visited Sana'a to turn a new page in the relations of his government with the YAR.

71. Katz, 'Camels and Commissars'.

72. Stookey, *Arabian Peninsula: Zone of Ferment*, pp. 106–7.

73. Ibid.

74. It should be noted that Sana'a–Moscow relations were limited from 1970 to 1979 as a result of the Saudi–US influence in the YAR. When both its 1970s allies ignored YAR military needs, Sana'a responded to Soviet initiatives to resume cooperative relations. In 1979 Moscow provided the YAR with arms needed to maintain stability in the country, though the former's relations with the PDRY continued to be the same.

75. Author's interview with engineer Mou'djib al-Malazi, London, 8 November 1989.

76. Ibid., quoting Ambassador William Rugh 1983–87.

77. Yemen Hunt Oil Company, *In an Era of Great Accomplishments*, p. 7.

78. Author's interview with Tom Meurer.

79. Ibid.

80. Ibid.

81. *Oil and Gas Investor*, vol. 7, no. 8, March 1988.

82. *World Oil*, April 1988, p. 33.

83. Ibid.

84. *Al-Thawrah*, Sana'a, 17 January 1982.

85. *Forbes*, 22 February 1988.

86. Yemen Hunt Oil Company, *In an Era of Great Accomplishments*, p. 7.

87. Author's interview with Meurer.

88. *World Oil*, April 1988, p. 33.

89. These names were taken from Arabic letters that head several chapters of the Holy Koran.

90. *World Oil*, April 1988, p. 33.

91. Author's interview with Ambassador Rugh.

92. The fourth of July is the American National Day of Independence.

93. *World Oil*, April 1988, p. 33.

94. Ibid.

95. *Al-Thawrah*, Sana'a, 26 September 1985.

96. *Oil and Gas Investor*, March 1988.

97. Yemen Hunt Oil, *In an Era of Great Accomplishments*, p. 12.

98. Ibid.

99. *World Oil*, April 1988, p. 36.

100. *Washington Post*, 11 December 1987.

101. *Financial Times*, London, 27 November 1987.

102. Author's interview with Tom Meurer.

103. Ibid.

104. Author's interview with Marjorie Ann Ransom, former US cultural attaché in the YAR, Washington, DC, 8 February 1990. In early 1990 she was USIA Yemen desk officer and executive assistant to the counsellor, US Information Agency.

105. Ibid.

106. Quoting Assistant Secretary of State John Kelly in a press conference, Washington, DC, 24 January 1990.

107. As mentioned by a Yemeni official to this author who talked on condition of anonymity. He also mentioned that an official letter was sent to the Yemeni government expressing the same views.

108. Yemeni sources who insisted upon anonymity, Sana'a, 1988.

109. Katz, 'The Saudis, Again, are the Bullies on the Block'.

110. Ibid. Katz referred to reports from the area that talked about a Saudi invasion of South Yemeni villages following the 1986 events in Aden, and Saudi support to Dhofaris against the Sultan of Oman, ibid.

111. *Financial Times*, London, 18 December 1985 and 1 May 1986.

112. Ibid.

113. *International Herald Tribune*, 25 December 1985.

114. According to the American Embassy in Sana'a, by this time there were 171 American employees of US government agencies working in the YAR: the embassy

staff, the AID mission, the Office of Military Cooperation, the Defence Attaché Office, the Marine Security Detachment, the US Information Service and others, See Embassy telegram to the Secretary of State, No. R 290452Z, March 1986.

115. USIS, *Arrival Statement of Vice-President George Bush*, Sana'a, 10 April 1986.

116. USIS, *Excerpts from Remarks by Vice-President George Bush at Dinner Hosted by Vice President al-'Arashi*, Sana'a, 10 April 1986.

117. *Al-Thawrah*, Sana'a, 11 April 1986.

118. USIA, *Press Conference Statement by Vice-President George Bush*, Sana'a, 11 April 1986.

119. See US Embassy telegram to the State Department, No. O 160746Z, April 1986.

120. US Embassy telegram to the State Department, 'transcript of Bush Remarks at Embassy groundbreaking ceremony', No. O 111024Z, April 1986.

121. *Al-Thawrah*, Sana'a, 10–13 April 1986.

122. *Al-Thawrah*, Sana'a, 10 April 1986.

123. *International Herald Tribune*, 20 May 1986; *al-Nahar*, Beirut, 19 May 1986.

124. See various reports in *al-Rai al-'Aam*, Kuwait, April 1986.

125. *ME/8228/A/10*, 9 April 1986.

126. *ME/8232/A/5*, 14 April 1986.

127. *FBIS*, 5 May 1986.

128. *ME/8233/A/5*, 15 April 1986.

129. Preferred not to be mentioned by name.

130. Author's interview with YAR Foreign Minister Dr 'Abdul-Karim al-Iryani, Sana'a, 19 September 1988.

131. Author's interview with David Ransom.

132. Dobert, 'Development of Aid Programs to Yemen', p. 109.

133. Marjorie Ransom said that her country was no longer interested in 'putting so much money in big projects abroad; we are interested more in training people, a road is good, but to train people to build a road is much better'.

134. Author's interview with Dr al-Iryani.

135. Ibid.

136. *US AID Annual Report*, Sana'a, 1988.

137. Author's interview with Marjorie Ransom.

138. Dobert, 'Development of Aid Programs to Yemen', p. 112.

139. *USIS Bulletin*, Sana'a, 10–12 April 1986.

140. Author's interview with Ambassador al-'Aini.

141. *USAID Presentation to Congress*, 'YAR', 1985.

142. Ibid.

143. Barakat, *Masadir Tamwil Khutat al-Tanmiyah*, pp. 798–9.

144. Author's interview with Dr al-Iryani.

145. *USAID Congressional Presentation 1991*.

146. *USIS Bulletin*, 11 April 1986.

147. Ibid.

148. *USIS Bulletin*, 25 January 1990.

149. Ibid.

150. *Business America*, 16 July 1979, p. 16.

151. CPO, *Loans and Assistance Annual Report*, Sana'a, 1988.

152. *Financial Times*, London, 18 December 1985 and 1 May 1986.

153. Ibid.

154. *US Federal News Service*, 24 January 1990.

155. *USIS Bulletin*, 25 January 1990.
156. Ibid.

5. The US and unified Yemen

1. The leadership of newly united Yemen agreed on a thirty-month period, during which they would prepare for free parliamentary elections to be held in the country before 21 November 1992. They called this time the transitional period. This interval was extended 184 days; the leadership promised to hold elections on 27 April 1993. On the background of unification, see Dunbar, 'The Unification of Yemen: Process, Politics, and Prospects'; Halliday, *Revolution and Foreign Policy: The Case of South Yemen, 1967–1987*; Burrowes, 'Oil Strike and Leadership Struggle in South Yemen: 1986 and Beyond'; Gause, 'Yemeni Unity: Past, Present and Future' and 'The Idea of Yemeni Unity'; Katz, 'Yemeni Unity and Saudi Security'. Among the numerous sources on the common background and politics are Bidwell, *The Two Yemens*; Halliday, *Arabia Without Sultans*; and Peterson, 'Nation-Building and Political Development in the Two Yemens', in B.R. Pridham (ed.), *Contemporary Yemen: Politics and Historical Background*. The main studies of South Yemeni politics are Lackner, *P.D.R. Yemen: Outposts of Socialist Development in Arabia*; Ismael, *P.D.R. Yemen: Politics, Economics, and Society*; and Stookey, *South Yemen: A Marxist Republic in Arabia*.

2. The KSA, which in 1947 had signed a defence agreement with the US, requested US help.

3. According to Dr al-Iryani in a lecture at the Royal Institute for International Affairs, London, January 1991.

4. A recent documentary report by the British Thames Television revealed that Brigadier Fahd Ahmad al-Fahd, the head of Kuwait's intelligence security services had 'agreed at a meeting in Washington with William Webster, the US CIA director, in October 1989 that it was important to take advantage of the deteriorating economic situation in Iraq in order to put pressure on that country's government to delineate the two countries common borders'. See *Guardian*, London, 4 April 1991.

5. Ambassador Arthur Hughes, *USIS*, Washington, 11 September 1991.

6. Ambassador David Mack delivered the opening statement in Arabic, Sana'a television.

7. *New York Times*, 5 June 1992.

8. *Al-Thawrah*, 17 July 1992.

9. On his return to Sana'a.

10. On 28 October 1992, a Yemeni delegation arrived in Riyadh to participate in the second ROY–KSA preparatory meeting on the border issue. ROY Minister of State of Foreign Affairs Abdul-'Aziz al-Dali met KSA Foreign Minister Sa'ud al-Faisal in New York just a few days before the Riyadh meeting. It was the first meeting at this level since the Kuwaiti crisis.

11. The exploration for oil in Yemen began in 1938 when the governor of Aden granted the Iraqi Petroleum Company (IPC) an oil concession to cover the southern governorates of Yemen; in 1953 the West German Deilmann Bergban signed an agreement to explore north Hudeidah. He pointed out that several Western companies had terminated their explorations at the following areas: Pahoc/Pamoc, North Hadramaut, 1967; Syapco, South Sanau, 1976; Siebens, Socotra, 1980; Technoexport, North Sanau, 1984; Agip, Alghayda-Sayhut, 1985; IPG, Balhaf, 1987;

Braspetro, Hoowarin-Ghayda, 1987; Hunt, Hudeidah (offshore), 1988; Yepco, Belhaf, 1988; Total/Texaco, al-Mukalla, 1990; Elf, Aden-Abyan, 1989; Texaco, Central Plateau, 1990; BP, Tihama, 1990. 'Abdul-Sattar O. Nani, 'Activities of Oil Exploration and Production Board', unpublished report, Ministry of Oil and Mineral Resources, Sana'a, 1993.

12. *Al-Naba'*, 20 August 1992.

13. The development of gas needs an investment of approximately $US10 billion, which only a giant company can provide, according to the Yemeni armed forces weekly newspaper, *26 September*, 25 November 1993. It expected that Yemen's annual income from such an investment would reach $1.3 billion beginning of 1994.

14. *Al-Hayat*, London, 26 November 1993.

15. Yemen's Oil Exploration Board sources, November 1993.

16. American Occidental owns 30 per cent of the company's shares. Personal communication, David Warburton.

17. Other US businesses are NCR Corporation Sell computers, Sheraton, Touche Ross, Bank of America (a partner and manager of International Bank of Yemen), Frank B. Hall (owns 10 per cent of United Insurance Company), and Sana'a International School.

18. Author's interview with 'Uthman Ahmad 'Uthman, deputy chairman of ROY Corporation for Oil Exploration, Sana'a, 26 May 1992.

19. It is important to note that oil had given both the ex-PDRY and YAR an important reason to unite.

20. *Al-Sharq al-Awsat*, London, 31 December 1991.

21. *USIS*, 11 September 1991.

22. Yemeni opposition sources claimed that the Bush administration had advised Sana'a not to proceed with radical democratic change in the Yemeni arena that would shake the stability of the neighbouring kingdom and that Sana'a should not oppose Iraq, in order to prevent the national element in the country from taking over.

23. American media coverage was limited to a few stories by Nora Bustani of the *Washington Post*, Dean Fisher of *Time*, and the *Voice of America*, plus a *New York Times* editorial praising Salih's proposal for a US-style presidency. On the other hand, the BBC, Japanese newspapers, *Frankfurter Allgemeine*, and the *Financial Times* ran series' and profiles. Even the *Jerusalem Post*, according to *Mideast Mirror*, 13 May 1993, enthused that: 'The Yemeni elections, not the Madrid process, will be viewed by history as the turning point on the road to Arab–Israeli peace.'

24. USIA/ Sana'a, unclassified cable.

25. Remarks at the American Institute for Yemeni Studies, 21 April 1993.

26. The author's interview, published in *Yemen Times*, 16 May 1993, p.16

27. Iris Glosemeyer, 'The First Yemeni Parliamentary Elections in 1993: Practising Democracy', Sana'a, August 1993, p. 11.

28. Carapico, 'Elections and Mass Politics in Yemen'; al-Madhagi, 'Min Adjli Aliyyah Muhayidah lil-Rikabah 'ala al-Intikhabat: Wudjhat Nazar', Sana'a, April 1993.

29. Eric Watkins, *Financial Times*, London, April 1993.

30. Interview, *Yemen Times*, 16 May 1993, p. 16; see also Carapico, 'Elections and Mass Politics'.

31. Ambassador Hughes' remarks at YAFA Symposium. In the meantime, university professors and lawyers organizing a Saudi Organization for Sharia Rights were arrested for crimes including smuggling of tapes of Yemeni political campaigns

and parliamentary debates. See 'Abd al-Amir Mousa, 'Lijnat al-Difa' 'an al-Hukuk al-Shar'iyah. Keif kamat wa il yn Taseer?' *Al-Djazeera al-Arabia* (sic) no. 29, 1993, pp. 8–9, and other articles in the same journal devoted to the committee and the issue of Sharia rights in Saudi Arabia.
32. *Al-Thawra*, 13 August 1993, p. 1.
33. Speech at Sana'a University.
34. *Yemen Times*, 19 September 1993, p. 2.
35. *Al-Hayat*, 21 November 1993, *Al-Thawra*, 23 November 1993.
36. Pelletereau remarks in Kuwait on 11 May 1994, *USIS*.
37. In an interview with Al-Sharq Al-Awsat, London, October 1994.

Conclusion

1. Author's interview with USSR ambassador in 1988, Viniamin Popov, Sana'a, 21 September 1988.
2. Author's interview with Ambassador al-'Aini.
3. US Department of Defense, *Area Handbook: The Yemen Country Studies*.
4. Author's interview with Ambassador al-'Aini.
5. Author's interview with Ambassador Lane.
6. Ibid.
7. *USAID Presentations to Congress 1982–1986*.
8. Ibid.
9. Author's interview with Marjorie Ransom.
10. Author's interview with Ambassador al-'Aini.
11. Sana'a, 19 September 1988.
12. Author's interview with the deputy prime minister and chairman of the YARCPO, Dr M.S. al-'Attar, Sana'a, 6 September 1988.
13. According to the minutes of the meeting held in Sana'a, 23 November 1990 between Baker and Salih.
14. Ironically, James Baker's law firm later advised Yemen in its border negotiations with Saudi Arabia – advised by Henry Kissinger and associates.
15. Cited in Fu'ad Ibrahim, 'Risalat al-Intikhabat al-Yamaniyah 'ala al-Mamlakah', *Al-Djazirah al-'Arabia*, p. 23, citing Salih's 4 May 1993 interview with *al-Khalidj*.
16. Ibid.
17. *Al-Watan*, Kuwait, 15 October 1992; *Yemen Times*, Sana'a, 24 October 1993.
18. Author's interview with Ambassador Lane.
19. For more details see Nadji, *al-Tarikh al-'Askari li al-Yaman 1939–1967*.
20. Photocopy of statement obtained from the US Embassy, Sana'a.
21. On economic conditions, see International Monetary Fund, 'Republic of Yemen 1993 Article IV Consultation', Sana'a: 18 September 1993.
22. In the words of Manfred Wenner in a commentary letter to me on the first draft of this book, May 1990.

Bibliography

Unpublished material

Boals, Kathryn, *Modernization and Intervention: Yemen as a Theoretical Case Study*, Ph.D. thesis, Princeton University, 1970.

Burrowes, Robert, 'The Other Side of the Red Sea and Little More: the Horn of Africa and the Two Yemens', 1990.

Al-Hilw, M.I., *al-Siyasah al-Kharidjiyah al-Yamaniyah fi al-'Ahd al-Djumhuri*, Ph.D. thesis, King Saud University, Riyadh, 1985.

John F. Kennedy Library's oral history interviews with: US ambassador in the KSA and minister to the Yemen in 1962, Parker T. Hart; US ambassador to the UAR in 1962, John Badeau; Chester L. Cooper, a liaison officer to National Security Staff from the CIA 1961–62; George McGhee, US under-secretary for political affairs in 1962.

McClintock, David William, *Foreign Exposure and Attitudinal Change: A Case Study of Foreign Policy Makers in the YAR*, Ph.D. thesis, University of Michigan, 1973.

Minutes of Talks between President Saleh and US Secretary of State James Baker, 24 January 1991, Presidential Archive, Sana'a, Republic of Yemen; Minutes of Yemeni Leadership's talks with President Saddam Hussein 1991–92, Presidential Archive, Sana'a, Republic of Yemen.

National Security Files: correspondence between the US Department of State and US embassies in the YAR, KSA and the UAR released to the author under the US Freedom of Information Act for the period 1962–90.

Petro Finance Market Intelligence Service, *Yemen: Border Disputes and Relations with Saudi Arabia*, Washington, DC, May 1992.

UKFCO Records on North Yemen–US contacts 1902–57.

US Embassy/Ta'iz Study, 17 April 1965.

Washington Yemen Legation Statements, Washington Middle East Institute's files on Yemen.

White House Central File, Box no. 6, J.F. Kennedy Library, CO 320 Yemen.

White House Central File, Box no. 5032.

'Yemen': an administrative history prepared by the US Department of State for the White House at the close of the Johnson administration, LBJ Library.

Yemen Ministry of Interior Statements, Sana'a, 1992–1993.

YOMINCO, *The Geological Activities in North Yemen Since 1912* (compiled by Isma'il Musa), Sana'a, 1982.

Al-Zindani, Mansour, *Yemen Relations with the Two Superpowers*, Ph.D. thesis, University of Cairo, 1988.

Official publications

Yemen

Central Bank Annual Report, 1972–1990.
Central Planning Organization, Statistical Yearbook 1981–1990.
— Loans and Assistance Annual Report 1975–1990.
Ministry of Information, Speeches and Interviews of President Saleh, 1978–1986; al-'id al-Fiddi li al-Thawrah al-Yamaniyah, 1988.
— The Yemeni Revolution 3rd Year, Cairo, 1965.

Other Yemeni publications

Isma'il, 'Abdul-Fattah, The Political Report, Unification Congress (11–13 October 1975), Aden, 1975.
Yemen Hunt Oil Company, In an Era of Great Accomplishments, 1987.

United States

American Council of Voluntary Agencies for Foreign Service, Development Assistance Programs of US-Non-Profit Organizations, Yemen, February 1980.
Department of Commerce, Bureau of Foreign Commerce, Basic Data on the Economy of Yemen, no. 60–2, part 1, January 1960.
Department of Defense, Area Handbook: The Yemen's Country Studies, Washington, DC, 1986.
Department of State, Treaties and Other International Agreements of the United States of America 1776–1949, vol. 12, no. 1235.
Department of State, Treaties and Other International Acts Series 1535, 4286, 4346 and 4413, 1949–59.
Department of State, Bureau of Public Affairs, Gist, April 1979.
Department of State Bulletin, 1950–1990.
Documents on American Foreign Relations, vols 9 and 13, 1946–47.
Foreign Relations of the United States 1955–1957, vol. 13, Washington, DC, 1988.
Proposed Arms Transfers to the YAR, Hearing Before the Subcommittee of Europe and the Middle East of the Committee on Foreign Affairs of the House of Representatives, 96th Congress, 1st Session, 12 March 1977, Washington, DC, 1979.
Proposed Expansion of US Military Facilities in the Indian Ocean, Hearings before the Subcommittee on the Near East and South Asia of the Committee on Foreign Affairs, House of Representatives, Ninety-Third Congress, Second Session, 21 February; 6, 12, 20 March 1974, Washington, DC, 1974.
Public Papers of the Presidents, Jimmy Carter, vol. II, 1978.
Al-Rashid, Ibrahim (ed.), Yemen Under the Rule of Imam Ahmad, Chapel Hill, NC, 1985.
Sana'a US Commercial Office Bulletin, Sana'a, May 1988.
Sinclair, Reginald W. (ed.), US Documents on the History of South West Arabia: Tribal Warfare and Foreign Policy in Yemen, Aden and Adjacent Kingdoms 1920–1949, vols I and II, Salisbury, NC, 1976.
United States Arms Policies in the Persian Gulf and Red Sea: Past, Present, and Future, Report of the American Staff Survey Mission to Ethiopia, Iran and the Arabian Peninsula, 85th Congress, 1st Session, December 1977.

United States, *Papers Relating to the Foreign Relations of the United States, 1927* (3 vols), Washington, DC, 1942.
USAID Congressional Presentations, 1957–90.
US Arms Control and Disarmament Agency, *World Military Expenditures and Arms Transfers* (series 1971–86), Washington, DC, 1983.
USA–YAR Cooperation for Development, USAID Office, Sana'a, 1987.
US Census of Population, 1980.
US Congress, Senate, Committee on Foreign Relations, *Fiscal Year 1980 International Security Assistance Authorization, State Department Briefing on the Situation in Yemen*, 96th Congress, 1st Session, 1980.
US Congress, Senate, Committee on Foreign Relations, *US Security Interests and Policies in South West Asia*, 96TH Congress, 1st Session, 1980.
US Congressional Record, Senate Records, vol. 109, part 10.
US Embassy in the YAR, *USIS Bulletin*, 1979–86.
US Peace Corps Report on Yemen, 1986.
Weekly Compilation of Presidential Documents, 27 June 1966.

Saudi Arabia

Foreign Ministry, *Saudi–Imam Yahya Relations (The Green Book)*, Mecca, 1934.

United Kingdom

British and Foreign State Papers 1934, vol. 137.
Great Britain Parliamentary Papers, 1934, No. 34 Cmd, 4 July 1952.
House of Commons, Parliamentary Debates, vol. 666, 31 October 1962.
Trevaskis, KCMG, OBE, Sir Kennedy, *The Future of Arabia*, London, 1966.

United Nations

United Nations Official Records of the Second Session of the General Assembly, Plenary Meetings of the General Assembly, verbatim record, vol. I, 80th-109th Meetings, 16 September to 13 November 1947.
United Nations General Assembly, Seventeenth Session, Official Record, 1962.
United Nations Development Program, *Background Paper for a Country Program for the Yemen Arab Republic*, Sana'a, March 1973.
UN Document No. S15650 Concerning Conflict in Yemen, 9 April 1964.
UN Yearbook 1963, New York, 1965.

Others

International Bank for Reconstruction and Development, *Yemen Arab republic, Development of Trade and Economy*, Washington, DC, January 1979.
Lloyds Bank Group, Economic Reports, *Yemen Arab Republic*, London, 17 February 1986.
National Westminster Bank, *Yemen Arab Republic*, London, September 1985.
World Bank, *Yemen Arab Republic: Development Traditional Economy*, Washington, DC, 1979.
World Bank, *YAR: Current Position and Prospects*, Washington, DC, June 1985.

Author's interviews

Al-Ahmar, 'Abd-Alla Bin Hussein, Paramount Sheikh of Hashid Tribal Confederation, Sana'a, 1983.

Al-'Aini, Muhsin Ahmad, YAR ambassador in Washington 1990 and ex-prime minister and foreign minister, Sana'a, 13 July 1988 and Washington, DC, 7 February 1990.

Al-Akwa', Muhammad 'Ali, military leader of the 1967 '5 November Movement', Sana'a, September 1987 and September 1988.

Al-Ashtal, 'Abd-Alla, PDRY ambassador to the UN and chairman of the UN Security Council in February and March 1990, New York, 5 February 1990.

Al-'Attar, M.S., YAR deputy prime minister, minister of development and chairman of central planning organization in 1988, Sana'a, 6 September 1988.

Burrowes, Robert, author of the *Yemen Arab Republic: the Politics of Development 1962–1986*, Washington and London, February and May 1990.

Carapico, Sheila, president of American Institute for Yemeni Studies, Richmond, VA, February 1990.

Al-Iryani, 'Abdul-Karim, YAR deputy prime minister and foreign minister 1983–90, Sana'a, 19 September 1988.

Lane, George, US ambassador to the YAR 1978–81, Worcester, MA, 16 February 1990.

Al-Malazi, Mou'djib, London, 8 November 1989.

Popov, Vinyamin V., USSR ambassador in the YAR in 1988, Sana'a, 21 September 1988.

Ransom, David, ex-American deputy head of mission in the YAR and director of the Arabian Peninsula Affairs Bureau in the US State Department in January 1990, Washington, DC, 8 February 1990.

Ransom, Marjorie, former US cultural attaché in the YAR, Washington, DC, 8 February 1990.

Rugh, William, US ambassador to the YAR 1983–87, Washington, DC, 9 February 1990.

Sabrah, 'Abdul-Salam, former deputy prime minister and one of the main organizers of the 26 September 1962 revolution, Sana'a, 4 September 1988.

Sallam, Muhammad 'Abdul-'Aziz, YAR ambassador in the UN in 1990 and foreign minister in 1967, New York, 20 February 1990.

Seelye, Talcott, director of Arabian Peninsula Affairs in 1962, Washington, DC, 19 February 1990.

Seif, Muhammad Kaid, deputy leader of the Ta'iz 1955 coup in the MKOY and member of the first YAR Revolutionary Commanding Council, Sana'a, September 1988.

Al-Shami, A.M., former member of the YAR Presidential Council 1970–74, and former foreign minister of the Yemeni royalists 1962–67, Sana'a, July 1983.

Stoltzfus, William, the US second chargé d'affaires in the MKOY, London, 1 June 1990.

Stookey, Robert, US chargé d'affaires in Ta'iz during the first few months of the YAR, Austin, TX, 30 January 1990.

Al-Sukkari, 'Abdul-Karim, YAR defence minister 1967–68, Sana'a, 1988.

Al-Sukkari, Hussein, the officer who attempted to kill the imam on the eve of 26 September 1962, Sana'a, 1988.

Tarsisi, 'Adnan, former personal secretary of Prince Abd-Allah, KOY ambassador to the world and the UN, Geneva/London, 14 March 1989.
Wolters, Curt C.F., USAID deputy program officer in the YAR, Sana'a, July 1988.

Books in English

Abir, Mordechai, *Oil, Power and Politics: Conflict in Arabia, the Red Sea and the Gulf*, London, 1974.
Ambrose, Stephen E., *Rise to Globalism: American Foreign Policy Since 1938*, New York, 1985.
Antony, John Duke, *The States of the Arabian Peninsula and Gulf Littoral: A Select Annotated Bibliography*, Washington, DC, 1973.
Aron, Raymond, *The Imperial Republic, the United States and the World 1945–1973*, New Jersey, 1974.
Badeau, John, *East and West of Suez, the Story of the Modern Near East*, New York, 1943.
— *The American Approach Towards the Arab World*, London, 1968.
— *The Middle East Remembered*, Washington, DC, 1983.
Badeeb, Said M., *The Saudi–Egyptian Conflict Over North Yemen 1962–1970*, Washington, DC, 1986.
Be'eri, Eleizer, *Army Officers in Arab Politics and Society*, New York, 1970.
Bell, J., *South Arabia Violence and Revolt, Conflict Studies*, London, 1973.
Bethman, Erich, *Yemen on the Threshold*, Washington, DC, 1966.
Bidwell, Robin, *The Two Yemens*, Boulder, CO, 1983.
Burrowes, Robert, *The Yemen Arab Republic: The Politics of Development 1962–1986*, Boulder, CO, 1987.
Bury, G. Wyman, *Arabia Infelix*, London, 1915.
Coon, Carleton, *Measuring Ethiopia and Flights into Arabia*, Boston, MA, 1935.
Cortada, James N., *The Yemen Crisis*, Los Angeles, 1965.
Dawisha, Adeed, *Saudi Arabia's Search for Security*, London, 1979.
Dequin, H.F.E., *The Challenge of Saudi Arabia*, Hamburg, 1976.
Douglas, J. Leigh, *The Free Yemeni Movement 1935–1962*, Beirut, 1987.
Fisher, S. N., *The Middle East: A History*, London, 1960.
Findlay, Paul, *They Dare to Speak Out*, Chicago, 1989.
Gaddis, John Lewis, *Strategies of Containment: A Critical Appraisal of Postwar American National Security Policy*, New York, 1982.
Garthoff, Raymond L., *Detente and Confrontation: American–Soviet Relations from Nixon to Reagan*, Washington, DC, 1985.
Gause, Gregory, *Saudi–Yemeni Relations, Domestic Structures and Foreign Influences*, New York, 1990.
George, Alexander L. (ed.), *Managing U.S.–Soviet Rivalry: Problems of Crisis Prevention*, Boulder, CO, 1983.
Grayson, Benson Lee, *Saudi–American Relations*, Washington, DC, 1982.
Halliday, Fred, *Arabia Without Sultans: A Survey of Political Instability in the Arab World*, New York, Vintage Books, 1975.
— *Threat from the East? Soviet Policy from Afghanistan and Iran to the Horn of Africa*, London, 1982.
— *Revolution and Foreign Policy: The Case of South Yemen 1967–1987*, Cambridge, 1990.

Heikal, M., *Nasser: the Cairo Documents*, London, 1971.
Helfritz, H., *The Yemen: A Secret Journey*, London, 1956.
Heyworth-Dunne, James, *al-Yaman: A General Social, Political and Economic Survey*, Cairo, 1952.
Hodgson, G., *In Our Time: America from World War II to Nixon*, London, 1977.
Hoffmann, Stanley, *Dead Ends: American Foreign Policy in the New Cold War*, Cambridge, MA, 1983.
— *Primacy or World Order: American Foreign Policy Since the Cold War*, New York, 1978.
Hofman, Michael, *Development Potential and Policies in the South Arabian Countries: YAR, PDRY, and Oman*, West Berlin, 1982.
— *The Importance of the Oil-Producing Countries of the Gulf*, West Berlin, 1984.
Holden, David, and Richard, Johns, *The House of Saud*, New York, 1980.
Hollingworth, Clare, *The Arabs and the West*, London, 1952.
Hosmer, Stephen T., and Wolfe, Thomas W., *Soviet Policy and Practice Toward Third World Conflicts*, Lexington, MA, 1983.
Hudson, Michael, *Arab Politics: The Search for Legitimacy*, New Haven, , 1977.
Hurewitz, J.D., *The Middle East*, New York, 1953.
— *Diplomacy in the Near and Middle East 1914–1956*, New York, 1956.
Ingrams, Harold, *The Yemen: Imams, Rulers and Revolution*, London, 1963.
Ismael, Tareq and Jacqueline, *P.D.R. Yemen: Politics, Economics, and Society*, London, 1986.
Johnson, C., *Superpower: Comparing American and Soviet Policy*, London, 1984.
Kay, Henry C., *Yemen*, London, 1968.
Kegley, Charles and Eugner, W.H., *American Foreign Policy: Pattern and Process*, London, 1987.
Kerr, Malcolm H., *The Arab Cold War: 1958–1964*, New York, 1965.
— and Yassin, el-Sayed (eds), *Rich and Poor States in the Middle East*, Boulder, CO, 1982.
Al-Khatib, M., *British Penetration and Imperialism in Yemen*, New York, 1958.
Kolko, Joyce and Gabriel, *The Limits of Power, the World and the United States Foreign Policy 1945–1954*, New York, 1972.
Korany, Bahgat and Ali Dessouki (eds), *The Foreign Policies of Arab States*, Boulder, CO, 1984.
Kostiner, Joseph, *The Struggle for South Yemen*, London, 1984.
Lackner, Helen, *P.D.R. Yemen: Outposts of Socialist Development in Arabia*, London, 1985.
Lenczowski, G., *The Middle East in World Affairs*, New York, 1980.
Link, Arthur S. and William B. Catton, *American Epoch*, vol. III, New York, 1974.
McCormick, M., *American Foreign Policy and American Values*, Itasca, IL, 1985.
McMullen, Christopher J., *Resolution of the Yemeni Crisis, 1963: A Case Study in Mediation*, Washington, DC, 1981.
Macro, Eric, *Bibliography of the Arabian Peninsula*, Coral Gables, 1958.
— *Yemen and the Western World Since 1571*, London, 1968.
Mahdjoub, M.A., *Democracy on Trial*, London, 1974.
Al-Mallah, Radjaei, *Yemen Arab Republic*, Worcester, 1986.
Mansfield, Peter, *The Arabs*, London, 1985.
Maurice, East (ed.), *Why Nations Act: Theoretical Perspectives for Comparative Foreign Policy Studies*, London, 1948.

Middle East Yearbook, London, 1979.

Mondesir, Simone L. (compiler), *The Yemens: A Select Bibliography*, NC, 1977.

Nadji, Sultan, *Selected and Annotated Bibliography on Yemen*, Kuwait, 1973.

Nakhleh, Emile, *The United States and Saudi Arabia: A Policy Analysis*, Washington, DC, 1975.

Novik, N., *Between Two Yemens: Regional Dynamics and Superpower Conducts in Riyadh's Backyard*, Tel-Aviv, 1980.

Nye, Joseph S. (ed.), *The Making of America's Soviet Policy*, New Haven, CT, 1984.

O'Ballance, Edgar, *The War In Yemen*, New York, 1975.

Page, Stephen, *The USSR and Arabia: The Development of Soviet Policies and Attitudes Towards the Countries of the Arabian Peninsula 1955–1970*, London, 1971.

— *The Soviet Union and the Yemens*, New York, 1985.

Peterson, J.E., *Conflict in the Yemens and Superpower Involvement*, Washington, DC, 1981.

— *Yemen: The Search for a Modern State*, Baltimore, MD, 1982.

— 'Nation-Building and Political Development in the Two Yemens', in B.R. Pridham (ed.), *Contemporary Yemen: Politics and Historical Background*, London, 1984.

— *Defending Arabia*, New York, 1986.

Philby, H. St. John, *Arabian Jubilee*, London, 1954.

— *Saudi Arabia*, London, 1955.

Pridham, B. (ed.), *Contemporary Yemen: Politics and Historical Background*, London, 1984.

— *Society and Culture in Contemporary Yemen*, London, 1985.

Raban, Jonathan, *Arabia: Through the Looking Glass*, London, 1979.

Al-Rashid, Ibrahim, *Yemen Enters the Modern World*, Chapel Hill, NC, 1985.

— *Yemen Under the Rule of Imam Ahmad*, Chapel Hill, NC, 1985.

Rehmy, 'Ali 'Abdul-Rehman, *The Egyptian Policy in the Arab World, Intervention in Yemen 1962–1967: A Case Study*, Washington, DC, 1983.

Reilly, Sir Bernard, *Aden and the Yemen*, London, 1960.

Rihani, Amin, *Arabian Peak and Desert: Travels in al-Yamen*, Boston, MA, 1930.

Rosenau, James (ed.), *The Scientific Study of Foreign Policy*, New York, 1971.

Safran, Nadav, *Saudi Arabia: The Ceaseless Quest for Security*, London, 1985.

Sanger, Richard H., *The Arabian Peninsula*, New York, 1954.

Schmidt, Dana Adams, *Yemen: The Unknown War*, New York, 1968.

Al-Shoureki, Ibrahim, *The Bloody Strife in Yemen*, Tehran, 1965.

Sinclair, Reginald (ed.), *US Documents in the History of South West Arabia: Tribal Warfare and Foreign Policy of Yemen, Aden and Adjacent Tribal Kingdoms 1920–1927*, Salisbury, NC, 1976.

Smith, G. Rex (compiler) *The Yemens*, California, 1984 (monograph).

Sorensen, Theodore, *Kennedy*, New York, 1965.

Spanier, John, *American Foreign Policy Since World War II*, New York, 1985.

Stookey, Robert, *America and the Arab States: An Uneasy Encounter*, New York, 1978.

— *Yemen: The Politics of the Yemen Arab Republic*, Boulder, CO, 1978.

— *South Yemen, a Marxist Republic in Arabia*, Boulder, CO, 1982.

— (ed.), *Arabian Peninsula, Zone of Ferment*, California, 1984.

Sullivan, Michael, *International Relations Theories and Evidence*, New Jersey, 1976.

Thomas, Bertram, *Arabia Felix*, New York, 1932.

Trihon, Arthur S., *Rise of the Imams of Sana'a*, London, 1925.
Twitchell, Karl, *Saudi Arabia*, Princeton, NJ, 1958.
Wenner, Manfred, *Modern Yemen 1918–1966*, Baltimore, MD, 1968.
Williams, W.A., *America and the Middle East: Open Policy. Imperialism or Enlightened Leadership?*, New York, 1968.
— *The Tragedy of American Diplomacy*, Cleveland, OH, 1971.
Yemen: 3000 Years of Art and Civilization in Arabia Felix, Frankfurt, 1988.
Yodfat, Aryeh, *The Soviet Union and the Arabian Peninsula*, London, 1983.
Zabarah, Muhammad, *Yemen, Traditional Versus Modernity*, New York, 1982.
Al-Zindani, 'Abdul-Wahid, *Arab Politics in the United Nations*, New Delhi, 1977.

Books in Arabic

'Abd-Allah, *Memoirs*, Beirut, 1987.
'Afif, Ahmad Djabir, *al-Harakah al-Wataniyah fi al-Yaman*, Damascus, 1982.
Ahmad, Yusuf Ahmad, *Al-Dawr al-Misri fil Yaman*, Cairo, 1981.
Al-Baidani, A., *Azmat al-Ummah al-'Arabiyah wa Thawrat al-Yaman*, Cairo, 1984.
Al-'Azm, Nazih, *Rihlah fi Bilad al-'Arabiah al-Sai'dah*, Cairo, n.d.
Al-Baradduni, A., *al-Yaman al-Djumhuri*, Damascus, 1983.
Barakat, A., *Masadir Tamwil Khutat al-Tanmiyah al-Idjtima'iyyah wa al-Iktisadiyyah fi al-Djumhuriyyah al-'Arabiyyah al-Yamaniyyah*, Damascus, 1981.
Al-Djurafi, A., *al-Muktataf min Tarikh al-Yaman*, Cairo, 1951.
Djuzeilan, A., *Al-Tarikh al-Sirri li al-Thawrah al-Yamaniyah 1956–1962*, Beirut, 1986.
Fakhri, A., *al-Yaman: Madiha wa Mustakbaluha*, Sana'a, 1988.
Fawzi, M., *Harb al-Thalath Sanawat: Mudhakkirat*, Beirut, 1983.
Ghaleb, M.A., *Nizam al-Hukm wa al-Takhalluf al-Iktisadi fi al-Yaman*, Cairo, 1962.
Gulobofskaya, Elina, *Thawrat September* (trans. M. Tarboosh), Beirut, 1972.
Al-Haddad, M., *Tarikh al-Yaman al-Siyasi*, Cairo, 1968.
Hamroosh, A., *Kissat Thalatha wa-'Ishreen Yuliu: Abdul-Nasser wa al-'Arab*, Cairo, 1983.
Al-Haysani, Khadidjah, *al-'Alakat al-Yamaniyyah al-Sa'udiyyah*, Cairo, 1983.
Heikal, M., *Abdul-Nasser wa al-'Alam*, Beirut, 1972.
Heikal, M., *Sanawat al-Ghalayan*, Cairo, 1988.
Nadji, Sultan, *al-Tarikh al-'Askari li al-Yaman 1939–1962*, Beirut, 1985.
Numan, M., *al-Atraf al-Ma'niyah*, Aden, 1965.
Sai'd, Amin, *al-Yaman: Tarikhuhu al-Siyasi mundhu Istiklalihi fe al-Karn al-Thaleth al-Hidjri*, Cairo, 1959.
Salem, Sayyid Mustafa, *Takwin al-Yaman al-Hadith*, Cairo, 1984.
Salem, Sayyid, *Wathaik Yamaniyah*, Cairo, 1982.
Al-Shamahi, 'Abd-Allah, *al-Yaman: al-Hadarah wa al-Insan*, Sana'a, 1972.
Al-Shami, A., *Ahmad Hamid al-Din*, Beirut, 1965.
Al-Shuhari, M., *Abdul-Nasser wa Thawrat al-Yaman*, Cairo, 1967.
Al-Thawr, A.A., *Thawrat al-Yaman 1948–1968*, Cairo, 1974.
Qasimiyyah, Kheiriyyah et al., *Al-Siyasah al-Amrikiyyah wal-'Arab*, Beirut, 1982.
'Umar, Sultan Ahmad, *Nazrah fi Tatawwur al-Mudjtama' al-Yamani*, Beirut, 1970.
Al-Wazir, Zeid, *Muhawalat li Fahm al-Mushkilah al-Yamaniyah*, Beirut, 1971.
Al-Zubayri, M., *al-Imamah wa-Khataruha 'Ala Wahdat al-Yaman*, Aden, n.d.

Articles

Al-Azhari, M., 'Aspects of North Yemen Relations with Saudi Arabia', *American Affairs*, vol. 15, no. 3, 1984, pp. 277–86.

Badeau, John S., 'U.S.A. and U.A.R.', *Foreign Affairs*, no. 43, January 1965, pp. 221–46.

Baldry, J., 'Anglo-Italian Rivalry in Yemen and 'Asir', *Die Welt des Islams*, vol. 17, no. 1, pp. 156–96.

Bissel, Richard, 'Soviet Use of Proxies in the Third World: The Case of Yemen', *Soviet Studies*, vol. 30, no. 1, 1978, pp. 87–106.

Brecher, H., 'Charles R. Crane's Crusade for the Arabs 1919– 1939', *Middle East Studies*, January 1988, pp. 42–55.

Brown, William R., 'The Yemeni Dilemma', *Middle East Journal*, Autumn 1963, pp. 349–67.

Burrowes, Robert D., 'Oil Strike and Leadership Struggle in South Yemen: 1986 and Beyond', *Middle East Journal*, vol. 43, no. 3, Summer 1989, pp. 437–53.

Burrowes, R., 'The Yemen Arab Republic and the Ali Abdalla Salih Regime', *Middle East Journal*, vol. 39, no. 4, Autumn 1985, pp. 775–95.

Carapico, Sheila, 'Elections and Mass Politics in Yemen', *Middle East Report*, no. 185, November 1993.

Cook, James, 'Yemen Felix Redux', *Forbes*, 22 February 1988.

Coon, Carleton S., 'Southern Arabia a Problem for the Future', *Moslem World*, no. 37, April 1947, pp. 155–6.

Crane, Charles R., 'A Visit to the Red Sea Littoral and the Yemen', *Journal of the Royal Central Asian Society*, vol. 15, January 1928, pp. 42–67.

Dawisha, A., 'Intervention in Yemen: An Analysis of Egyptian Perceptions and Policies', *Middle East Journal*, vol. 29, Winter 1975, pp. 47–63.

Dobert, Margarita, 'Development of Aid Programs to Yemen', *American Arab Affairs*, no. 8, Spring 1984, pp. 108–16.

Dunbar, Charles, 'The Unification of Yemen: Process, Politics, and Prospects', *Middle East Journal*, vol. 46, no. 3, Summer 1992, pp. 456–76.

Friedlander, Jonathan (ed.), *Sojourners and Settlers*, California, 1988.

Gause, Gregory, 'Yemeni Unity: Past, Present and Future', *Middle East Journal*, vol. 42, no. 1, Winter 1988, pp. 33–47.

— 'The Idea of Yemeni Unity', *Journal of Arab Affairs*, vol. 6, no. 1, Spring 1987, pp. 55–81.

Gazit, M., 'President Kennedy's Policy Toward the Arab States and Israel', *Journal of Palestinian Studies*, vol. 15, no. 1, 1985, pp. 150–1.

Grimaldi, F., 'Yemen Without Hamdi: No Change Expected', *The Middle East*, no. 15, pp. 10–11, 15.

Halliday, Fred, 'Counter Revolution in the Yemen', *New Left Review*, no. 63, 1973, pp. 3–25.

— 'Yemen the Unfinished Revolution: Socialism in the South', *MERIP*, no. 81, October 1979.

— 'Russians Help to Defeat Left-wing Guerrillas', *Guardian*, 3 May 1984.

— 'The Yemens: Conflict and Coexistence', *The World Today*, August–September 1984, pp. 355–6.

— 'The Arabian Peninsula Opposition Movement,' *MERIP*, no. 130, February 1985, pp. 133–9.

— 'The Contest for Arabia', *MERIP*, vol. 15, no. 2, 1 February 1985.

— 'North Yemen Today', *MERIP*, no. 13, February 1985, pp. 3–9.

Heymann, Hans, 'American Aid to the Middle East', *Fortnightly Review*, February 1984, pp. 96–101.

Hoogstral, Harry and Robert E. Kuntz, 'Yemen Opens the Door to Progress', *National Geographic Magazine*, vol. 101, February 1952.

Horton, Philip, 'Our Yemen Policy: Pursuit of a Mirage', *Reporter*, 28 October 1963, pp. 28–35.

Hoskins, H., 'Background of British Position in Arabia', *Middle East Journal*, vol. 1, no. 2, April 1947, p. 137.

Ibrahim, Fu'ad, 'Risalat al-Intikhabat al-Yamaniyah 'ala al-Mamlakah', *Al-Djazirah al'Arabia*, no. 29, June 1992, pp. 23–5.

Jenkins, Loven, 'North Yemen Between East and West', *Newsweek*, 24 March 1980, pp. 16–17.

Katz, Mark, 'Sana'a and the Soviets', *Problems of Communism*, vol. 33, January–February 1984, pp. 21–34.

— 'North Yemen Between East and West', *American Arab Affairs*, vol. 8, Spring 1984, pp. 99–107.

— 'Camels and Commissars', *The National Interest*, Winter 1988–89, pp. 121–4.

— 'The Saudis, Again, are the Bullies on the Block', *Wall Street Journal*, 9 October 1989.

— 'Yemeni Unity and Saudi Security', *Middle East Policy*, vol. 1, no. 1, 1992, pp. 117–35.

Kemp, Peter, 'Oil Breeds Confidence in Sana'a', *Middle East Economic Digest*, 19–25 September 1987, pp. 8–9.

Law, John, 'A Pawn in Nasser's Dream of Empire', *United States News and World Report*, vol. 54, 31 December 1962, pp. 44–9.

Liebesny, Herbert J., 'International Relations of Arabia: The Dependent Areas', *Middle East Journal*, vol. 1, April 1947, pp. 148–68.

Lynch, John, 'The Superpowers' Tug of War over Yemen', *Military Review*, vol. 61, no. 3, March 1981, pp. 10–21.

Malone, Joseph, 'America and the Arabian Peninsula: The First Two Hundred Years', *Middle East Journal*, vol. 30, Summer 1976.

Malone, Joseph, 'The Yemen Arab Republic's Game of Nations', *The World Today*, no. 27, 12 December 1971.

Mosher, Lawrence, 'Nasser's Drive for South Arabia', *The Reporter*, 9 February 1967, pp. 24–7.

Parlov, N., 'British Aggression in Yemen', *New Times*, vol. 2, 1950, pp. 15–16.

Peterson, J.E., 'The Yemen Arab Republic and the Politics of Balance', *Asian Affairs*, vol. 12, October 1981.

Philips, Wendell, 'Exploring Queen of Sheba Land', *Collier's*, 7 and 14 April 1951.

Rich, Warren, 'North Yemen: Land of the Queen of Sheba Struggles into the 20th Century', *Christian Science Monitor*, 12 January 1983.

Roucek, J.S., 'Yemen in Geopolitics', *Contemporary Review*, vol. 202, December 1962, pp. 310–17.

Ruszkiewicz, John, 'How the US Lost its Footing in the Shifting Sands of the Persian Gulf: A Case History in the Yemen Arab Republic', *Armed Forces Journal*, September 1980, pp. 64–8.

Sanders, Sol., 'How the West is Losing a Strategic Middle East Crossroads', *Business Week*, 11 February 1980, p. 50.

Seale, Patrick, 'The War in Yemen: Did Nasser Lure the US out on a Limb?', *New Republic*, vol. 198, 26 January 1963, pp. 9–11.

Serezhim, K., 'US Policy in the Middle East', *New Times* (Moscow), vol. 24, 13 June 1947, pp. 5–18.

Sergeant, R.B., 'The Two Yemens: Historical Perspectives and Present Attitude', *Asian Affairs*, vol. 9, Fall 1973, pp. 3–16.

— 'Perilous Politics in Two Yemeni States', *Geographical Magazine*, vol. 51, August 1979, p. 769.

Stark, Freya, 'Yemen Chose to be Poor', *Asia and the Americans*, vol. 154, February 1946, pp. 78–80.

Stark, Joseph A., 'The United States and the Yemen Crisis in 1962', *Columbia*, 1969–70, pp. 245–65.

Stookey, R., 'Social Structure and Politics in the Yemen Arab Republic', *Middle East Journal*, vol. 28, no. 3, 1974.

— 'Red Sea Gate-Keepers: The YAR and The PDRY', *Middle East Review*, Summer 1978, pp. 39–47.

Taher, Ribhi, 'al-Harakah al-Wataniyah wa Atharuha 'Ala Harakat 26 September', *Dirasat wa Shihadat lit-Tarikh*, vol. I, Sana'a, Center for Yemeni Studies, 1986.

Van Hollen, Christopher, 'North Yemen: A Dangerous Pentagonal Game', *Washington Quarterly*, vol. 15, Summer 1982, pp. 137–42.

Walker, Bernard, 'The War in Yemen', *Near East and India*, vol. 43, no. 1234, January 1934, p. 457.

Wolynsky, Alexander, 'Bungle in Yemen', *Nation*, vol. 228, 15 March 1980, p. 293.

Wriggins, Howard, 'Political Outcomes of Foreign Assistance: Influence, Involvement, or Intervention', *Journal of International Affairs*, vol. 22, 1968, pp. 217–39.

Journals and newspapers

YEMEN *Al-Nasr, 14 October, Al-Thawrah, Saba News Agency, 'Adan News Agency, Al-Hikmah, Al-Djumhuriyah, Yemen Times, Al-Tashih, Al-Tadjamu', Al-Mustakbal, Al-Naba, 26 September, Al-Hak, Al-Ayyam, Al-Balagh, Sawt Al-'Ummal, Al-Masir, Al-Sahwah, Al-Eslah.*

UNITED STATES *American Arab Affairs, Armed Forces Journal International, Air International, Arab Studies Quarterly, Business America, Collier's Magazine, Christian Science Monitor, FBIS, Federal News Agency, Forbes, Foreign Reports Bulletin FRB, Mideast Mirror, Military Review, Voice of America, Journal of Arab Affairs, Middle East Policy, Middle East Report, National Geographic Magazine, National Interest, New Republic, New York Times, Oil and Gas Investor, Oil and Gas Journal, Problems of Communism, USIA, World Oil, Washington Post, Washington Star, Wall Street Journal.*

KUWAIT *Al-Rai al-'Aam* and *al-Siyasah.*

SAUDI ARABIA *Al-Djazirah Al-'Arabiyyah, Al-Madjallah, Al-Nadwah, Al-Shark al-Awsat.*

EGYPT *Al-Ahram.*

LEBANON *American University of Beirut Bulletin, Hawadeth, Al-Hayat* (now in London), *Al-Kifah al-'Arabi, Al-Nahar, Record of the Arab World.*

CYPRUS *Middle East Economic Digest* (MEED), and *Middle East Survey* (MES).

UNITED KINGDOM *Arab Report and Record, BBC Summaries and World Broadcasts, Daily Telegraph, Deadline Data, Fortnightly Review, Financial Times, Guardian, Independent, Journal of the Royal Central Asian Society, Military Balance, Middle East Affairs, Middle East Journal, Observer, Reporter, Sunday Times, New Internationalist, Times.*

GERMANY *Frankfurter Allgemeine.*

FRANCE *International Herald Tribune.*

ISRAEL *Jerusalem Post.*

CHINA *Hsinhua News* and *New China News.*

Index